# The
# GEOFF BELL Story
## – from farm worker to
# MILLIONAIRE

Geoff Bell revolutionised truck drivers' accommodation by building Carlisle Truck Inn and running it for 10 years. He built up a fleet of 15 Volvo F86s running night and day and helped forge the modern-day road haulage industry. Then he was defrauded by a chartered accountant, Michael James Bland, a professional fraudster from Carlisle.

ISBN 978-1-78222-797-7

Book design, layout and production management by Into Print
www.intoprint.net
+44 (0)1604 832149

# Contents

1   Village childhood . . . . . . . . . . . . . . . . . . . . . . 5

2   On the road . . . . . . . . . . . . . . . . . . . . . . . . . 12

3   Learning the ropes . . . . . . . . . . . . . . . . . . 27

4   Life's licences . . . . . . . . . . . . . . . . . . . . . . 37

5   Growing the fleet . . . . . . . . . . . . . . . . . . . . 47

6   New homes on the horizon. . . . . . . . . . . . 61

7   Meeting the Truck Inn challenge . . . . . . . . 74

8   Family footsteps . . . . . . . . . . . . . . . . . . . . 87

9   Next generation trucks . . . . . . . . . . . . . . . 99

10  New horizons . . . . . . . . . . . . . . . . . . . . . . 108

11  Property international . . . . . . . . . . . . . . . . 122

12  On tour. . . . . . . . . . . . . . . . . . . . . . . . . . . 136

13  Transport transition . . . . . . . . . . . . . . . . . 155

14  Family downs and ups . . . . . . . . . . . . . . 172

15  Courtroom game . . . . . . . . . . . . . . . . . . . 187

    Appendix 1 . . . . . . . . . . . . . . . . . . . . . . . 196

    Appendix 2 . . . . . . . . . . . . . . . . . . . . . . . 201

    Appendix 3 . . . . . . . . . . . . . . . . . . . . . . . 239

    Appendix 4 . . . . . . . . . . . . . . . . . . . . . . . 278

## Acknowledgements

I wish to start by thanking my wonderful, loving, caring wife Celene, for her encouragement and support she has given me, to complete this book. I also want to thank her for standing by me all these years, going through more than 25 court cases in different countries. Also to my son Chris, for standing by me also through these disastrous years, and the help on finding those old photographs.

*The young Geoff Bell could see a wonderful world in front of him – just needs to be grasped – and he gets started as soon as possible.*

# Village childhood

I was born in Little Bampton, about 11 miles west of Carlisle, in 1939. Little Bampton was a small village with seven farms, nine small houses, a State Management Pub, the Tam O Shanter Inn, and no shop. My father was a blacksmith and his workshop was at one end of the pub and our small house was at the other end. My mother did work for the local farmers; so we were never short of food, with the farmers dropping of potatoes and vegetables and my mother always cooking. But I soon learned that money was in very short supply.

I'm telling this story to give the young ones an idea of what can be done from leaving school at 15 to work on a farm for £2, 7/6 per week, from starting with absolutely no money, to owning a fleet of 15 Volvo articulated trucks, a Rolls Royce and with cash in the bank. I did this by 1969 at the age of 30 and I had no loans or borrowings; everything was paid for.

By 1977, at the age of 37, I had built and opened the first purpose-built Truck Stop, which I named Carlisle Truck Inn; it became a success overnight with over 200 trucks per night and still all without any loans or borrowings.

By 1987, at the age 47, I had sold the Carlisle Truck Inn to BP Oil and I had become a millionaire.

In this unbelievable story I will tell you how my trusted chartered accountant defrauded me of my fortune; and how, after more than 25 court cases, I did get a judgement on him for £6.2 million.

* * *

There were five in our family, with me being the youngest one; my two older sisters were married and gone; my older brother was in the army and my other brother was about 18 months older then me, but we were different.

I would always be working on building my four-wheeled carts in my dad's workshop and then testing them out down the two very steep hills called Lanshaw we had just around the corner.

I don't know if my mother and father planned our family but it sure worked. Our small house was only big enough for the four of us, being my brother myself, mam and dad; my other siblings had left the house.

On entering the house, there was a small room used for both dining and as a sitting room with a fire grate burning coal or firewood and fitted with an oven and crane-type arm for hanging the big kettle on. This big kettle was used for washing up and filling the old tin bath we had to use to bathe in.

There was no electric or main sewer in the village, so we had to go outside up the side of the house to the dry toilet. The house had a very tiny kitchen and I now wonder how my mother made such good food in it.

To go upstairs from the living area, we had to pass through my parents' small bedroom and up the stairs to two small bedrooms. My brother and I stayed in one room and the other was for my other brother when he was on leave from the army.

My friends were Eric and Ernie Miller in the village and we did spend a lot of time together. They had three other brothers older than them. The family had a farm but only one son would work at home while the others were working away.

School was at Kirkbampton two and a half miles away. We used to cycle there every day, come rain, hail or snow. When we were 11 years old we got the bus from Kirkbampton to Burgh By Sands secondary school, but still had to cycle the two and a half miles each way.

When I was about eight years old I started going to Mr Joe Rudd's farm. It was a family run farm with Mr and Mrs Rudd, two daughters and the son; another two daughter were married and gone.

I got very interested in the two Fordson Tractors they had so I would go at nights and Saturdays and by the time I was 10 years old I could handle those tractors in the fields.

In all the school holidays I would be on the farm, and they would take me to the fields with the tractor to plough with the three furrow Ransom plough. I became a specialist at it, getting the furrows dead straight and making perfect finishings.

When not at school I spent all my time at the farm I was not interested in sport only tractors.

When I was about 13 years old I took on a paper round. The Nestlé milk collection truck would drop the papers off for me at about 7.30am on Sunday mornings and I would load up my News of the World paper bag which was very heavy.

My first stop was Ploughlands – three farms and a cottage – then onto Longrigg – one farm, two houses – then head up to Oughterby, dropping papers at the school house on the way past.

Oughterby had quite a few farms and houses and all the kids were going to the same school as me so I knew them all. Next I went onto Fisher Gill farm, home of Tommy Vary and his brother-in-law Tommy Gillespie; they were great fun and always trying to wind me up and hold me back.

Next I was on my way up to Aikton and I was dropping papers off at Water Flosh on the way past. Aikton was quite a big village with lots of farms and houses; after delivering there I had to return home to reload.

After a fast reload and delivering in our village, I then went down West Lane to West Field House farm, which was the Patinson's farm. The son, Stan Pat as we called him, was well-known for buying all kinds of machinery at Lanark monthly sales.

Going down the lane to West Field House farm was about quarter of a mile with wide grass verges at each side; now you are picturing lovely mowed grass each side, but surprise! It was completely covered with old tractors and machinery that would not work.

Stan Pat's father was a great man who would grow some 40 acres of potatoes each year, and in the October school holidays he would have his potatoes harvested. He would collect pickers from the local villages, including me and my friends and many women. We would pick in pairs and we all had a measured distance to collect into wire baskets, and Tot Graham with the horse and cart would collect and empty the baskets into the cart and then he would tip the cart into a big long heap. This was a non-stop operation which worked very well.

The biggest problem was that in the morning it took Stan Pat, the son, half an hour to get the tractor going. It was an old Fordson and what we could not understand was that all the tractors down the lane were also all non-starters.

The pay for picking was 10 shillings per day, plus they supplied the food; this was very good money in 1952 we were all there for one week.

Back on my paper round, I'd be down the lane onto the road to my next delivery, which was Barnes farm next door to the Patinson's, then onto Biglands, another village made up of mostly farms with a few houses. Quite a lot of these farmers were Grahams and Bimsons – all very nice people who I got to know very well and I still see them around today and have a word with them.

*This is the type of Fordson Tractor I worked with, but those Mr Rudd had were all on rubber tyres. From when I was 10 years old at the Rudd's farm in our village at Little Bampton, I could plough and do most things with these tractors.*

After Biglands I went to my last village Gamelsby, again made up of mostly farms with two or three houses, and again there were lots of Grahams families; I became friends with the likes of Allan Graham, Ritz Graham and his brother Nory. Another well-known individual in the village was Tish Graham and his brother Ed. I could number many more and they were all good to me.

But my favourite in Gamelsby was my last delivery at the McCracken's sweet shop, where I used to load up my paper bag with sweets and custard creams, dropping sweet papers all the way back home.

After leaving Gamelsby I would pass the fields where Tish Graham was growing vegetables to sell in Carlisle market. I would park my bike inside the field away from view of the road and pick the pea pods into my big newspaper bag; pea pods were my favourite, I loved them.

The next Sunday, when delivering in Gamelsby, Tish asked me:

Were you steeling my pea pods last week?

No it was not me.

You are telling lies, you left a track of empty pea pods from here to Little Bampton.

I was guilty as charged.

\* \* \*

My father was very good man and a well-known Cumberland Westmorland wrestler in his early days. He was retired from that but was now invited to the local sports in the area to be a judge at these events. The local village sports were held on Saturdays in the summer.

From when I was five years old until eight, my Dad would take me with him. We would go on our bikes and he would take the lead and I would follow him close behind. On those days, it was very interesting to see all the sports being played.

When I was about 14, my older brother Reg left school and went to work at Mr Baird's big dairy farm at Wampool near Kirkbride. Mr and Mrs Baird had eight children – four boys and four girls – but only one son John had left school, so they needed extra help until the next son Gilbert left school.

I became very good friends with the family and used to bike down there on Sunday afternoons. A few of us we would go around to Kirkbride and other places.

I left school at 15 years old and got a job on the farm at £2.7s 6d per week and I lived in on the farm. The family was very good to me and the food was excellent, all home grown and fresh.

Mr Rudd was a very clever man. He could do anything and I learned a lot from him. Everything had to be done correct. For instance, if I erected a fence which was not quite level, he would say

Come on old son and we will have a look at that fence and put it right.

So it was all done in a very smooth way that made me make sure everything I did was as near perfect as possible and this stayed with me all of my life.

Mr Rudd was like the local vet. He assisted other farmers with help on livestock and also with butchering pigs in the season all around the area – four a day on Mondays, Wednesdays and Fridays. He was bringing back lots of black pudding and sausages of all kinds. He would also make gates, then put the hinges into the stone gate posts with melted lead. Mr Rudd's only son Lorry was a strong man, always working and very cleaver also. They were mainly dairy farmers but also with quite a few sheep to breed lambs.

Every cow had a name. Lorry could go out into the fields and tell you which cow was the mother of every offspring; also he could go among the sheep and he knew who the mother was of all the grown-up lambs.

Mr Rudd was unbelievable. At night he would go around one or two fields with his car checking the sheep or livestock, and on his way back home he would pull up at the pub and have a half beer and whisky with water and get on the piano and sing – a multi-talented man.

When I was 16 (on 28 February 1955) I got my licence for a motorcycle. All the lads in the village over 16 had motorcycles. Jack, Tommy and Joe Miller had Triumph Speed Twins – beautiful balanced twin engine. Eric Miller had a BSA 350, Billy Granger had a A7 BSA. My brother Reg had a Triumph Thunderbird.

All the lads in the village were customers of a motorcycle dealer in Carlisle, a Mr Graham of Strand Road; they took me to see what he had and in my price range was a BSA 350 for £45. This was okay but, with only probably less than a pound to my name, I would have to ask Mr Rudd if he would buy it for me.

In those days you worked on the farms on six-month hires so normally you only got pocket money each week, then got paid out at the end of the six-month period. So when I decided to get the motorcycle I had to ask Mr Rudd if he would buy it for me and he could take the money from me at the six-month end; this he agreed to.

I went with the lads to Carlisle to get the bike, paid Mr Graham the £45 and then off we motored. Well, what a new world I came into that I did not know existed. Assisting me was my brother Reg and Eric Miller, both experienced riders.

We would go into the Lake District. It was so exciting for me but I had difficulty keeping up with them on my first day.

I had to try and keep up because I did not know where I was. It was some experience. I was so excited but scared to death around those corners trying to keep up. They pulled up at one of the village cafes and we had a coke.

I told them they were going too fast for me, but we were all having a real good laugh and enjoying the day.

* * *

In 1956 when I became 17 years old I moved to another farm at The Lathes near Kirkbride. The farmer was Gordon Dixon and his wife was Mary. I was then on £6 per week, living in, all food included. I was moving to a very different environment and would be using all I had learned from my previous boss.

Gordon Dixon's was a dairy farm, It had a new type of byre for 40 milk cows with enough space in the centre to get the muck spreader in, not like the many small byres that Mr Rudd had with the centre isle just wide enough to get a borrow in and cobblestone surface, Gordon's byre was all cemented out and had a cooling house at the end with all the washing-up facilities.

I was hired to look after the milking, see to all the calves and in general be in charge of everything. Being very well groomed by Mr Rudd and his family, I had no fears whatsoever about what I was letting myself into.

I moved into the Lathes Gordon's farm on a Saturday after lunch, met Mary Gordon's wife and she showed me my room – a nice big room with a double bed and with a bathroom next door. How exciting; I would now have access to a proper bath. Then Mary took me into the farmyard to meet Adam McCracken.

I expected to see Gordon the boss for instructions, but it was Adam who showed me around the farmyard and told me about all the stock and the feeding material methods. At about 4pm Adam would start about getting ready for milking time. We got started milking the 40 cows and also a small byre with about 12 cows.

We got finished and washed all the milking units and

fed all the stock by about 5.30pm. We did finish a lot earlier than when I was at Rudd's because we had to start at 5.30am as the milk collection was at 7.30am.

We then went in for the supper Mary had made. Gordon was back but had never come into the farm buildings to see what was going on. Gordon Mary Adam and myself all sat around the table; it was very good food and very enjoyable with all the chat going on; we were all laughing. Gordon was a right character, full of fun. When Mary was coming around filling up our teacups , Gordon put his hand up Mary's legs and pulled her knickers down. I didn't know which way to look because I'd never seen anything like this before. They were both laughing their heads off, even Mary. All she said was "stop it Gordon", so I had to let my laughter out.

Adam lived at Gamelsby with his family in the sweet shop I called at on my paper round two years previously. I had packed the paper round up when I left school. Adam actually worked on the council looking after the gutters and roads around the Lathes area five days a week but he did part-time for Gordon on the farm at weekends. He would bike all the way back and forward to his home.

After dinner I had a nice bath, got changed and I was up and onto my motorbike to see my pals, just up the road where Baird's farm was. Gib could use the farm Ford 10 van with bails of straw in the back to sit on, so there would be four or five of us up to the Joiners Arms pub at Aikton. You had to be 18 to get a drink and most of us were 17 so we were let into the back room to have a few nut brown ales; then onto the Little Bampton dance; after that I went back to my new home on Gordon's farm.

On my first Sunday I was up sharp at 5.30am. Adam was already there but no sign of Gordon. Adam had the engine started for the electric generator – no mains there in those days. It was a Lister diesel engine with a hand start which was very hard to crank over and you needed all your strength.

We got all the milked byres cleaned out, all the calves fed but there was no sign of Gordon or Mary, so I said to Adam:

*What about breakfast?*
*We will have to go in and make our own.*

So we went into the kitchen. Adam knew the ropes and went into the larder; he came back with bacon, eggs, sausages and bread. The cooker was fired up for six eggs, bacon, sausage and fried bread; we were hungry after two and half hours hard work. With all the cooking done, we sat down and enjoyed our breakfast with a lovely pot of tea.

After breakfast we went back to finish off around the farmyard. Being Sunday, we were off until about 3.30pm and then back in for milking. Adam was back to help me at night but on the Monday morning I would be alone. I knew pretty well now how things worked and was more or less settled in and not in the least worried about anything.

After we finished work on Sunday night, Adam and I went in the house for dinner. Mary had a good meal for us. Mary, Gordon, Adam and myself were all at the table and it was all fun again. Gordon was full of unbelievable banter. I was in another world completely different from Little Bampton.

After dinner I got changed and went up to Baird's farm to see Gib and Ed. Quite a few of us gathered there on a Sunday night – Chris Hall, Joe Kenny, Fred Abbott, Stan Pat. In the summer they would play cricket. I did not join in – I was not into cricket – but Gib was crazy on it.

Later at night we would have a fry-up, making egg and chips. They had a big Aga cooker and a large kitchen and very large dining room for the workers. Baird's farmhouse was large they had eight children, Mr and Mrs Baird were very nice people. I never heard them shout in all the time I spent there. There was always someone visiting but I never heard anyone getting told off.

On the Monday morning I was up with the larks at 5.30am on my own. Adam had gone on his own job. I managed all the milking, washed up, mucked out fed the calves and all the other stock. Gordon would come out with me after breakfast and tell me what was to do on the land. He had a good tractor which I liked, a Ford Power Major with front loader. He had an eye for good machinery and I think he was more interested in machinery than farming.

\* \* \*

Gordon had a Bedford 10 ton truck and one day he said to me

*Do you want to go with the driver to Prudhoe, Newcastle for a load of lime?*

I said "yes", and off we went, got loaded up. All the way back I was thinking this is what I want to do, to be, a truck driver.

When we got back to the farm I went straight to Gordon, who asked

How did it go?

It has just made my mind up that I want to be a truck driver.

Gordon was then doing haulage for M&H Towel, Agricultural Merchants, Carlisle, but he also wanted to get into lime and fertiliser spreading that Towels would sell to the farmers.

The local machinery rep for County Garage Carlisle, the main Ford dealer, was a Wilf Clifford. He would call at Gordon's farm and would come in for lunch with us all. He was a character, so we had two of them together; what a laugh we would have.

During one visit Gordon asked about a new Atkinson Lime spreader and a new Ford Power Major to marry up to the lime spreader. Mary went mad:

Where are you going to get the money from? We cannot afford those things.

Anyhow Gordon always ordered what he wanted and after a week or so a new tractor and a new lime spreader arrived. So after milking at nights I would go and spread the lime and fertiliser, which I loved to do.

Gordon was getting more orders in from Towel's and needed another truck so he ordered a new Ford Thames Trader from County Garage.

The new truck was for me to drive so it had to be under three tons unladen weight for a driver under 21 years old. It was fitted with a 20-foot flat wooden body and the sides were what we call 'drop on sides' which were removable for weigh-in at the police weighbridge to get the proper road tax bracket. Gordon arranged for me to take it to the weigh-in and said if you don't get it under three tons you can't drive it , so it's up to you to get it under three tons.

Well, I took everything off that was possibly legal with only about half a gallon of diesel in. So into the police weighbridge, handed in the papers trying to keep calm and couldn't stop thinking if it is over three tons I will not be able to drive this truck.

Waiting for the weigh ticket to be given over to me, a voice came from the weighbridge window "here you are son:. I was nervous to read the contents but I could see that my worries were over -just under three tons. I was on the road and was one very happy young lad.

I started driving full time for Gordon and went back to live with my mother at Little Bampton. She was very happy to have me back. I would be away early in the mornings. If I was going to ICI Billingham, I would want to be there first in the queue to load up, so I would be up at 5am to be there before 8am, get loaded with 10 tons of bagged fertiliser, and then back to Carlisle or the Wigton area to deliver to farms. We did a lot of bulk slag in the autumn and through the winter so I needed the sides on for this.

Basic slag was waste from the steel works, just like black dust. When we had loaded this slag we would bring it back and it was to spread on the fields of the farmers who had ordered it. It was all to shovel from the truck into the spreader which would hold about two tons.

The farmers wanted it spread mostly half a ton to the acre. When our truck was empty I would be as black as a crow, in my hair all over my face, impossible to comb my hair. It was very hard to get your hands clean. It got into the truck cabs and all over. I wore a boiler suit that I took off when I had unloaded. We collected this slag from steel works all over – Lackenby Steelworks, South Bank Steelworks, Middlesbrough, Skinningrove, Corby Weldon Steelworks, near London.

I was making very good money – £13 per week clear with all taxes paid – but working very hard for this. On a normal working day I would be up at 5am, over to Middlesbrough, load up back into Cumbria, shovel the 10 tons into the spreader (five spreader loads) and spreading it onto the fields. Then back into a farm to pick up a load of baled hay, load it onto the truck eight rounds high. Loading these bales up to eight rounds high could only be done by drivers like me that had the farming experience. Once loaded, I would then deliver it to the farmer that had purchased the load, mainly in the Cumbria area.

Gordon had another driver, Freddy Miller, driving a Bedford truck but I was doing more work than him so I said to Gordon

*Why is Freddy getting the same money as me and not doing as much work?*

*Gordon was not interested and would not talk about it.*

In those days there were a quite a few contractors doing this same contracting. John Rumney from Thursby had a contract with Graham's Agricultural Supplies Penrith and he approached me to work for him; he knew I could drive the truck and also handle the tractor and spreader; most men could only drive the trucks and knew nothing about spreading. On the other hand tractor spreader men did not drive trucks.

John Rumney offered me £16 per week clear, so I thought "well, same job, why not? I spoke to John Rumney and said I would start the following week and he agreed. So I spoke to Gordon and said I was leaving and would work one week's notice. He exploded. I started my last week for Gordon and within two days he approached me and said

*You are not going to work for f--king Rumney I will F--king kill him.*

So the next night John Rumney called me and said he could not start me because Gordon had been onto him.

* * *

So here I was, 19 years old, looking for a job. I got started on a farm with Mr and Mrs Curruthers, Pow Hill Farm, Kirkbride, which was very near to my friend's farm Baird's of Wampool. The job was more or less tractor and general farm work; they did the milking and looked after the stock. It was very boring actually and not what I wanted. But the farmer and his wife who lived opposite gave me a lot of fun. Pais Brown was his name and what a character. I used to go over at lunch hour and have plenty of banter with him and his wife. Also at nights I was over to Baird's farm with my mates Gib, Ed and the others.

I only stayed at the Curruthers farm for a few months. My next job was for John Dixon, Gordon's elder brother.

His farm was Low Houses, Wigton. He was a dairy farmer and also a horse trainer, a real gentleman; I knew him from being at Gordon's. I lived in with them with all food included. My job was not involved with the livestock but was more general and tractor work and also to drive the horse box truck with the trainers and jockeys.

John Dixon's son John did all the milking and looking after the herd and calves. He was fully dedicated to the dairy, and of all the dairy men I have known I think young John could get the most milk out of each cow for the cheapest input. Father John and young John had their own mix of cattle food, not the expensive normal cattle food made by the likes of BOCM, Carr's Mill, etc.

Working at Low Houses was like being freed from jail after being at Pow Hill. John had about 30 horses in training so there were plenty of people around the farmyard all day. There were stable lads, one jockey, John the blacksmith, and horse owners popping in and out.

I would take the race horses and trainers out for gallops twice a week in the large Ford Diesel horse box, once to the beaches to gallop in the sand, and once to a normal gallop area. Also I would take the appointed horses to the races all over the UK.

I did not gamble at all because I learned from one of the stable lads Peter. He got paid every Thursday and by Monday morning he was broke; he had to make a sub every week. John the boss never gambled.

The jockey there was Johnny O'Hara, an Irishman. We became very good friends and we had lots of fun. I had a Ford 8 van which we often used to go to dances. Every week there were dances at Waverton, Rosley, Wigton and Thursby. Johnny was a small guy who did not drink, but had plenty of courage, so he did not need the drink. He would ask any girl to get up and dance. There was a farm up the road called The Beck. The family were Bonesses, also a horse family, and the daughter was called Ann, a very smart young lady who was Miss Cumberland. Well Johnny would always get her up to dance, which she did, because they had something in common, the horses. Johnny thought he was in with a very good chance and he never gave up on her, but I told him that he had more chance of going to the moon than getting off with Ann; it turned out I was right. But he was still in the race and he married the daughter of Mr Atkinson, another horse trainer from Carlisle.

* * *

I enjoyed my time in Wigton but it was time to move onto my next plan. On the farms you agreed a six-month hire. My hire with John Dixon was up at the end of September 1961. John asked if I was staying on for another six months? I said

*John, thanks for asking me but I think you know what I want to do.*

*I think I do, you want to go truck driving full time.*

*Yes I will be 21 years old on 28 February next year and can drive any heavy goods vehicle.*

He wished me well and good luck.

My idea was to get a truck driving job with Fred Brown after hearing he was paying the best wages. I had met Fred Brown before when I was working with Gordon Dixon. My van broke down one night outside his bungalow at Bank End, Thursby, where his depot was. I knocked at his door and he answered and I told him I had broken down and could I use his phone to call my pal to pick me up? He invited me to use the phone and also allowed me to stay in until I was picked up. We got chatting and he knew who I was and where I was working; we got on fine.

So I dropped in at Fred Brown's depot to speak to him.

He was then living with Gordon and John Dixon's sister Irene so he knew exactly what I had been doing. He knew I was after a driving job but could not put me on HGVs until I was 21 so he said I could go on the tractor and spreading until I was 21, so I accepted the job and started after I had finished at John Dixon's and moved back home to live with my mother.

My first day was an 8am start at Brown's. Fred had a tractor and spreader ready and gave me a farm address – Brocklebank Farm, Brocklebank, Wigton. He said he would take his van and meet me at the farm to tell me what to do. We met at the farm and I followed him for a mile or so into the fields and then he stopped. I stopped behind him, got off the tractor and could not believe my eyes. There was this big long high stack of bagged slag, must have been 100 ton. Fred said

*There you are – good first job for you.*

*He showed me all the fields that were to be treated at half a ton to the acre.*

*I will come and pick you up about 4.30pm.*

So off he went. I had this first job polished off before Fred expected and it showed in my first week's wages.

\* \* \*

After a couple of weeks I had a new tractor and new Atkinson spreader complete with a set of ramps. The ramps were a real dream but needed the trucks to be tipper trucks. With the tipper trucks they reversed up the ramps and tipped direct into the spreader. Normally in a day we would have about four-10-ton trucks to spread, but some were not tippers; the flat trucks were all to shovel off into the spreader. Fred had about 10 spreading units going – quite big business. He had about 10 trucks in all, but used a lot of subcontractors to bring in the fertiliser, and slag. He did a lot of lime spreading, which was best for the tipper trucks where they could back up the ramps and tip into the spreaders.

George Bowness, Fred's foreman, told me never to knock the tractor out of gear down the hills. One day I was coming back to the depot with my outfit down Warnel Bank – a very steep hill. What did I do? I put it out of gear. Off I went, full speed ahead. Then the road became very bumpy. I looked behind and the spreader had come adrift, crashing into the hedge. I was very lucky and just damaged the front corner of the spreader. The problem I had was that I could not find the pin which slotted in the tow bar to connect the spreader. So I had to walk away over to the nearest farm and get a tow pin from the farmer.

When I arrived back at the depot George Bowness was there.

*What have you done?*

*I did what you said not to do, knocked the tractor out of gear.*

*Get in your van and go home before Fred comes in.*

The next morning I was in for 8am and Fred was waiting, and I was waiting to see what my future held there. Fred said

*Get in that truck. It is loaded with 14 tons of fertiliser for WCF Cockermouth. Tip there, then phone in to see what you have to do next, but do not ring and say you smashed it up.*

Well, what a surprise. I could not believe it. This was what I wanted. I was back on the road again.

The truck was a six-wheeler Albion Truck with the very same engine as the four wheeler, and could not pull my hat off, yet I did a lot of work with this old girl; it was snail pace up the hills and did not want to stop going down – brakes, what brakes? She didn't like to start either. The cab was coach built by Bobby Hind from Carlisle. I think they used the wrong plans – it was a hen house on wheels.

It had built in air-conditioning drafts coming from

every direction. I never found the heater. But anyhow the best thing about the old girl was that I was earning top wages and was the best paid man at Fred Brown's, picking up £21-23 clear every week.

Some months later I called into see Gordon and Mary Dixon one Sunday afternoon. Gordon said he could do with me back to manage the farm so we talked about what the wage would be and I agreed. The next day on the Monday I gave my one week's notice to Fred. He said

*I hope you are not going to work for that f—ing Dixon I will call the licensing office and report him for using those farmers' licences on his trucks for doing all kinds of other work.*

I phoned Gordon on the Wednesday and he said he could not go through with the job offer; he did not explain to me what Fred Brown had done or said. Gordon and Fred were at loggerheads for years about his sister Irene living with Fred. Gordon was very pally with Irene's husband Joe Nelson, a farmer.

On Thursday morning I spoke to Fred

*Hi Fred I will not be leaving now, can I stay on?*

*No, once someone has given their notice that is it, no coming back.*

*Okay.*

I carried on doing various jobs on the truck before I set off on my journey. Just before I started the truck Fred came over and he said

*That will be OK, you can carry on working here.*

I stayed with Fred until I was 22 years old. I then got an offer from a friend of mine Willie Dickinson. He was selling lime for Adam Lythgoe and had a truck and a lime spreader on, also a subcontractor with a truck hauling to his spreader. He offered me more than I was getting at Fred Brown's if I would drive the truck and do the spreading. I took up his offer and started with him. His subcontractor was a man called Charlie Ingledow who had worked with the electricity board all his life. His wife Ann ran their boarding house in London Road, Carlisle. Charlie had been given the chance to take early retirement and got a nice lump-sum pay off.

So Charlie decided to buy a brand new Thames Trader tipper with no truck experience at all. He got started with Adam Lythgoe and hauling to Willie Dickinson's spreader. I started with Willie., Charlie and I would run together for loads then come back to various farms and spread our loads. Charlie had had no experience on trucking but we always got the jobs done, he was great to work with – plenty of banter and fun.

I used to go out with them on Saturday nights around Carlisle's social clubs. They had long-time friends Tommy and Ann Dowell. Tommy was a truck driver at Robson's of Carlisle. Many years later their son Billy Dowell came to drive for me on a Volvo F86 with tipper trailer.

I was with Willie for some time but he was wanting to buy another truck so he asked me to go with him to McKenzie's truck sales at the Stripes, Cumwhinton, near Carlisle.

He had got his eye on an overworked six wheeler Dodge and he asked:

*What do you think of that?*

*I am driving your old Bedford flat wagon and having to shovel all the loads off, Charlie has a tipper and tips his off with no shovelling attached, and it is a new truck. My advice is to get a new truck like Charlie with a tipper on and we will do more work than if you get another flat truck with no tipper on.*

Willie went ahead and bought the old Dodge, so I decided to leave. When I left Willie on the Saturday he then started one of his brothers to do my job. The brother started on the Monday and got killed on the first day when he had an accident with the tractor – what a tragedy.

After leaving Willie I decided to have some time off

and did quite a bit of work with Alan Harrison, who had a scrap yard at Oldoth. Alan was a very clever man and we got on very well together and became big pals. I did learn a lot from him that rubbed off on me and led me to thinking about starting with my own truck. Alan had one truck, a four-wheel Albion. He did work for Fred Brown in the winter when the slag job was on. I got to know him through working at Brown's when we would meet on the road regularly over Bowes Moor. He would be coming behind me from Middlesbrough and would see all this smoke miles ahead and know it was me.

My old Albion had the same engine as Alan's truck but was six to seven ton heavier so the engine was struggling, putting black smoke out like a train. We would stop in a layby and get into my lunch box my mother had prepared for me. My mother had a big square biscuit tin – I mean big! She would fill this to the brim every day with boiled eggs, tomatoes, sandwiches, everything, and I had a big flask. So Alan would jump into my cab and have a snack with me. We would be talking about what we should do in the future, throwing ideas about and how we could make money; we were both on the same wavelength.

I called round to see Gordon and Mary Dixon and Gordon asked me if I would come back and work on the farm and I said "if the money is right". By then I could drive an HGV and the driving paid better than the farming, so we haggled away until I got what I wanted, Mary, Gordon's wife, was unimpressed and did not agree but Gordon was the boss. So we agreed I would come back on the farm and live in, all food included, and my wage would be met and they would pay the tax.

So I left my mother again and went back to the farm. By then Gordon had about five Commer two-stroke 10-ton tipper trucks, one eight-wheeler ERF, a 20 ton tipper. He had done very well. Towell's Agriculture Merchants farm supplies, who Gordon was working for, had really achieved good sales but the problem was that this was Gordon's only customer. If Towell's was quiet, so was Gordon.

Back in those days to haul for anyone, you had to have an "A" licence; then you could work for any company all over the UK. Thesel licences were like gold dust. Say someone was retiring and a licence came up for sale, it most likely would be on an old worn-out four-wheeler 10-ton truck and the owner would be asking £2,000.

So the likes of Fred Brown Gordon Dixon and many more were all operating with "B" licences which were restricted to conditions on the licence. For instance, Fred Brown's "B" licence would read, Goods For WCF and Own Goods, which meant that he could only carry goods for West Cumberland Farmers and they must be goods he owned himself (Fred had bought goods to resell). Fred did a lot of sales of fertilisers and slag to the farmers so he was carrying his own goods. Gordon's "B" licence would read Goods for Towells Agricultural Supplies and own goods.

So I was back on the farm, up at 5.30am, no problem for me, same old system. Since I'd last been on the farm, Gordon had bought another small farm next door which we used to call McSweeney's farm. He had a married couple in the house. The husband worked for Gordon and his wife did jobs for Mary. They were a German couple. Gordon said Bruno would work under me on the farm; he would do all the mucking out for me and any job I asked. But he was clueless and hard work for me. In those days Gordon was always wanting to improve his farm by laying concrete, extending buildings, building a bigger silage pit. I was very handy at this and Bruno was like my labourer, but he was hard work for me and hopeless. Gordon would have a load of ready-mixed concrete coming in for laying. Bruno was on the barrow and I was laying the concrete. Well, he was useless. I would have a panel all levelled off, then Bruno would come along, let the barrow fall off the timber and all over my lovely finished panel. Bruno would throw the barrow into the concrete and say "f***ing barrow".

Anyhow Gordon was very good to work for and all the fun and banter was still there. After a few months Gordon came to me and said

*Can we talk.*

*No problem.*

*Mary is always going on about what we are paying you and it is too much for us to pay out.*

*What would you like me to do?*

*Mary says Bruno could take over the farm work now and you could go back driving. What do you think?*

*Well I can do anything.*

*I was thinking of getting my own truck.*

*But look, Gordon, Bruno is not fit to look after the cows, he has not got a clue. It has taken me all this time to get the milk consumption up and Bruno will ruin all my work and you will lose out.*

*Well, this is what Mary wants.*

So we agreed.

So I went back home to my mother and father and, as always, they were pleased to see me. I started driving for Gordon again, but was now looking to start with my own truck. I needed work for a truck before buying one, so I went to one or two agricultural agents to see if I could get to work from them on their "B" licence system, but no luck.

I found a man called Billy Stoddard at Hallbankgate who had two trucks and he wanted to sell one; it was a 10-ton Ford Thames Trader tipper with a "B" licence on. The "B" licence was very good – 120 miles radius to carry building materials and farm requisites, which allowed me to work for any company that wanted these materials moved. Bill was asking £1,000 so I said I would take it. He said he would change the "B" licence into my name, which could take a few weeks, so it gave me time to get the money sorted out. I sold my van, an Austin A35, and, with the money I had saved, I then had £350 in the bank.

Next I made a trip to see my bank manager at the Midland Bank, English Street, Carlisle, thinking this is just a formality. I had been with the bank for eight years and never borrowed anything. I was introduced to the manager, a man I had never met before, explained what I was wanting to do and needed a loan. He started

*That's OK, we will need your father as a guarantor.*

*But my father and mother have no money.*

*What about your boss Gordon Dixon?*

*I think Gordon will need a guarantor.*

No loan from Midland Bank. Next stop Bowmakers HP finance. I went into see the manager and it was the same story: I would need a guarantor. So over the next couple of weeks I tried more HP companies but without success – no loans possible.

* * *

In 1963 when I was still 24 years old, on one cold Sunday afternoon, Billy Stoddard's girlfriend, a very nice girl called Nan, arrived at our house and came in. My mother as usual made tea and her home-made rock buns (mind they were rock hard buns). Nan said

*Billy has got the licence back and all changed into your name, so I have come for you to collect the truck.*

*Nan up to now I have not been able to borrow the money.*

*Look Billy said come and collect the truck.*

So off I went with her.

To get to Hallbankgate from Little Bampton you go through Carlisle and onto Brampton, then another few miles heading on the Alston Road. We arrived at Billy's house and I explained to him that I would not be able to take the truck because I was unable to get a loan yet. He said to take the truck and pay me when I had made the money. No argument from me on that.

So I took the truck back home with me, thinking all the way home "what will I do tomorrow?" With not knowing that I was getting the truck, I did not have any work planned. The weather had been very wet over the past couple of weeks so there would be no slag spreading. At that time of year, when the frost is in the ground, there are plenty of loads of slag to be had, so I worked out a plan for the morning.

On Monday morning I drove down to Gordon's and borrowed some wagon sheets; he sorted me out with what I needed. Then off I set to the Thistle Transport office. Thistle Transport did all the work for British Gypsum

Cocklakes factory, a very big factory with lots of loads going out daily all over the UK. Thistle Transport had a lot of trucks but not enough to do all the work so they used a lot of subcontractors. Fred Brown and Gordon Dixon could not do these jobs because their licences did not cover this material. So what you did was park on their big park outside the transport office and report to the transport manager, a Donald Alcorn.

I introduced myself, gave him my "B" licence particulars and he opened me an account to do work for them. "OK, " he said, "where would you like me to load you for?" I said "Glasgow or Edinburgh area". With this area in mind, Gordon would load me back from Scotland with brewers grains. Donald said "Okay, wait on the park and I will call you when a load comes in." Late afternoon Donald called me, "Here is a ticket go up to the Cocklakes office, hand them this ticket it is a load for Kirkcaldy." My first load! I thought "what an achievement I have got started".

I went into the Gypsum factory, white dust everywhere. I got loaded up with all different types of bagged plaster and I looked like a flour grader, all white. I telephoned Gordon from a call box – no mobiles in those days.

Gordon I am loaded for Kirkcaldy have you anything from back from Alloa tomorrow?

Yes, go into Alloa distillery and pick up a load for John Dixon, Moor End Thursby.

Okay thanks.

I set off early morning to get there for opening time 8am. In those days you had to go around by the Kincardine Bridge because there was no Forth Bridge. I found after a few miles she wasn't so positive at stopping or slowing down, so the brakes need attention and she was also dodgy at starting.

I was up to Kirkcaldy, found the building merchant, got unloaded, then back down to Alloa to the distillery. Got loaded up okay, 10 tons of wet grains now heading for home. I came down through Armadale, through Whitburn and down towards the A8, a very busy main road between Glasgow and Edinburgh. I stopped at the halt sign and the engine stalled. I pulled the starter switch-nothing. I tried again, tried again. Nothing, the battery was dead flat.

It was getting late in the day so dusk was arriving. There was a filling station on the roadside there and I noticed a Landrover filling up with fuel. I approached the driver and asked him if he would give me a tow to start the truck. I said I had a heavy wire tow rope and a special tow hook on the front of the truck. He said OK and he reversed up to the front of my truck and his Landrover was actually on part of the busy road. I attached the tow rope to the tow hitch on the back of his Landrover, then attached it to my truck.

The next thing I knew I woke up in hospital. I did not know where I was, my head was all bandaged up and I felt a mess and out of it. When I eventually came round and starting thinking, the conclusion I came to was: a vehicle must have come between my truck and the Landrover and hit me. No-one ever came forward to explain to me what had really happened; the police were not involved. If they were, they never spoke to me.

After a couple of days I was ready for discharge. My older Brother Tom came up to Scotland and drove me and my truck home. We found the truck parked at the filling station where the accident took place. No-one explained who towed the truck off the road or gave any other information. My brother Tom drove down from Armadale, delivered the load of grain to John Dixon's farm and parked the truck on the green beside our house. Tom lived at the other end of Little Bampton.

I had couple of days to recuperate and do a lot of thinking. I decided to get hold of one of my friends who did a lot of fitting work for Gordon Dixon, a man called Big John Liddle; he was a big strong fellow with hands like shovels and what a character. I would get him to check the truck over and tell me what repairs it needed. This was the list: needs brakes completely relined, new battery, new starter, dynamo needs repairing. John's advice to me was to take the truck back it was going to cost me a lot of money to put in good order.

I agreed with John's analysis of the truck but I was also thinking that I still wanted to have my own truck. If I took it back, where would I go next? No-one , banks or HP, would loan me money. We had no phone in the house so we used the call box on the green outside our house. I phoned Billie and told him what repairs the truck needed and I would have to bring it back. My mother had kept in touch with Billie's girlfriend Nan and kept her up to date with what had happened to me. To my surprise, Billy Stoddard said

*Take it into the County Garage Carlisle truck department and see the foreman Alec Edgar and he will sort it out for you.*

*Billie I cannot afford to pay all these repairs with just starting off.*

*Just take the truck in I will sort it all out.*

I took it into the County Garage and met with Alec Edgar who was expecting me and he had a couple of fitters right onto the job. Alec became a very good friend of mine over the years.

I phoned in the next day and he said to come and collect it the following day. It would be all ready. I picked it up the next day and it was a different truck. I was ready to go. Over the next couple months I did various jobs for various companies. With the "B" licence I had, I could load both ways, for example take steel from Workington down to Scunthorpe and load slag back for Fred Brown or Gordon Dixon or Eddy Stobart.

When I was working for Fred Brown, a new young office lad called Lance Hetherington started.. He was very sharp and soon became transport manager. I always got on very well with Lance he was one of those rare characters and very clever. Fred Brown out of the blue got a contract to haul gypsum rock from British Gypsum Kirby Thore to Dunbar, to a new cement plant, tipping 24 hours a day. He needed quite a lot of trucks on this job so I was one of them, and also my very good pal Alan Harrison. I was more or less full time on this job for two years, apart from about two or three days a month hauling perlite from a boat in Silloth docks to British Gypsum Cocklakes and Kirby Thore. My last load would be to Kirby Thore then I would load up with gypsum rock for Dunbar. I had a man, Ian Strick from Silloth, who did my night runs to Dunbar.

My normal day was to leave home up to British Gypsum Kirkby Thore for 7.30am. Loading was very fast from an overhead shoot. I drove up to Dunbar through Carlisle, Longtown, Langholm, Hawick, Kelso, Coldstream, Duns, then up to Granthouse onto the A1 and up into Portland Cement Factory Dunbar. Unloading was a five-minute job with this tipper. Now I retreated back to British Gypsum Kirby Thore to reload, then back to Carlisle, say about 4.30-5pm. My night man Ian Strick would then set off about 5.30-6pm. We always changed over behind the County Garage where there was plenty of space and any fast repairs could be done. They were the main Ford agents and were open 24 hours for repairs. County Garage was a top-class repairs garage with about 20 first class fitters.

With two loads a day to Dunbar, one on Saturday and Sunday, total of 12 loads a week, I was doing well. It was £13 per load so £26 per day. People were all talking about Geoff Bell making this big money. I met Billie Stoddard on the road one day and I said

*Billie can I pay you part of the truck off.*

*No, give it to me altogether.*

Within a few weeks I paid him the £1,000. The old truck was more or less worn out so I got a new Ford Thames Trader. County Garage changed the body and tipper gear over onto the new truck to save money. The total cost was £1,000. I got it on HP from Forward Trust Finance, part of the Midland Bank Group. The loan was for one year and the interest was then 5% so it was £50 to borrow the money, £1 per week. I think that was a very good deal, going from an old worn-out truck to a new updated model.

I was on top of the world because this new truck was tip top, with air brakes, and Minimec fuel pump. I was very comfortable to drive with a nice cab interior. My cousin Clary Cowen was a fitter at the County Garage but on the car side. He was always a friend of the family and also my brother Tom's best pal. He would always help us when we needed a car, so I spoke to him and told him I could do with a little run-about. He soon came back to me and said

*Our next door neighbour is getting old and he has been advised to stop driving, it is an Austin 7, perfect condition. He wants £15 for it.*

So I went with Clary to see the car and it was as he said, perfect. So I paid the £15 and came home with it, no problem.

Things were going very well still on the Gypsum job for Fred Brown, and money was coming in. So back I went to see Clary.

*I am looking for a better car can you have a look around for me?*

I used to see Clary regularly because my night driver Ian Strick would meet me at the County Garage each night to take over and tip the truck at Dunbar. Within a couple of days Clary had his eye on a car for me, he said

*One of the directors at the County Garage Tom Ingles is getting a new car and his old one is for sale.*

Clary took me to have a look at the car. I could not believe my eyes. It was perfect. I said to Clary "what a bird puller that is" and we both laughed our heads off. It was a Ford Zephyr Zodiac with every extra you could mention – overdrive, sun shade, badge bar, silver wheel trims, interior ladies mirror, front bench seat, column gear change. I said to Clary

*How much?*

*Tom Ingles said for you a special price of £100.*

So I got the car what a thrill I was over the moon.

*Geoff's Ford Zephyr Zodiac.*

I was 25 years old on 28 February 1964. I had applied for another truck to be added to my "B" licence and had already been adding goods to my licence and stretching the radius of miles I could go. I was getting pretty clued-up on how to get these haulage licences. You had to apply to the Government Transport Commission Department. Then they advertised it in what was called the Application and Decisions booklet which was sent to all the hauliers in the UK. So any haulier could object to you acquiring that licence. If this did happen, you had to go in front of the transport courts and fight it.

Applying for a "B" licence was in a different league than applying for an "A" licence which was a monopoly. I planned my application to go in over the Christmas period when hauliers would be on holiday. Anyone objecting had to do it inside two weeks of publication. A letter came in the post from the Transport Department. What was it to be – good or bad news? I read the letter "Your application for an additional "B" licence has been granted". Success.

My plan was to get into flat haulage and to buy a second-hand Ford Thames Trader. I got one from the County Garage Carlisle with a 20-foot body. It was a very clean truck and seemed in good condition. John Blacklock came to drive it, a lad about 22 that had worked on the farms like myself. I knew him very well his father had a farm at Studholme. I got a job hauling goods from Liverpool for Carr's Agriculture Mill, Silloth, Cumbria, taking pulp wood back down to Bowater paper mill Ellesmere Port.

In 1964 I met a young lady called Lorraine Murray who lived at Black Bank near Longtown with her parents, and by coincidence her father was a haulier -mainly livestock and the odd truck on for British Gypsum. We planned to get married in December 1964 so we started looking for a house, going with my accountant Mr Fred Nixon to one or two auction house sales. I thought the houses we looked at were not in good order and were too dear. My accountant Mr Nixon was also Mr Murray's accountant. He said he would ask Mr Murray if he would contribute to get a house. I said not to ask. Anyhow a few days later Mr Nixon said he had spoken with Mr Murray and the answer was "no". Mr Murray had said we should get a council house.

One night in November I was driving from Carlisle back home and coming in to Kirkbampton I saw this bungalow with a 'for sale' sign on. I stopped and knocked at the door and a Walter Purdam came to the door. Walter was a builder I had known him for some years. I said

*Hello Walter I didn't know you lived here. Are you selling the house?*

*Yes, I have built this bungalow so we are moving on.*
*It is lovely and warm in here, how do you get it so warm?*
*Central heating.*
*What is that?*

He showed me the system boiler and how it worked with all the radiators; it was all new to me but very comfortable. He took me around the house, which had three bedrooms, kitchen, dining room and a large sitting room. We could not fault the house, and it was all new.

*What price are you asking?*
*Well, it is more or less sold at £4,000, but they have not paid a deposit yet.*
*I will give you £4,100.*
*Come and see me on the way by tomorrow night.*
*I will.*

The next night I called in and Walter said that we could

have the house for £4,100 I said

*OK, I will get onto my solicitor and send you the 10% deposit.*

Working for Fred Brown, being single and fuel being very cheap, I didn't need much money, so I used to leave it on. I had a summary every month so I knew what Fred owed me. If I needed money, I would ask Fred or Lance. The next day I called in to see Fred and told him I was getting married and was getting a house and could he give me £1,000 for the deposit? He said it was fine, no problem. So I was all set up. I would have about £1,400 worked for at Fred Brown's so I was OK.

After paying the £1,000 deposit on the bungalow, I needed another £3,000. Mr Nixon my accountant said he had a farmer selling up and retiring and would get the £3,000 loan for me, which he did.

*Geoff and Lorraine got married on 12 December 1994.*

We got married on 12 December 1964, drove down and had a week's honeymoon in London. We came back and got settled into our bungalow and on 28 October 1965 our daughter was born; we were all very excited and we named here Angela Lorraine Bell.

In early 1966 the Dunbar job came to an end, which left a big hole to fill. The railway had installed facilities in the Dunbar factory to handle the rail wagons. Fred Brown had not enough work to keep me going with my tipper truck. My other flat truck was still on the timber down to Ellesmere Port and Carr's goods back. I went back to my fertiliser spreading, I got a spreader from Gordon Dixon and bought a Fordson Major tractor. I had envisaged the Dunbar job coming to an end soon because I could see the Dunbar factory was busy erecting the facilities for the rail. So I had in my spare time been building ramps in our back garden. I had bought a welder and collected all the steel from various scrap yards. I needed ramps to reverse the tipper truck up, then tip direct into the spreader. That way there was no more shovelling and this was much faster.

I was spreading for various companies. If I was in the Brampton area spreading a load for Towel's agricultural agents, I would phone Millican's to see if they had anything to spread there. He would say "yes, John Abbot, North Farm, Brampton, needs two 10-ton loads of lime from Harrison's Lime works, Shap".

I carried on a few months but, although I was making money, I could not see any future in this to expand; this was very dirty job and out in all weathers. On 28 September 1966 our second child was born, a boy. We now had one of each and felt very lucky and again excited. We named him Christopher Geoffrey Bell.

*Our two children Angela and Christopher.*

My plan was to sell the tipper and get another flat truck. I sold my spreading equipment and traded my tipper in for a six-wheeler Ford D Series with a 24-foot flat body. I started hauling timber for Millican's from various forests down to Ellesmere Port and loads back to the Edinburgh/Glasgow area. In 1967 I also traded the four-wheeler Ford Thames in for a Leyland Retriever six-wheeler. Both trucks were on the same job. I was driving one and I had a driver on the other.

I was really wanting to get an "A" licence and I heard that Willie Dockray at Abbeytown was slowing down a bit, for semi retirement and word was he was selling an "A" licence. I phoned him and he said he would come to our house and see me. He came to see me in a couple of days. I knew him and had spoken to him over the years, he was a very nice chap but fit to travel, clever sly operator and fit to pull the wool over your eyes.

*Well, Willie, how little do you want for this old worn out Albion Review?*

*What do you mean? This truck has been kept in first-class condition.*

*Is that right, then you will give me a year's warranty on it.*

*No cannot do that on a second-hand truck.*

*What is the price then?*

*£1,800 pounds with the "A" licence.*

*Willie, I will give you £1,700 but I can only pay you in 12 monthly payments. Also I will want to test the truck.*

*O, come over tomorrow and you can check it over and give it a test run.*

Next day I went down to Abbeytown to Willie's yard, checked and tested the truck, which seemed fine. Although with older hard-worked trucks, it is always a bit of a gamble, nevertheless I told Willie I would take it. We got all our papers sorted out – just needed the "A" licence changed into my name which was not a problem. I arranged to have the truck picked up in a couple of days, which gave me time to start a driver. So I had three trucks on the road.

One of my best pals Eric Miller had emigrated to Canada to work on a farm. He worked there for six months and never got paid so he could find no alternative but to join the Canadian merchant navy. When he came out, he was wondering what to do so I said

*Buy my Albion six-wheeler, I will change the "A" licence from the Albion and put one of my "B" licences on for you.*

*How much would you want for that?*

*£1,300.*

*I have not got that kind of money.*

*Get started and pay me back when you can.*

We worked a plan out so that he would pay me back. I got him started on the same job as me

We were running together and one day Eric and I had unloaded in Ellesmere Port and we phoned this clearing house in Liverpool for return loads to Scotland. The manager said go into United Glass St Helen's and they will load you for Scotland. So we went into United Glass, more or less a newly built glass-making factory. We loaded up for Dumbarton, Glasgow, with new empty whisky bottles for the J & B Scotch whisky bottlers. After we were all sheeted up and ready for home, we went to the canteen for our late lunch, a top-class lunch for one shilling and six pence. I said to Eric

*I am going in to see the transport manager and ask him if I can come in here direct to load back, are you coming in with me?*

*No we might get barred if the clearing house finds out.*

*Well that's a gamble I will have to take.*

I went into reception and asked to speak with the transport manager. I explained to him I was coming regularly down to the Lancashire area, could he load me back into Scotland. Without hesitation, he said

*We can, give us a ring the night before you are coming in, we will give you the details of where we will be loading you for. Just hang on five minutes, my secretary will take your details and give you our rates schedule.*

So good job done. I left the office and outside explained to Eric what had gone on, and suggested he go and get in direct, but he would not go in.

The haulage rates were very good and they paid me by the pallet, so the more pallets I got on the truck the more I earned. On the pallets were just empty new whisky bottles so they were not so heavy. This is where I would score with the artic because the trailer was 32 feet long.

So it was going well with United Glass St Helens. I was getting my loads back all the time. My planning was back in action. I would trade the Ford six-wheeler in to the County Garage for a New Ford D Series artic tractor unit with a Cummins engine. So I would have to order a 32-foot tandem trailer to pull behind the tractor. I had been eyeing trailers for a while and liked the Boden trailer, so I ordered a new trailer from the factory in Bolton in Lancashire. The new Ford tractor was soon ready for collection. I collected it from the County Garage Carlisle and headed down to Bolton for my new trailer. I'd also arranged to load from United Glass St Helens for Scotland.

Sometimes you get lucky. When planning to go into artics I knew that going into the woods was a no-go area. So I had got a contact to call Steins, the fire brick manufacturers, who had factories in and around the Glasgow and Edinburgh area. They made fire bricks for the foundries in the steel works. I called the transport manager, a John Benny, and I explained who I was and that I had an artic 20-tonner and a six-wheeler 14-tonner, and that one would be coming into his area each day. I was looking for loads down to Lancashire as I was hauling for United Glass St Helens. He said

*OK, always give me a call 4.30pm the day before you are coming and I will tell you what we have.*

*I am up tomorrow with the artic.*

*Come into Manuel works and get 20 ton for Irlam.*

*Okay, thanks.*

Less than 10 minutes on the phone, unbelievable, all fixed up. Now where is Steins Manuel works, and where is British Steel Irlam? I mapped out Steins, okay, Linlithgow very handy. Where is Irlam? Again, couldn't be more handy for St Helens – job's a good one.

I was up at the crack of dawn into my new artic on 1 March 1969. My mother had heard I was getting an artic truck and begged me not to get "one of those death traps". She asked my brother Tom to talk me out of it because she had heard that they jack knife and drivers get killed. Anyhow, I was heading up into Scotland, no problem with the traffic moving and mostly trucks at that time of morning. Then suddenly, approaching Beattock summit, we all came to a stop. I could see truck tail lights for miles ahead – it was black dark. I wondered what the problem was, got out of the cab and immediately fell on my backside. The road was like glass, all iced, all over.

We were stuck there for 45 minutes and it got me wondering if my mother was right. The gritter eventually came spreading grit all the way up the Beattock summit road. In another 10 minutes we were all moving completely clear; all the ice was gone. I arrived at my destination, United Glass store Cook Street, Glasgow, got the covers all off, pulled into the warehouse and had two pallet trucks unloading me, one at each side – job done. Now over to Steins, Manuel works, Linlithgow, to load 20 ton of fire bricks for Irlam, Manchester.

I pulled onto the weighbridge and then went into the office to meet the transport manager, John Benny. He took all my particulars and I had a nice conversation with him; It was the first time I had met him. He sent me to bay number six to load 20 ton for Irlam, so I backed into bay number six, the pallet driver rapidly put 10 pallets of bricks, two ton per pallet, onto my trailer, equals 20 ton. I pulled back onto the weighbridge, got my delivery tickets and sheeted up the load. I then went into the canteen and got my lunch – very good food, one shilling and three pence.

After lunch I drove back down home to Kirkbampton, very excited about the job. The next day I went down to Irlam Steel Works, Manchester, unloaded and then back into United Glass loaded for Scotland again. Meanwhile my other truck the Leyland six-wheeler 14-tonner was onto the same job – fire bricks and United Glass. While I was down unloading and re-loading in the Lancashire area, he would be in Scotland unloading the glassware and loading at Steins for the Lancashire area.

In June 1969 I went on a Sunday to Tait's of Haydon Bridge to test drive a Volvo F86 tractor unit. These trucks were just beginning to be imported from Sweden. Bobby Tait took me on the test run with a loaded 20 ton trailer on. I drove it up and down a few hills and I was very impressed. It was comfortable, with a very quiet turbocharged engine, eight speed synchromesh gear box, tilt cab. Not like most of the English trucks that had crash gear boxes. So I decided to trade my Leyland six wheeler in for a new Volvo F86 tractor unit.

On 1 July 1969 I started with the Volvo F86 and another new 32-foot Boden trailer, so now I had two artics doing the same job – United Glass from St Helens and Steins fire bricks from Scotland, a very regular job. The new artic Ford I got in March was giving me bits of trouble, so I was quite regularly into the County Garage for starter trouble and window wiper motors. It was under warranty which was a good job, and they were very quick at repairs I had no downtime. In September I was coming out of St Helens loaded with whisky bottles for Scotland in the Ford Truck, and suddenly there was an awful big rattle up in the engine and it came to full stop. Engine trouble.

I telephone Cummins engines who luckily were just up the road. They towed me into the workshop and on examination said I needed a new engine. The truck was still under warranty so that was fine and in a couple of days I was back on the road with the new engine fitted.

I was making good money. I had paid cash for the trailers but had one year's finance on each of the tractor units. So I started my planning again. I would apply to add three more vehicles to my "A" licence. This was very rare because the big companies had a monopoly and they did not want an upstart like me to spoil that.

I applied to the transport authorities and they put it into the Applications and Decisions circular that was sent to all hauliers in the UK. I knew I would have plenty of objections so I was ready loaded up with ammunition. There were no solicitors in Carlisle that knew anything about applying for "A" licences. It was more or less unheard of. I had supporting letters from Steins fire brick manufacturers and also from United Glass.

The objections came in from Robson's, who had about 200 trucks, from Jack Watt who had 150, British Road Services, who had hundreds, and a small local haulier down the road Pearson Brothers, with about seven trucks. I spoke with my solicitor, a Bill McKenna, about going to the traffic courts. He said

*I know nothing about "A" licences.*

*Don't worry I know the ropes, I just need you to go with me and do the talking to the judge, it looks better if you are with me.*

The letter arrived from the licensing department about a court hearing in Penrith Courts, for the Application from Ian Geoffrey Bell to acquire three additional "A" licences, the application to be heard by the Honourable Northern Area Licensing Judge. So Bill McKenna and I went into the court at Penrith. First on the stand was Robson's.

*Judge: What is your objection to Mr Bell's licence?*

*We have enough trucks in the UK.*

*Judge: Mr Bell what do you say to this?*

*Well your honour you have the letters in front of you from United Glass and Steins saying they need more trucks and are having difficultly getting extra trucks, and also your honour United Glass have just recently started using Robson's and they can not supply enough trucks.*

*Judge: Mr Robson, is this correct what Mr Bell is saying?*

*Yes recently United Glass have been asking for trucks, we have only just started to work for them.*

*Judge: Then why are you objecting?*

*Well we always object to newcomers.*

*Judge: Sit down Mr Robson and thanks.*

*Next came Mr Watt.*

*Judge: Yes Mr Watt what is your objection?*

*There is enough trucks around without getting more licences.*

*Judge: Do you do work for Steins or United Glass?*

*No Sir we do not.*

*Judge: OK Mr Watt that will be all.*
*Next up British Road Services.*
*Judge: Yes what is your objection?*
*Well we object to all new applications, there is enough trucks to cater for all transport needs.*
*Judge: Do you haul for United Glass or Steins?*
*No Sir.*
*Judge: Very well thanks, you may sit down.*
*Next Mr Pearson.*
*Judge: Why are you objecting Mr Pearson?*
*There is plenty of cattle trucks around, we don't want any more.*
*Judge: But Mr Pearson, Mr Bell is not going to haul cattle or sheep.*
*Well there is enough cattle trucks about.*
*Judge: He is not going to carry cattle or sheep, do you do work for United Glass or Steins?*
*No we only carry cattle and sheep.*
*Judge: Mr Pearson thanks and please sit down.*
*Judge: Mr Bell is granted his three additional "A" licences court now adjourned.*

I was over the moon with my achievement. Now more planning to be done.

The Ford artic was still giving trouble with starter motors and window wiper motors, but was still under warranty. In February 1970 coming down from Scotland the engine was getting noisy and then there was a big loud bang and the engine stopped – trouble. I phoned the County Garage Carlisle and they and towed it in; next day another new engine was required. In a couple of days a new engine was fitted and I was back on the road still under warranty. In July the same happened again. This time, no more engines. I got another new Volvo F86 tractor unit. I visited the foreman at Robson's transport who ran a lot of Ford trucks and I sold it to them for £350.

In August 1970 I started with the new Volvo and was very pleased. It was going very good with United Glass and Steins, regular work with no problems. Over the next couple of years I added two more Volvo F86 tractor units and updated the four trailers to Crane Fruehauf 38 footers from 32 footers – the law had changed. We could now get another four pallets on from United Glass, getting more revenue as we were paid by the pallet. My idea was now with the trailers paid for and the Volvo units on one year's HP, I would not get number five truck until I could pay cash.

Within a very short time the Volvo units were almost paid for. Tait's business was haulage with tipper trucks but they had seen an opening to get the franchise to sell and service these Volvo trucks. Tait's were three brothers Bob, Bill and Dougie, very nice people and first class at servicing and spares. They said sales were getting very good and if I was expanding I should order well ahead. I took the bull by the horns and ordered four trucks per year. With hindsight, I had done the best thing. Within a very short time there was an 18-month waiting list.

Within a few months my last Volvo unit would be all clear of HP, so my next Volvo unit was on its way. The law had changed again and the trailer length was now extended to 40 foot. I changed the four trailers I had and got five new 40 foot Dennison trailers from Northern Ireland and paid cash for them. I got these with container locks fitted. The movement of goods was changing fast from loading goods from docks, to goods in containers. The United Glass and Steins job was very good but I was getting prepared for other things. Having five Volvo trucks on now and every-thing paid for and on good jobs, the money was coming in very nicely.

I had five drivers on now, while I was doing the office work from home and doing the odd night runs to St Helens for a changeover. I was parking the trucks at Kingstown beside my father-in-law's garage, so I was looking for my own yard and garage with an office. It was very difficult to find a yard, because the council in those days did not want truck depots on Kingstown Trading Estate. I found a site at Willowholme Industrial Estate which was leased from the Carlisle City to Ringtons Tea, so I got a lease from Ringtons Tea. The site was bare land so I applied for planning permission for a new garage, 40 foot by 60 foot, which came through with no problems. Crendon Concrete put the structure up for me and I paid cash. George Graham, a contractor next door to my site, finished all the building work on it for me.

*My wife Lorraine and daughter Angela in Mother and Child at Butlins entertaining. After the theatre there were the well-decorated showbars, good entertainment and dancing every night.*

I was doing quite well and tried to take the family on one or two weeks holiday each year, normally to Butlins. It was good fun with plenty to do and good entertainment. Lorraine did not like the accommodation, but we only had to sleep in the rooms because we were out all day and all meals where served in the restaurant. Through the day there were all kinds of competitions and sports going on, and after dinner there was the theatre, always very good.

George Graham was very slow at finishing the garage and it took him much longer than I expected; but this helped me because he was asking for the money as he went along in dribs and drabs, so when he did eventually finish the job, I was all paid up, no borrowings.

The garage turned out well, with a 40-foot inspection pit, 60-foot flat bay, my small office, small stores and two small toilets, all inside the garage. I bought a second-hand 5,000 gallon diesel tank so I was all set up.

We moved into the new garage and the office. I now had six Volvo tractor units and I needed a HGV fitter to service the trucks and do repairs. For many years I had got to know one of the County Garage foreman fitters very well and I'd asked him one day if I were to get a garage, would he consider coming to work for me, and he'd said he would. So I went to see him and wondered if he was still in the same frame of mind to come and work for me, as he was working for a well established firm.

This fitter was called Fred Titterington, excellent fitter and we got very well over the years.

Hi Fred how are you, I have got the new garage finished and ready to roll are you still interested in coming to work for me?

Let's meet tomorrow at your garage, have a look around and we can talk about it there.

So Fred came round, was very impressed with the garage and said

*Your trucks are all very new vehicles and will not need many repairs, mostly just routine servicing. I could do your trucks and could bring a lot of my customers here and do there repairs and servicing.*

So we agreed that I would pay him so much each week to do my work and any money he brought in we would halve. I had bought all the equipment we needed for the garage so it was well equipped. Over the years with all these old trucks I had owned, I was getting very handy at repairs and servicing and if needed still did quite a bit of fitting. When I had got into the new garage I sprayed all the new trucks myself, and any fitter that came to work for me I would show them how to do paint spraying. I started spraying with no training. Just like everything else I was doing, I was self-taught. You soon learn. The first new Volvo tractor unit I sprayed, I went to the local factors Thomson and Browns, spoke to the storeman

*Hi, I need a spray gun and enough carnation red paint and thinners to spray a tractor unit.*

He gave me the goods.

*How much thinners do I mix with the paint?*

*Fifty-fifty.*

I was on my way. I used to paint the old wagons by hand and the carnation paint was very good for hand painting.

So back to the garage on a Saturday afternoon when all the workers had gone home, I had a new truck all masked up ready for spraying, new spray gun unwrapped, mixing paint and thinners fifty-fifty. Off I go – back and forward, nice strokes like I had watched the spray painters do many times before. Well, the paint is running off down the side of the truck doors. So then I was thinking this advice I had been given was totally wrong. Too much thinners. So fast thinking had to be done. What next? I thought if I keep on spraying and watch carefully then the surplus paint would run down onto the floor. Surprise surprise, it did actually, turn out to be a very good job. I would spray the new trucks on Sundays, or early morning before 9am.

The government changed all the regulations for HGV and all the "A" and "B" licences were abandoned; every truck owner with these licenses was issued with an operator's licence, could operate as many trucks as he wanted. The rules were very strict you had to prove your maintenance records and if you hadn't got your own garage, the ministry of transport needed to know who did your maintenance. They would come around regularly to check your records; you also had to show you had capital to maintain the vehicles.

With the six Volvo artics on the road, I bought an old Leyland Comet tractor unit from Johnston's of Gilcrux, West Cumbria. It was old and needed a bit of tidying up and painted in my colours. We got it all tided up in my garage. I wanted it in United Glass St Helens for loading trailers with; it was not needed to go on the road, only in the factory. I had bought two more new Dennison trailers to leave at St Helens. I employed a driver down at St Helens to load trailers in the factory. Some of my trucks that had unloaded further down the country than Lancashire, maybe Birmingham, would come back into United Glass, drop their empty trailer and pick a ready-loaded one up and get back home to Carlisle.

But at night there would always be two of my loaded trailers sitting loaded for Scotland. I had one regular night driver but also many part-time night drivers. Two trailers loaded with fire bricks would go down to St Helens, drop their trailers off, pick the loaded ones up that were loaded for Scotland and back to Carlisle. The next day the first man unloaded, say in Irlam Lancashire, and would then drop his trailer into United Glass, pick up a loaded trailer with fire bricks – one that was dropped off there the night before – and take it to the destination to unload. When unloaded, he would drop that empty trailer into United Glass, pick up the other loaded trailer with fire bricks on and unload that one; then back into United Glass, drop it off, pick up a ready-loaded one for Scotland and back home to Carlisle.

Everything was going very well for me. I now had 10 Volvo trucks and 14 40-foot trailers. I was now hauling for quite a lot of companies, I tried to pick jobs that were quick turnarounds and could tip and load 24 hours a day and keep the trucks earning. I had plenty of night drivers to call on. Being one of the first hauliers having 40-foot trailers with container locks on, I was doing a lot of work for container shipping companies. Overnight they changed from 30- foot containers to 40-foots when the new regulations came in and caused a shortage of 40-foot trailers.

I did a lot for Seatrain, who were a big shipping company which moved from Felixstowe Port to Greenock Port where we could tip and load 24 hours a day.

Also I did a lot for Sealand Container shipping, who were based in Liverpool docks and used to have all their containers on their own chassis. They would give me something like 10 of these units at weekends to take from Liverpool to Grangemouth. The job was to take an empty tractor unit from Carlisle down to Liverpool, pick their trailer up with an empty container on, drop it into their Grangemouth depot and back to Carlisle with the empty unit. One man could do the round trip so if I had to move 10 over the weekend, I would cover all those by doing night shifts. One unit could do two round trips per 24 hours.

These Sealand containers were tanker containers for carrying bulk liquid goods, which would come from the USA into Liverpool with a certain bulk liquid, then needed to go to Grangemouth to their special washing facility to get washed out before loading bulk Scotch whisky back for the USA.

Fred my fitter was getting more of his work coming into the garage and with me getting more trucks, it was becoming unworkable. We made an agreement that Fred would get his own garage and take all his customers. I did not want to do outside repair work because I wanted to give my trucks first priority. I started a new fitter Jimmy Gibson. I knew Jimmy from when he used to go into Moorhouse pub with his mate and we would all share a laugh together. He was a first-class fitter and we got on well together.

I had got a new 164 Volvo car and my wife got my other one, so I gave Jimmy, my wife's old one to use for breakdowns and as a runabout for parts, and for his own use. In 1972 I bought a Crane Fruehauf bulk tipper trailer and added another Volvo tractor unit. I started carrying bulk lime for Harrison's lime works Shap, to their store in Wigtown, Scotland; it could do two trips a day with a night driver going up at night.

I was pleased that everything was going to plan. The plan I made back when I started was that I would only buy number five truck when I had the cash, and I was still using this philosophy: pay cash or don't buy. So 11 trucks and cash in the bank I was still on the look out.

Carr's Agricultural at Silloth were giving me loads for my tipper back from Glasgow to their feed mill in Silloth, and became regular, Carr's were also needing a bulk trailer to bring wheat feed from Newcastle to Silloth so I ordered a specially built bulk trailer from Richardson Brothers, Stoke on Trent. I had the four trucks a year ordered with Tait's, so when the new bulk trailer was ready from Richardson's, this was number 12 truck on the road.

Tait's now had a Volvo franchise in Carlisle which was very handy for good spares and a good garage facility; the Volvo trucks had a 12 months full warranty so any warranty work was done there in rapid time. I found with running the Volvos I had little or no lost working time.

*My first tipper trailer Crane Fruehauf 32 cubic yards.*

\* \* \*

Within a couple of years I had five tipper trailers, working a lot for Carr's of Silloth and other jobs I had picked up. Things were going very well, all paid for and cash in the bank. So I had 15 Volvo trucks working and I was thinking "my drivers are driving around with expensive equipment, so why have I not got a nice vehicle to drive?" I had no expensive hobbies, I was always working, no office staff; my wife would type the bills every month end from my ledger that I recorded and priced every day, and added up at the month end. Quite a lot of companies I worked for were self-billing so that was very handy and easy.

So a Rolls Royce it was! I looked all around far and wide to get a new one but it was not possible; there was an 18-month waiting list. So I found one at Reg Vardy's in Newcastle, 11 months old. I thought "what an achievement I have made it from just a few years ago working on a farm for £2, 7 shillings and 6 pence a week to a Rolls Royce."

We had no garage at our bungalow, My uncle and auntie ran the pub at Little Bampton and were retiring and he had a lot of hens and hen houses. He was an immaculate man and the hen houses were creosoted every year. One was a very large hen house and I said to my uncle David:

*What are you going to do with the big hen house?*
*Do you want it?*
*Yes.*
*Well come and take it.*
*How much do I owe you?*
*Nothing, just taking it away will be a big help.*

So with a couple of my drivers on a Saturday afternoon we picked it up and dropped it off in our bungalow back garden at Kirkbampton.

When I got the business built up and stopped driving on full-time basis, I would often go down to the pub at Moorhouse for the last hour for a couple of pints with the lads, including my pal Peter Short. We called him Shorty but he wasn't short, rather about 6 feet tall and about 25 stone and could drink about 15 pints a night. We were in there one week after I had brought the hen house back home and Willie was in, who was a joiner, and I said

Willie, could you do me a job.?

*Yeah, what is it?*

*Well I have a hen house to erect in the back garden.*

Shorty said

*You can't keep hens in your back garden.*

*It's not for hens.*

*Well what are you going to do with a hen house?*

*To put the Rolls Royce in.*

Well, laughter all round the pub.

I got Willie persuaded to come and erect the hen house and fit the end with double doors so I could drive in. We put an extra layer of strong timber where the wheels would travel – job done and tested, no problem. It was a very tidy garage.

Jimmy Gibson my fitter moved on to work for himself so I started a new fitter Chris Lewis, a top-class man from Volvo. I gave him Lorraine's Volvo car for breakdowns, collecting parts and for his own use. My garage was absolutely spotless, no oil on the floor and all tools had their place. We needed lots of different tools to complete any job that was needed to be done on the Volvo. There was no job we could not do- full gearbox rebuild, engine rebuild, rear axle rebuild, turbo rebuild. Volvo said it is not possible to repair turbos. Was it not? Well we did.

All going well, 15 trucks out working, all paid for, no debt and money in the bank.

# 6: New homes on the horizon

Saturday morning was always a very busy day with trucks all making their way back and needing little jobs done. All trailers got their brakes adjusted every Saturday. Also we had the most up to date hot water steam cleaner, and a young lad from the village would come with me to steam clean all the tractors and trailers every Saturday. One Saturday morning Derek Leslie popped in to see me. He was a builder that had a partner Tom Beck and they had built a lot of houses.

*Hi Derek, how are you what can I do for you?*

*I have come to sell you a house.*

*No, I don't want to live on a housing estate, and any how this is our busy day, can you come back on Monday.*

*No, it is not on a housing estate it is my house.*

*Oh, well come in , why are you selling your new house? It is magnificent.*

*Well, I am having trouble with my partner and my money has stopped coming in.*

I explained to him I had bought a small farm at Moorhouse with 60 acres of land. The farm buildings and house were all dilapidated, so I had planning to demolish the old buildings, build a new house and keep the 20-acre field beside it, then sell the other 40 acres off. Derek said to come and have a look the next day, Sunday, and see what I thought. I knew the house because I gave Derek some soil when I was clearing my site to build the new garage; he needed some filler. So I was up at the house a few times while he was building it; it was a very fine house.

My wife and I went up on the Sunday and had a look

around, and it was what we wanted, very nice. We settled on a price £30,000.

A couple of weeks previously I had been into see my solicitor Bill McKenna. He had got me one or two little investments over the past couple of years. I said

*Bill have you any investments of interest at the moment? I have enough trucks now I need something else.*

*Well, the only thing I have been looking at is this half built Truck Stop at Kingstown it is in liquidation and they are looking for a buyer, why don't you have a look at it.*

So I did go up and have a look around. It was half-built with no roof on, no windows. But it was a very big place, 12 acres in total – a 10-acre truck park, two acres for hotel and fuelling area. It was all fitted out with eight fuel pumps. Being in the truck business I said that I thought it would work.

Anyhow we agreed to buy the house and get the deposit paid. Then I told Derek about this truck stop half-built at Kingstown and, being a builder, I thought he would be a good partner for me. He said it looked like a good idea and he would have a look at it the next day with me. So we looked around the place together and both agreed it should work. We found out Armstrong Watson the accountants had it for sale for the liquidator at the office in Penrith. I made an appointment to see them the next day in Penrith at 9am. We arrived 9am sharp, they gave us a few details. The price was £35,000. From my enquiries around, it had been standing empty for two years and there had been over 55 people looking at the property but no buyers. Everyone said it would not work. We offered £30,000 and the accountant said to come back in one hour. We had a coffee around the corner and then back into his office. "Sorry, no confirmation yet, come back in at 11 am." We went back around to the cafe for tea and scones. Back at 12pm but there was still no more news about our offer.

"Come back at 2.30pm." We had lunch, more tea, roast beef on the menu, very good, read the daily paper front to back three times over. Back in the office at 2.30pm but no news. The accountant told us the hold-up was because one of the money lenders could not be contacted to give the go-ahead. I said "Well if we don't get a deal today, I will not be here tomorrow." He said to come back in at 5pm and it was good news: "I have permission to sell at £30,000 but you have to pay £5,000 within a week" "Okay."

Part of my idea to go for the Truck Stop was that I badly needed a larger depot for my trucks. I had been looking around but with no success. I signed a few papers stipulating that I needed planning permission from the council to erect a garage and run my transport business from there, otherwise the deal would be off and I would get my deposit back, Derek did not sign anything.

So back to Carlisle I asked Derek give me his cheque before the weekend and I would drop it in at Armstrong and Watson's office in Carlisle. The weekend came, no Derek and no cheque, I phoned Derek

*Where is your cheque.*

*I cannot get the money released from the company at the moment.*

*I will have to go and pay the deposit.*

So I went into Armstrong Watson's on the Monday and paid them. I knew quite a few of the partners there because they were doing my weekly PAYE for my drivers on their new computer system. So I asked them if we could start doing work on the building and they said "yes" and put the permission on paper and we both signed.

Then next day we had a meeting with Carlisle's Town Mayor and another of my solicitors from Burnett's, Donald Livingston. The Truck Stop was being built on council lease-hold property with a 99-year lease. So we were negotiating the lease and I requested a four-year rent-free lease to give us time to get the thing going. I told the Mayor I would need planning permission to build a garage and office to be on hand to run both businesses from there. He agreed on that. We asked permission to start doing the work on the place and he granted us that without a problem. But he needed time to think about the ground rent. I could see the Mayor had taken a liking to me and I got on very well with him. The council had been stuck with this site for five or six years and needed the Truck Stop open. The big problem in Carlisle was all the trucks at night had parked right in the centre of Carlisle on the Sands centre and were using the vast number of bed and breakfast places in town. There would be at least a 100 trucks per night on that park. The council were under pressure to move them to the Truck Stop, but it had lapsed into liquidation, and the council needed the Sands site for a new leisure centre.

* * *

The company that started building the Truck Stop was called Vanguard Inter Stop Ltd. At that time the government were going to subsidise these Truck Stops as they knew truck drivers were having to put up with shabby overnight stop accommodation. But after this company had started building work, the government decided to withdraw the subsidy, so the company stopped and went into liquidation.

We decided to start a week on Monday to get the roof put on so I said to Derek

*This is where you come in you are the builder get the men to start on Monday.*

Come Friday Derek had no men lined up, and I was not impressed. So over the weekend I lined up some lads who had done some work for me building the new garage and had built me an extension onto our bungalow, all self-employed good lads. So I said to Derek

*The lads will meet you at 8am on the site at the Truck Stop, so you can tell them what to do.*

*OK, I will be there.*

Monday Morning the lads phoned me at 9am

*Geoff, where is Derek?*

I called Derek's house and his wife answered the phone/

*Doreen where is Derek?*

*Oh he is not well.*

Probably been on the drink.

I went up to the lads and we ordered the roofing material and they got a start, Derek arrived in the afternoon and within a few days the roof was watertight and finished. The next job we were to plaster some panels in the room that was going to be the bar area; it was a big room and had about 10 large glass panels going from floor to a very high ceiling, and in between each panel was about six foot of bare bricks. So I had arranged for a lad Willie who was a plasterer and his gang to come and do this job on Saturday. I had already shown Willie the job and told him to plaster it in old English design. I had already had the plaster delivered, and told Derek to be there at 8am to see the lads. I had the trucks to organise so I got up to see Willie about 12 midday; they had just finished the job and I said that it looked top class and it was. I always paid the men when they had finished the job. Up to now I had paid for everything and Derek had paid nothing out.

Derek called me up late afternoon on Saturday and said

*I have just been up to the Truck Stop and Willie has put the plaster on wrong side up.*

*What do you mean? I think it is perfect.*

*The old English curves are the wrong way up.*

*I don't know, you are the builder, you should have been there. Listen we need to talk can I come over to your house tomorrow*

*about 2pm and have a talk with you and your wife?*

*Yes no problem.*

I had heard on the grapevine that Derek's problem with his building company's partner, was that Derek was on the drink. I had only learned this over the past week or so. I made some enquiries. Jimmy Gibson, my ex fitter, was the brother of the foreman of Derek's building firm Tommy Gibson. Jimmy knew the story and it was correct. Derek was on the drink and was being shunted out of the building company

I arrived at Derek's house at 2pm and had my wife Lorraine with me. Derek's wife was a nice woman and she made tea and biscuits for us. I got onto that very delicate subject of drink and of course both denied it. We left with me thinking this arrangement would not work for me with Derek hanging on. He had been no help up to then, even holding me back, and not yet paid a penny out, not even paid me back his half of the deposit.

I went home, did some thinking, and talking with my wife. The plan became clear. I would phone Derek and tell him I could not work with him and he could take the place on himself or I would take it on. So that was my decision. I phoned him and said what I wanted to do. He said

*Okay I will come back to you.*

Within a couple of hours I got a call from Dougle Kyle, Derek's accountant. I knew Dougle, who said

*Derek cannot take the job on he has too many problems with his building firm so you go ahead and the best of luck.*

So that was all sorted out my head was already clearing.

\* \* \*

I started some self-employed men I had known for some time – all good lads , experienced and reliable. I told them I would take them on to complete the job and I expected it to be ready for opening in one year and would pay them every week. There were six of them. Brian Graham was a joiner and his mate was Bass. George Rice was an electrician and his mate was Jacky. They were all good workers; none of this 9 till 5 thing. It was daylight until dark. I also had a good plumber, John Bell and his son from Brampton.

The Truck Stop had three floors, second and third floors with 20 bedrooms, ground floor with 20 bedrooms, plus all the facility areas, cafeteria, kitchen, large bar area for 200 people, small shop, two offices, television room, shower room, ladies and gents toilet, games room. It also had its own lighting plant in case of electricity breakdowns.

I was in the Civic Centre one day at a meeting with the council planning and the Mayor was always there, when one of the chaps said

*You know Laing's have all the windows and doors for the Truck Stop stored away.*

*Okay I will get onto them, thanks for that.*

The council were bending over backwards to help me.

Laing's were a very large construction firm based in Dalston Road , Carlisle, I went up to the offices and met with a Mr Robinson who was a very nice chap and we seemed to hit it off straightaway. I said

*I have bought the Truck Stop and they tell me you have all the windows and doors for the building.*

*We have.*

*Well, how little will you take? I have taken on a massive job here for a small individual, so be kind to me.*

*£12,000 and we will be losing money.*

*Wow, too much for me. I am only opening the first floor so it will be cheaper for me to buy them elsewhere.*

*Look I will come down to £10,000.*

*No, too much for me, I will offer you £8,000.*

*Go on then, it's a deal.*

Then I had the cheek to ask if I could pay a thousand a month He said he would sort that. I paid him a cheque for the first £1,000 and on the way out I said

*Um, would you be able to deliver them to the Truck Stop?*

Well we had to laugh.

*You are in the haulage business and you are asking me to deliver?*

*Well, my trucks are all very big and could be difficult getting into your storage sheds at Kingmoor.*

*Okay then we will do that.*

They delivered a few days later and I could not believe how many there were. They filled what was going to be the cafeteria, stacked up high to the ceiling. The windows were all aluminium and the doors were all solid, lovely grained wood with narrow panels of fire glass fitted.

My first plan was to fit all the windows on all floors to keep the weather out. This was the joiners' job. George and his mate would go about putting the electricity in; when he started we had no electric, I had applied to the electricity board to connect, but up to now it had not arrived. So George had started on the job and I said to him

*We have no electric yet.*

*No problem.*

Within half an hour we had electric.

*George, how did you do that?*

He had wired into the lamp post. George served his time at the electric board so he had contacts.

I would go up from my office in the garage every day at lunchtime – my lunch was a sandwich whilst on the move. I had my 15 trucks to look after and I had the men to keep busy, to see they all had what they needed, electrical material, joinery material, and plumbing material.

We had no plans to go by so we would all discuss together what material would be best for each individual job. Such as, what size of gas boiler for the water heater in the kitchen area? What size for the surrounding areas being the bar, cafeteria, and games room? We all put in our penny's worth, and when we had come to the decision, I made my list.

I got all the plumbing material from Yorkshire Heating Supplies. The manager was Jacky Atherton, who I had known for many years and he was good to deal with. He got everything I asked for. I bought everything myself that went into that project. When we were ready to lay the first floor with finished concrete it was time to call Willie back. Willie worked full time for Laing's and was a top-class builder who could do anything. For this job he would bring a gang of lads on a Saturday morning. He would come and look what I wanted and tell me how much concrete we needed. This was a big job to do all the ground floors, so he would do one on Saturday and finish off the next weekend. The ready-mixed concrete plant was next door to my garage at Willowholme so I knew all the workers well because they delivered the concrete to my garage when I built it. I ordered the ready mixed concrete to be delivered at 8am Saturday morning. I went up at 7.45am and Willie was already there with his gang of lads, with barrows, shovels, trowels. This flooring had to be perfect to lay fitted carpets on. The ready-mixed truck arrived on the dot of 8am. Willie got to work I returned to the garage to organise the trucks. I returned at 12 midday, all done. This first half flooring was the bottom bedroom block. It was quite a big job because there were 20 bedrooms and quite a long corridor. Willie always wanted to be finished at 12 noon. I knew this, so I was always there on time.

*Willie what do I owe you?*
*He told me and I paid him.*
*So Okay for next Saturday?*
*Yes.*
He then reminded me how many square yards of

concrete we needed to finish all the rest of the floors on the bottom floor, it was a very large area. The next Saturday morning all bottom floors were finished, excellent job.

I paid all my workers every week and paid my suppliers when the invoices arrived, which saved me filing all the invoices until the statements arrived and I could remember more easily what I had bought and the price rather than waiting a few weeks for the statements to come. For example, If I had a tyre rep coming in who said "we have a good offer on Michelin tyres this week", I had a large desk day diary and I would immediately put his quoted price in my diary. It was the same with all the reps. Many times I would get the goods delivered but when the invoice came, it was not the price the rep had quoted, so I would be on the phone explaining this and asking them to either change the invoice or pick the goods up.

I had now put my plans in for planning permission to build a new garage at the Truck Stop. It did not take long to get the permission. I knew what I wanted, I had put it all on the plan. It was a larger garage than the last one, with two nice sized offices and a drivers' tea room, a room for filing cabinets for the trucks and trailer maintenance sheets, two 50-foot inspection pits and a flat area for a complete tractor and trailer, a large store at the back for spares and tyres.

George Rice my electrician asked

*What kind of garage were you thinking of building?*

*A new steel construction one.*

*My friend I do work for at Kingstown Engineering is taking buildings down at Doves.*

*Yes, I have looked at them but they are too low to get loaded trucks in.*

*He can make it any height you want. Have a word with him and see what you think.*

I did meet with Kingstown Engineering and he was on

the ball. I told him what I wanted and he said that it was no problem and he could make it the height I wanted. I gave him my plans and he said he would work me a price out.

The way I was doing it was double-skinned roof, then come down the side of the building double-skinned and leave eight-foot clear from the ground and this area would be all bricked around. Double-skinned means you put double sheets of cladding with material in-between, which keeps the heat in and stops it dripping in the cold weather.

All the relevant paperwork was now done on the buying of the Truck Stop. I paid the balance of £25,000 – all my own cash and no borrowings.

I was starting to work on the kitchen and a chap called to see me. He said

*I am from a kitchen firm and have all the plans for this kitchen.*
*Well you can give them to me.*
*No we will fit the kitchen for you.*
*What is the price?*
*£17.000.*
*It is almost the price I paid for the place.*
*I can't move on that price.*
*Good day to you.*

The first thing the kitchen needed was a big extraction hood and I knew the very fellow that would make it for me. It was Ivor McKenzie, an engineer but who also had a few car franchises in Carlisle and also a big garage next to my garage at Willowholme with the Commer truck franchise. His biggest interest was engineering and he had a workshop at the Stripes, Cumwhinton. I called him and he came out and measured up for it, said he would make it in aluminium, no problem, knew exactly what I wanted. It arrived two weeks later- what a piece of work, very large. I paid him and my lads fitted it. George got a big second-hand suction fan to fit in the kitchen hood,

Then I needed a cooking range, a stainless steel double sink with double drainer, a big oven range, also a big Bamboree, all needed to be gas. In town there was a big company called Pioneer which was a family firm owned by Mr Jenkins. His son and daughter were also coming into the business. They had restaurants all over town and used to make most of their own equipment. My mother knew them well because she used to do work for them. They had a butchery business and delivered to all the restaurants and hotels around Cumbria. I was told by one of his workers that they had a large store in Cumwhinton with all kinds of used kitchen equipment, so I went to see Mr Jenkins and I told him what I was looking for. He said to get in touch with his foreman at Vallum House and he would show me what they had in the store. Vallum House was a restaurant and small hotel owned by Mr Jenkins and we used to go there sometimes with the Volvo people.

I got in touch with his foreman and we arranged to meet at the store the next day at 12.30. He took me in the store and what a surprise, there was everything. He asked what I needed I told him and he had everything except the Bamboree. I said to Mr Jenkins

*What do I owe you?*

*£25 per article*

Well I was over the moon and paid him. I said

*Can we collect these things tomorrow?*

*Yes, here is my phone number call me when you want to come and collect.*

That was an excellent deal.

We collected all the kitchen equipment and my lads put it all in position. The plumber plumbed in all the gas and water supply. Next I needed Ivor back to measure up for the stainless steel worktops around the kitchen. Within a couple of weeks we had the worktops back from Ivor all paid and fitted. What a fabulous job – stainless steel all round and a big range in the centre that you could walk around. All I needed now was a big Bamboree to put in the serving area. I found a man that sold second-hand kitchen equipment and he had the very thing I wanted for £90. So the total for the kitchen was a long way from the £17,000 I was quoted by the kitchen firm.

* * *

In December 1976 we moved into our house at Dalston and got the bungalow sold for £20,000. The new house had cost £30,000 so it had only cost £10,000 to change and all paid for. The bungalow was very nice but this was in a different league. It was new, had five bedrooms, big kitchen, big living room, spare living room, dining room, play room, double garage, and a large garden with greenhouse. So after the Christmas holidays in January 1977 our children Angela 10 and Chris nine would be going to a new school in Dalston. They did not like the idea of going to Dalston as all their friends were at Kirkbampton as they were born there. But they got started at the new school and very soon settled in.

All my friends and my drivers except one said I had done very well with the haulage business but this Truck Stop would be my big downfall. The one exception was Alan Jones, one of my drivers. Even the Mayor one day had whispered to my solicitor, Donald Livingston, that he was very unsure if it would work. But it was very funny that I had no doubts whatsoever. I had the experience of staying in some of these overnight places for drivers all over the UK and we called them dumps. They had five and six drivers to a room and no baths or showers, one toilet for a dozen people. So how could I go wrong? I was going to provide five-star treatment for drivers. We all needed it, and not before time.

John Bell and his son were busy in the bedroom area fitting the 20 bedrooms with baths and showers in the baths. The bedrooms were made up of singles and doubles, all with bathrooms. Central heating was in every room and we had a small room where we fitted the gas heating system. We decided to fit two small gas burners rather than one, so that if one broke down the other would manage.

In the main cafeteria, bar, games, and kitchen area, we had a separate boiler house with two gas boilers to operate the hot water and heating system.

I had to think about the fire regulations and George the electrician was well geared up for this; we had a small room in the reception area and he was planning on building his own system.

The fire officer had been to see me and I introduced him to George, and I said to him that he should tell George anything that had to be done and he would do it. So when I went to court for my drinks' licence, and singing and dancing licences I didn't want any objections. We had plans of what the fire officer had requested and were sticking to that.

All was going to plan but time was ticking on. We got started erecting the new garage on the Truck Stop site. I was kept busy keeping the trucks going, with 15 trucks and six night drivers so the money was coming in. I was doing all the office work myself and buying all the material for building the Truck Stop. Funny, it was no problem for me. I knew what I wanted to do, and I knew how it should be done. I had no-one to answer to or argue with me. I was going my own way. Some businessmen I knew were going to their accountants or bank managers for advice. What would accountants or bank managers do for me? They didn't know anything about Truck Stops. What could they do for me in the transport business? When I started and went for a loan, they threw me out of the door. A bank manager could not build up a transport business like me so how could they advise people?

My accountant then was a Mr Nixon, a real gentleman, but all he was doing was my tax at the year end. On the other hand, he did get me into some good pension schemes that did very well. Also he was an agent for General Accident and I had all my trucks and property insured with them. But I would have been better with a broker because I had to fill in all my own claims myself.

This was always a problem when credit squeezes came and the banks closed in on their clients and put many people out of business. In many cases it was the fault of the accountants. The clients would go to the banks for a loan to buy property or new machinery and the bank would say "no, we need proper projection figures of your business for the next two years". So the accountant would concoct a good profitable balance sheet for the next two years so the client would return to the bank and the bank manager would like what he was reading and give the loan. The accountant was not a businessman, nor was the bank manager, I would say 95% of them have never run a business. So when things go wrong and the bank wants its money back, you have no comeback on your accountant because the contract you signed when he started working for you stipulated that any work he is not responsible for.

I had agreed a price with Kingstown Engineering to erect the shell for the new garage and they were well on the way with this. I had arranged with the two lads that did quite a lot of work for me at the other garage, to do all the brick work around this garage when the shell was completed.

Brian and Bass the joiners were starting to build the bar and it was going to be a very long bar. Brian said to me

*How do you want this bar made?*

We had no plans so I said

*Well just as you think.*

*Well Bass will know he has stood propping bars up most of his life.*

We all laughed and I said

*We will rely on Bass.*

When they had finished the bar it was spot on. It was a big job with shelves under the bar. Then the back wall was all boarded for the optics, with a worktop along there with shelves underneath. I was doing quite a lot of haulage work from a firm called Krono Span, who had a big factory at Chirk in Lancashire. They made melamine boarding for kitchens and all kinds of furniture. I had got a good deal with them to get seconds grade, which meant that one side was imperfect but the other side was perfect. I got about 30 tons of this. The bar was all built with this melamine, also one wall in every bedroom was boarded where the bed ends would be. It went all around the cafeteria. We used it everywhere and it looked very well.

Next for Brian and Bass was making the stage in the bar area, which was a large room which I was going to use to put bands on and other acts. George had a hand in this to put some spotlights on the stage. It all worked out fine.

I applied for my licences for drinks, singing and dancing and I was called to the courts to go through the process and had no trouble with the fire officer. We were not ready to open yet but when we were ready, we would give the authorities a few weeks' notice and the special licensing committee would come and inspect everything to make sure all was up to specification.

My wife and I chose all the ready-made curtains, chairs, bedspreads, pillows, and settled on charcoal hale-cord fitted carpets throughout. I ordered all the carpet from Franky Bowman and got carpet-fitters in at the weekend to fit it.

I spoke to the Pioneer foreman and asked him where he got his restaurant tables from as they were very strong. He said they made them themselves and to come up and he'd show me. So off I went to his workshop and he showed me, easy. I needed what he called an "andy angle" to assemble the tables. He would send the rep around to see me and the rep came in on the Monday and he showed me what I needed to make lots of tables. He ordered the parts for me and I paid him and he said the delivery would take just over a week. The carpets were all fitted, looked spot on, good job done.

I ordered the beds from the blind shop in Carlisle and they were all made on time and delivered. I was kept busy for a couple of Sundays hanging all the curtains. We also had a local TV shop in town deliver all the televisions for the bedrooms. George the electrician and his sidekick made all the special brackets to fit the TVs into.

I had done a deal with Scottish Newcastle Brewers to supply me with their beer, so their fitters were busy in the bar fitting all the pumps and coolers – a big job. We had a room just behind the end of the bar which made a good cellar and spirits store. This was all very handy and more or less very near the back door for deliveries. I advertised for a bar manager and did many interviews and chose a lady, who seemed just what I wanted – not too clever and a good listener. She would come in for a couple of weeks before opening to get the bar all ready, order all the drinks, beers, spirits, soft drinks, glasses, and do a thorough clean and polish up. We started one other part-time bar person.

I also had two security men starting to cover the two shifts 3pm until 11pm and 11pm until 7am. There was a gate house with a small office in the centre of the way in and out, with a tank trap that operated from the office so no-one could get in or out if they were up. The security man would collect the money from the driver for parking for the night. If he wanted a bed, he would have booked in, but many drivers slept in their cabs. Behind the security office there was quite a large room that only had three toilets in. So we altered that and put a stainless steel work top down each side, with six sunk-in wash basins on each side, with hot and cold water, shaver plugs and mirrors, which was for sleeper cab drivers.

I got two brothers to do the cafeteria, who were both chefs. One was a teacher at the tech college and the other would be full-time.

I had rented the fuel site out to Exelby Services. They operated a large bunkering operation all over the UK but had nothing in the Carlisle area and needed a site to cover the north. I kept one fuel pump for my own trucks. Having Exelby services on site would pull more truck into the place.

I had now set a date to open, so it was all go. Everyone said we would never get open on that date. The drink licence inspectors landed and gave me the go-ahead to open, no problem. We were to open on the Monday and on the Sunday morning we had no tables made and we needed lots for the cafeteria and the bar room. So we all started – the two electricians, two joiners, my young son Chris, and myself. My mates kept coming past, some of my drivers, all saying that we'd never get open the next day because the large bar area and cafeteria looked so bare with no tables in. But we proved them all wrong.

* * *

I had asked my friend from Anan, Billy Anderson, who had a nice little three-piece band, if he would come and play each night until we got it going. Then I would get organised with other bands to relieve him. He accepted. I always intended to have entertainment on each night, because the bar room was big enough for this.

We got opened on Monday 16 March 1977. I named it Carlisle Truck Inn. On the first night there was just a trickle of trucks, maybe 40 to 50 trucks. A few beds were let out and we also had a few army lads staying in the bedrooms, and a few contractors working in the area. The band started just after 8pm and did three half-hour spots. There were not many in the bar at that time of night, but with the bar finishing in those days at 10pm, I wanted the band to start every night at 8pm; then in time people would come in early. There were quite a few locals who came in on the first night so I was quite pleased. I would be in the office at the garage all day organising the trucks, and every night up at the Truck Inn.

Over the next two or three weeks, there were more each night but not as many as I would have thought. Mike

Miller, a chap I knew running a late night bar in town, was in for a pint one night, and he said

*Look, I am starting to get these Go-Go dancers from Newcastle and I was going to put them on about 11pm and they will do three-five-minute spots. If you take them earlier and then they come and do my place later, we would get them cheaper.*

*It's worth a try, I will take them five nights a week.*

We worked the price out, got started the following Monday, put them on for three spots between the bands and it went down very well; we had lots of locals come in.

We were advertising our entertainment in the local paper and also had a big noticeboard in the reception area, with two weeks entertainment on the board. My wife did all the posters and they were very professional and stood out well. Within two or three weeks the trucks were lining up to get in, unbelievable, Billy started his band spot at 8pm each night, and people were already coming in before 8pm to get a seat. We were getting more part-time staff to cope. I started arranging different bands; there were plenty

of good bands about and I knew a lot of these bands with
going to the clubs on our Saturday night out.

By this time the new garage at the Truck Inn was finished
and we moved in with no problem. Everyone had been

paid, so the job was going well. I already had a man lined up to rent the old garage so that worked out. Within four months we were getting really busy, and the two brothers in the kitchen could not cope. So I got a husband and wife team Nicky and Joan Faulkner; they were both chefs and soon got the job under control, starting the cafeteria at six in the morning until three in the afternoon, then open five until midnight.

We were then getting up to 250 trucks a night from Monday to Thursday, then Fridays about 150, but got a lot of locals in on Friday nights. We needed six bar staff serving and a full-time glass collector and washer; all the bar staff were part-time, mostly people I knew. We needed 300 pint glasses behind the bar at night to keep the job going, plus all the other different types of glasses; replacements were four dozen a week with breakages.

I would plan all the bands out months ahead and use Monday night's band also on Tuesday, Wednesday's band would do Thursday, then Friday's would do one night. Most of the bands were from Carlisle and around Cumbria, and some of them were top class.

Andy Park was a big Carlisle band agent and brought a lot of bands from all over for the social clubs in the Cumbria area. He would be in touch with me on a regular basis, letting me know what he had coming in the area, and regularly would go to the clubs to see various acts and if they suited my venue. The clubs were Friday Saturday and Sunday night venues, so on Mondays Tuesdays and Wednesday the bands had no work. So I would take the bands that suited the Truck Inn, put them up free for a couple of nights and get a good deal that suited us both.

*This is Bob Fish's band, Johnny Rocco and me. We did a small film for Border Television.*

*This was part of the filming for Border Television.*

I paid approximately £50 per night for a band. When I started I had to look around for bands to play at the Truck Inn and they were all a bit dubious about a new venue. But within a very short time bands were ringing me because they were guaranteed a full house. No band liked playing to a half empty place.

The games room was very popular. It had four pool tables, space intruder games, one-armed bandits. There were four coin telephone boxes but we had to have two more fitted, and they needed to be emptied every morning. There was also a television room.

\* \* \*

*Chris our son, Lorraine, Geoff & our daughter Angela.*

On most Sundays the two children and my wife and her mother and father would go out for Sunday lunch. But one Sunday we were alone with the children, so we went to see a fellow I knew at Glencaple near Dumfries and had lunch some place on the way up there. This man was called Walter Clark and he was a well-known upmarket car dealer so I was going up to see what he had in. We looked around at various cars, all very nice, lots of new ones and second-hand. Standing there gleaming was a brand-new Rolls Royce – beautiful. I liked the colours and everything about it, but I didn't let Walter know what I was thinking. My Rolls was in tip-top condition and had low mileage because I never went far in it; if I was going on long business journeys, I would take the Mercedes. I said to Walter

*How much would you want to change my Rolls for the new one?*

*Let's see, your's is in very good order no problems, say £6,000 to change.*

*No no, too much. My car has done nothing I will give you £4,000.*

*OK, give me £5,000 and it's a deal.*

We shook hands and closed the deal. I paid him the cash and made arrangements to collect it the next Sunday. We went up to Walter's at Glencaple on the following Sunday and collected the new Rolls. What a car! I was over the moon.

*Ian Iceton's wedding. He was my nephew and I was best man. We were very good friends, more like brothers. The reception was at The Castle Inn Hotel, Bassenthwaite, Keswick, and at night, dinner and dance at the Stocksman in Wigton. The band was a very popular excellent musician Mel Ellwood.*

The Truck Inn was open seven days a week at the start, with entertainment on every night, but as the years went on we closed on a Saturday night and reopened on a Sunday night at about 4pm, and only had entertainment on five nights a week.

I decided to start slowly fitting out the second floor so I got Brian the joiner back and a plumber Mike Evans and his pal Derek Swindle. I used Willie's lads on Saturdays to do all the floors. George Rice the electrician and his side-kick Jacky were back too.

These lads were all self employed and had other people they did regular work for so didn't mind them having days off to go to other jobs. It was not like when I started to first build the Truck Stop and I needed it open in one year.

There was not much money to be made out of bedrooms. The rooms had to be reasonable otherwise the drivers would sleep in their cabs and most trucks now were coming with sleeper cabs fitted. It was far more comfortable in a bedroom with bath and shower, central heating, television, more space than your cabs; but money talks. I knew I was in competition with the sleeper cab. I had to finish all three floors to make the project complete. I was already planning for the future. No successful project lasts forever. With a new business idea which I had done, people will eventually copy you. We finished the second floor, got it all opened – a very good job. So I decided to just keep the lads on and finish the third floor.

When I had all the three floors going and the place was really busy I got a call from the gas company, a Jeff

Thomson asking if he could e come and see me. He arrived and we had a coffee in the cafe and then he said to me

*Could you show me around and see how your bill for gas is so small. You are almost putting gas back up the pipe.*

So I showed him all our boilers and how I had time clocks and thermostats all set to my methods; he was dumb stuck how I had it all set up so efficient.

\* \* \*

I decided to take my son Chris to the Isle of Man TT motor-bike races. I had already booked our hotel well in advance as this was a very popular event and the hotels get fully booked. We sailed over and hired a car, booked into the hotel, then took the car and had a buzz around the place to get our bearings. After that, we parked up at the hotel, walked around and found a nice place to have dinner, then called in at a very busy nice-looking bar. The people were friendly and all chatting, and we finished up talking to the pilots of the Red Arrows. They were doing their acrobatics show over the race days; I was surprised how young these guys were. We finished up having a good night.

The next day we had a free day to have a good look around the island. I had a pal from our local village Kirkbampton, Wilson Robinson, who had sold his hotel, The Hill Top Hotel in Carlisle, and then went to live in the Isle of Man with his mother and father. We located the house and rang the bell. His father answered the door and invited us in for a cup of tea, Wilson was not there – in UK for a few days. We had a good talk and then went on our way.

We came across a small village with a cafe and dropped in for a coffee and sandwich, then next door we went into this games area and we were playing on this ball machine where you roll the balls down shoots; you have a horse going across the top and the first to the end wins. At the other end of the room we heard these lads playing the same game and laughing. We looked around and, to our amazement, it was our next-door neighbours – these lads were all keen bikers.

The next morning we were up sharp, had breakfast and then off to choose our spot for the races. When the races are on, all the roads are closed so you are stuck for the day. We chose to be on the inside track, where there are plenty of snack places and toilets. We got in a good position where we could see the bikes coming down the mountainside and into the corners, The first race started and this bike was coming roaring down the mountain and I am thinking "he is going to fast to take this corner". I was goose pimples all over, but he made it and so did all the followers. I never realised how fast these bikes could go and the riders were amazing.

The smaller bike races started first, then the 500cc last. The man I really was waiting to see was Mike Hailwood who had been champion lots of times. At half time we decided to change our position and were walking over the fields, getting over this fence and who was at the other side? Norman Wisdom! He said "Hello folks" and my son said "Hi Mr Grimsdale" and we all had a good laugh.

The next race was the 500cc in which they come along the straight into the two-bend corner absolutely flying. I was wondering how they did it and that I would not do that for all the tea in China. Who was the winner? Mike Hailwood. The sidecar race was very exciting watching, especially the fellow in the sidecar going from side to side as the corners came up rapidly.

In March 1981 Mike Hailwood and his kids would go for fish and chips in the Tamworth area, when a truck, coming up the wrong way, went through the barrier and into Mike's car. His nine year old son was killed and Mike died in hospital two days late. The truck driver got fined £100.

* * *

On the haulage side I had a driver called Alan Jones who had been with me for some years and was a top-class person. He was very gifted and could almost do anything -take phone calls for me, organise the trucks, do repairs in the garage. So I said to him one day

*Would you like to stop driving and come and work with Chris Lewis in the garage, do repairs and servicing and also drop into the office if I have to go out?*

*I would like that.*

So we agreed his salary, and he started with Chris in the garage and they got on like a house on fire.

Everything was going well, but then one day Alan Jones came into my office and said

*Chris wants to work less hours and wants to finish at 5pm and be home earlier at nights, so if he finished at five I will start later in the morning and work later at night to finish all the jobs.*

*That will not work, most of the trucks are coming in at that time of night and are needing small jobs done or to be serviced.*

Chris was a top fitter and I did not want to lose him, also a very nice fellow and we got on very well together. I spoke to Chris but I could see he had definitely made his mind up about finishing early, his wife was wanting him home early. Chris said

*Will Mick not come in the garage?*

Mick Philiskirk was a man who came for a job some time ago that was working at Tait's on Volvos and I knew him very well. I said

*Hi Mick, what are you doing?*

*Well actually I am looking for a job.*

*OK start on Monday in the garage.*

*No, I am looking for a driver's job.*
*Why is a good fitter like you going driving, are you sure?*
*Yes.*

So Mick started as a driver for me, an immaculate man with a truck. So I said to Chris

*I will ask Mick but I know his answer will be no.*

I did ask Mick and the answer was no. Chris left at the next weekend.

I was getting a bit uneasy even though things were going very well. Everything was paid for and money was coming in, but I had got the business as far I wanted to go, so with no more expansion I was going to be working for the tax man – tax was very high in those days. The tax allowance on trucks then was 100% in one year, so for a few years in say November I would estimate what money I would have in the bank at the end of December, which was my year end. Say I had estimated it would be £100.000, then I would buy 10 new Crane Fruehauf tipper trailers and pay before the end of December. At that particular time there was about a nine-month waiting list on these types of trailers so when they were built, selling them for a good profit was not difficult. But I was only delaying the problem and hoping that the tax system might change.

I was getting calls from many various city councils asking if I would build a truck stop in their areas to try and remove trucks from parking all over their towns at nights. But I always refused. There was no point because I had everything I wanted. I would only be working for the tax man. I did assist quite a few other people who wanted to build truck stops. One was Alan Sherwood, a big haulier from beside Derby, who came to see me a couple of times.

We got on well and used to meet up at the tipper conventions every year at Blackpool and then when it was moved to Harrogate. These were very good weekends – three nights at a top-class hotel in Harrogate with a full executive room for the family paid for by Volvo or Crane Fruehauf. We had a special gala night on the Saturday night with comedians like Ken Dodd and a top-class band. We went to these Harrogate weekends for years.

Alan Sherwood did build a truck stop at Junction 23 on the M1. I also had enquiries from Scotland to build. I said no but that I would assist. I was asked to go up to Inverness and advise a company that were very interested in constructing a truck stop there. They asked what would my fees be for this. I said just pay my fuel costs and hotel accommodation and I would you book my wife and I into a hotel for two nights on the way back at Aviemore. We fixed the dates, went up there, and all went well. We had a very nice few days off, and saw quite a bit of Scotland we had never seen before.

I had always kept an eye on the stock market and watched various companies and how they were performing and I slowly invested, mostly in blue chip companies for long-term growth.

Each year about October I would start asking my customers for a rates increase. It was normal for the haulage industry to get the rate organised to start in the new year. This year I was asking for a 10% increase but my customers started offering 5%. I refused that immediately. Some increased their offer to 7% with a struggle in the middle of November. In the last week in November I wrote to all my customers I did the flat haulage for and said if I didn't get the 10% increase in rates I would be finishing at the end of December. But I was still going to operate the tipper trucks. I got no reply from my flat customers so I gave all those drivers four weeks' notice to leave at the end of December. In the last week in December the customers were calling me that they would give me the 10%. I said

*Too late, I am finishing at the end of the year.*

I paid the drivers their redundancy and that was that.

\* \* \*

By January 1982 I had only the five Volvo artic tippers going, so Alan Jones was doing a bit of office work, truck servicing and repairs, and also doing a bit of work in the Truck Inn – he was very handy at making things. With all the three floors open at the Truck Inn, we had 100 beds available and could often get filled up. This took quite a bit of my time.

I had a contract with Lakeland Laundry Penrith for sheets and pillow cases. They came Mondays, Wednesdays and Fridays and supplied all the linen. I had eight cleaners, two for each bedroom floor, and two for the bar room, games room and all the main areas. All the cleaners were from the local housing estate and all had children at school so we collected them at 8.45am and dropped them home for 12pm because some had children coming back for lunch.

I always had something to fix. There would always be a hoover that had picked up a cigarette packet or a broken belt, toilets that were not flushing, taps leaking, door locks stuck. Alan Jones was very handy at this and would help me out if he had time. I also looked after all the cleaning material.

First job in the morning was putting the money ready to bank, then popping down in the Rolls to the Midland bank at English Street. In those days I'd pull up right outside the bank and run in and out in a few minutes. The reps knew to call on me at 10am in the mornings as I would be in the cafeteria having my snack and we would have a cup of tea together and plenty of banter. One year after I had finished with the 10 Volvo artics flats, I also finished with the tippers and closed the transport side down.

With the transport finished I had lots of equipment to sell. In total I had 16 Volvo artics, two new Volvo artics never been used, 16-40 foot used trailers, six used Crane

Fruehauf tipper trailers, seven new Crane Fruehauf tipper trailers and six new 40-foot Taut-liners. I just ran an advert in the *Motor Transport* paper every week. I was in no hurry to sell them, and if it took a few years then it might stretch my tax bill. The new Volvos were no problem selling, also the new trailers went fast, but some of the older flat 40-footers were very slow and took maybe more than two years, but in the end all got sold.

I kept investing in the stock market and again mostly blue chip for the long-term.

Alan Jones then came full-time at the Truck Inn and took a lot of maintenance jobs that I was doing. The garage now was not getting used and I still had all the equipment and tools in there locked in the big store. A John Jeffreys came to see me one day and was looking for a place to build weighbridges, and had heard that my garage was empty. I showed him the garage and he said "spot on for my job". I told him I wanted to keep one office there, the front one, and he agreed. We negotiated the rent and that was that.

One of the lads who played in a band at the Truck Inn, Alan Sessford from Gretna – a very good lead guitarist – had had a heart attack and was not able to go back to his old job, and was told he had to take a light job. He came to see me and said he was into the CB radios, and could he come on the park with a small caravan and offer a service to the drivers? I said "Okay. See how it goes then we can discuss the rent." He got started and became very popular and it did bring trucks in.

\* \* \*

In 1981 my daughter Angela was 16 years old and left school. I did ask her if she wanted to go further in her education but she said "no". So she started work at the Truck Inn. I gave her all kinds of jobs, office counting money, cleaning, not just easy jobs but I wanted her to be able to do every job, which she did. She came with me each morning in the Rolls.

She had a boyfriend from the village who had quite a big motorcycle, and I told her never to go on the back of that bike, and that when she was 17 I would get her a car. Anyhow, one day my pal said he had seen Angela on the back of a motorcycle. I approached Angela and with a struggle she did admit to me she had been on it, and she also informed me that maybe she would go on it again. I was fuming, without showing it, and I said

*I am waiting each morning for to take you to work so you might as well have your own motorcycle.*

So on the Saturday afternoon we stopped into Stan Warton's motor cycle sales at Kingstown, looked around, chose a nice little Yamaha and got all the gear, helmet, leggings, etc. I got her started and followed her home and she was OK. On the Monday morning I set her off first, passed her in Carlisle on Eden Bridge and then she arrived at the Truck Inn no problem. Now she was independent.

In 1982 my son Chris would be leaving school and in the summer he was working up at the Truck Inn. There were always jobs to do and he was handy at doing things – they were learning lots in school in those days, about how plumbing worked in houses with header tanks, and drawing plans. He had a few mates older than him and he would be fitting their radios and CBs. He had a racer bike and he had a CB on it. The aerial must have been six to eight feet long but he had it working fine. He said

*What kind of motorbike will I be getting when I am 16?*

*That is not difficult to work out is it? You'll be getting Angela's and she will get a little car.*

*What, I don't want that, it is absolutely useless.*

*Why, it's spotless, lovely bike.*

*It will not go, no power, I could walk faster.*

It was a restricted bike for 16 year olds.

*That's what you are getting.*

One Sunday he was in his friend's car, which had a trailer on and he was backing around to the garden area where Chris used the shed attached to the greenhouse for his workshop. I went out to see what was going on, I looked into the trailer and said

*Don't bring all this scrap here.*

*Scrap? This is my motorbike to build up, I don't want that de-rated bike of Angela's.*

Well, there were bits everywhere. Where he got this, I don't know, must have got it given. Anyhow, when he was not helping me at the Truck Inn or at school, he would be in his workshop. Just before he was 16 he had the old bike fired up and ready to go. He left the school, got the bike all tested and off he went.

Chris then started to work for me at the Truck Inn. Just like with Angela, I wanted him to do every job, and get to know how everything worked, where all the fuse boxes were, all the stop taps were, how to start the generator, how to run the bar and clean the beer pipes, how the central heating worked, and I could go on. And over time they both did get to know.

Alan would come to me at 11.45am at the office, and I would give him the money to drop in at the bank after he had finished dropping the cleaners home. I would tell him what there was to do, and we would discuss that; he would also tell me about other jobs that needed doing, and we would also have a chat about things. But I began to notice all that had stopped, so I said to him one day

*Alan what is the problem you don't even pass the time of day with me?*

*You have got your son Chris in here to take my job over.*

*Nothing of the kind, that thought has never entered my head.*

But there was no talking to him and he walked off. When he came back from the bank with the receipt, I said

*Alan, you walked away from me when I was speaking to you; you have been with me for many years and we have had no problems and I expect you to be here for many more.*

He walked off again and I followed him and stopped him

*Alan, if I cannot talk to you then there is a problem.*

He started to be very cheeky with me, so I said

*Alan, if you don't want to talk to me, do you want to leave?*

*It has come to that.*

*OK leave at the weekend I will sort your redundancy money out.*

So that was the end of a very good relationship. Alan had been a very good reliable worker.

Angela became 17 and I got her a car, a Volkswagen Jetta diesel. I took her out most afternoons to give a few lessons and she passed her test with no problems; she could now do all the banking, pick up and drop off the cleaners.

When Chris became 17 I got him a little Volvo car. He had put in for his test before he had got his licence, so I took him out each afternoon and he passed his test within a couple of weeks. So my son and daughter were both driving, picking the cleaners up on their way to work each morning then dropping them back home before 12 midday.

In 1982 the chap who was renting the garage at the Truck Inn, building weighbridges left and Fred Titterington came and rented the garage. He was my first fitter at my first garage at Willowholme when I had six Volvo artics. When Fred left me, he took his customers and started by himself and took on the DAF truck agency and had done well. He took partners on to do the DAF agency and in time they took over from him and he went back on his own, so he rented the garage from me.

Also in 1982 my accountant Mr Fred Nixon was semi retiring and I was passed on to a Bill Dodd at Dodd & Co. who had a few partners, but he would look after me. Bill had started the business in 1981 and we got on very well. After a couple of years or so a chap called Michael Bland, a chartered accountant, started as a partner with Dodd's and was working on my accounts, but Bill Dodd always did the meetings with me and introduced Michael Bland to me. Around the end of 1985 Bill was explaining to me that he would be leaving the partnership in about March 1986 to take a role in a different company, and would be giving more of my work to Michael Bland. As time went on I got on very well with Bland and by the time Bill Dodd was leaving at the end of March 1986, Michael Bland was then doing all my work.

We were still very busy at the Truck Inn with up to 250 trucks a night. My son and daughter would do shifts and were getting well into the job. I started being ambitious again. When there was a farm, about 250 acres, for sale beside where we lived, we had a look at that, but I was thinking that it was some 25 years since I was on the farms and it had all changed since then, so I didn't take the plunge.

However I was starting to look at trucks again and thought that because my two children had taken a lot of work from me, I could start in trucks again. This time I had the money to buy them. But I didn't want to be tied to the daily running of them. So my idea was to contact George Holiday, a chap I had known for years. He had always had his own truck business but had run into difficulties and had to pack it in. Barnett and Graham had taken his transport business on and George was managing it for them.

I went to Penrith to meet George and put my idea to him: my thinking was 10 artic trucks with 10 40-foot three axle flat trailers with container locks. No spare trailers like last time I was in the job, because it got to be a problem coping with extra loaded trailers. I said we could go halves and he could run the business and get a salary. I would not take a salary but I would be looking for contacts which I had done before and assisting all I could. He said he liked the idea, but would have no capital to put in. I said I would buy the trucks and trailers, to get the job started, and we could have half shares each but he would pay for his shares as we progressed. He said he was all for it because he hated working where he was. But he said he would have to ask his wife. I agreed and he came back to me and said his wife would like to meet with me, and would I come to the house. I said yes and I went up to the house one night and met his wife. We had a good discussion and she soon made her mind up and told George and said "If you want to join Geoff, it's up to you". So George and I decided to give it a go.

I got started getting prices for tractor units. Volvos was my choice, but I needed prices from DAF trucks and Scania. Scania were always dearer, Volvo not so bad but DAF were rely trying. It was 10 trucks, a good order. I was back and forward with these people playing one against the other. Scania were first out of the race. I preferred Volvo because I knew them from before and they were a good truck. I had already got a deal with 10 trailers from Crane Fruehauf so that was sorted.

Every time Volvo matched DAF, DAF would come back with a lower price. I was also wanting a deal that when each truck was one year old they would change it for a guaranteed price. Volvo actually could not match what DAF had to offer, so I settled on the 10 DAFs. The deal was £20,000 per tractor for the DAF 2800 unit all rigged up – fifth wheel, the full outfit; each tractor unit would be changed at 12 months old for £5,000.

George started in January 1984. DAF had only four trucks ready which were the DAF 2800, so we got started with four drivers with no problems. We picked up the new trailers from the Crane Fruehauf factory and picked four loads up for Scotland. The second four we got on 1 February were DAF 3300 units – an upgraded more powerful model and more expensive. The sales manager at DAF with whom I made the deal was George Cleasby. He said I was to pay a bit more for this model as it was quite a bit more expensive. But the mistake he had made was he had delivered them to us, lettered them with the Bell Holiday name on and finished to our specification, without asking beforehand. So I was sitting in the driver's seat. I said

*George, we made a deal – £20,000 each. Also you said you would deliver 10 trucks on 1 January and we only got four, so I am not paying you any more, we are still two trucks short of the 10. If you are demanding more money for these four, then take them back as I can get Volvos for the price you are wanting.*

So what choice had George got? It was take it or leave it time. He said

*Belly, you have got me this time.*

We had to laugh. What else could he do? I actually finished up with a good deal.

*George Cleasby, DAF trucks sales manager, and Geoff Bell. George passed away some time ago. He was a top-class person and I really miss him. We had some great times together. He was an unforgettable, unbelievable man, always happy.*

Two weeks later we were still waiting for two more, George at DAF's said they would be delivered 1 March. I said

*They will have to be the DAF 3300 model as the drivers will kick up if they don't have a 3300; you have given us a problem with not making them all 2800.*

*I will have to have a word with the powers above and come back to you.*

A few days passed and George did come back to me and said DAF was able to make the next two 3300. The DAF factory was helping with the deal. On 1 March the two DAF 3300 trucks were delivered, together with another surprise: one was a space cab which was normally £2,000 extra, so all in all we had finished up with a very good deal.

*Geoff Bell's second fleet of DAF trucks.*

So by 1 March 1984 we had the 10 DAF artics with 40-foot Container locks on the road. George picked up some of his old contacts, and I up picked up some of my old ones, so we were keeping busy. We got quite a good job from Enichem Southampton who made rubber for tyres. That was about three loads a day going to tyre manufacturers around the Midlands area, the Pirelli factory in Carlisle and Enichem factory in Grangemouth, which also had loads for us going south. We also did a lot of container work for various companies which I had known well from a few years before.

We got on to a regular job carrying steel ingots from British Steel, Clydesdale Works, Bellshill's, Glasgow, to British Steel division, Bromford, Birmingham, doing about seven loads a day and it was a 24-hour a day unloading. We were loading back to Scotland from Cadbury Schweppes, Bournville Factory Birmingham, containers or bricks back into Scotland, on a daily basis, a very good job. One of our drivers was Eddie Boyd who was a top-class driver and always winding everyone up. He called our firm the BBC. I asked "What is that Eddie?" He said "Bricks, billets and containers".

Well, it was time to go and see Walter Clark again up at Glencaple to see what cars he had in. I went up on a Sunday just to have a look around and all the cars were immaculate as usual. I'd got my eye on this new Rolls Royce again. Walter had a look at my one which was still immaculate and very low mileage. We haggled away as usual on price but came to an agreement in the end and I paid him. He would get it sorted out and I would collect the new Rolls the following Sunday. All excited, I went up to Walters at Glencaple, picked the new Rolls up, with no delay, and then had a nice luxurious drive back to Carlisle.

In 1985 we started replacing the DAF Trucks at a year old. £5.000 was the arrangement and my idea was to get one a month, which we did and this worked out well. We added two more DAF units so this was 12 in total. Other hauliers were asking me how I managed to replace my trucks every year. I replied that all repairs came under warranty so I had no tyres to buy because they last the year; all we had to do was regular servicing and oil changes, and Fred did that in my garage, so we had no other expenses or down time.

* * *

The Truck Inn was still going strong with up to 250 trucks per night. We were well organised and my daughter Angela and son Chris were well into it and giving me more time on other things. Angela, after cashing up at the Truck Inn, would do an hour or so on the books for the transport side. Chris would also be helping with the cashing up and after that would re stock the bar. On cashing up, one would be emptying the machines, pool tables, two bandits, six pay phones – in 10 pence coins about £60 per night. The space intruders could take £100 per week – we had three of them. Chris and I would do the repairs. After the cleaners had finished and been taken home, we would have our lunch in the cafeteria.

In the afternoons we only needed one person in the bar which we also used as reception for the booking in of beds. My sister Amy came in about 12 noon and the bar manager started at 5pm. Two of them managed up until 8pm, then we had six part-time bar staff come in at 8pm. Amy would then go home. The cafeteria closed at about 2.00pm until 4.30pm. Angela and Chris worked shifts so after lunch they would sort out that one of them would be on each other day.

I was still organising the booking of all the entertainment and I had that well organised. Angela was 20 years old and one Saturday afternoon back at home, I said

*What have you been doing today?*
*I have been looking for a house.*
*Why are you leaving home?*
*I would like a house of my own.*
*What have you seen?*

She told me and I said

*They are far too dear and are old houses. If you are so determined to get a house, let's go and see a builder I know, Tom*

105

*Beck. He is building new houses down in the far end of Dalston.*

I phoned Tom Beck and asked if we could look at his new-built houses. He said anytime and we agreed on 12 midday the next day. OK. Angela and I arrived on time and Tom took us around, found one that suited her – a new-build with three bedrooms upstairs, nice bathroom with shower. Downstairs it had a big living room and dining room; the kitchen was still to be chosen by the purchaser. I said to Angela

*What do you think?*

*It's lovely, way ahead of anything I have seen.*

*Well, Tom how little will you take from your next door neighbour?*

Tom only lived down the lane from us at Dalston. We battled over the price and the price to fit the new kitchen. At last we agreed, did the deal and I paid the deposit and the solicitor would sort out the rest. Within a couple of weeks Angela had moved in.

After a few months Angela decided to leave the Truck Inn. I could not understand why and Chris tried to talk to her out of it but she had made up her mind, even left the car.

I was very friendly for years with one of the BP bosses from London, Mike Godfrey. We often had BP lads come up from London on a Thursday to have a look around; they would land about 3pm in the afternoon, always about three or four of them, and we always had plenty to talk about. They were booked into a local hotel near the Truck Inn, and would always ask me out to have dinner with them at Newby Lodge restaurant. After dinner we would all go back to the Truck Inn for a few drinks; they always enjoyed the nights there with the entertainment, and Mike Godfrey came each time.

One day in the back end of 1986 Mike Godfrey rang me and said

*Look, BP is getting interested in going into truck stops, would you think about selling?*

*Everything is for sale at the right price.*

We talked for a while and I liked Mike very much and we got on well together. He said

*I will get back to you on this so keep it quiet.*

He got back to me within a couple of weeks and asked if he could bring a couple of BP men up to have a look around and talk to me. We agreed on the following Thursday and on the Thursday afternoon we showed the BP men around and we did a lot of talking. They asked me to join them for dinner as usual, then all of us came back to the Truck Inn for plenty of drinks; it was a very good night and everyone enjoyed themselves. Next morning they came into the Truck Inn for a bit more chatter and then off they headed back to London.

We were always closed for about two weeks at Christmas and New Year. All the factories were closed and no trucks were on the road. When we got opened up in early 1987, Mike Godfrey from BP was back up to the Truck Inn with more top guys from BP. They repeated the performance: landed on the Thursday afternoon, looked all around, plenty of questions, out for dinner, good chat. BP was very interested in the Truck Inn and they asked if I would sell. I said "yes at my price". We as usual finished up at the Truck Inn for the night with plenty of drinks, another very good night. Next morning there were more talks and they asked what price I was looking for. I said "£2 million" and they said they'd be back in touch, and off they went back to London.

At the same time, my wife Lorraine and I were drifting apart and had been for some time. She was living mostly with her mother. My thoughts were: I had built the Truck Inn from scratch, built the transport up with no money the first time round, and now I was back in haulage with 12 trucks and all paid for with several hundred thousand pounds in my stocks portfolio. But really for me it had been the challenge to build these businesses, now it was getting the same old thing every day and the challenge had gone. So I asked myself: was this the time to move on? Had BP just arrived at the right time?

In the next couple of months A Keith Cripwell from BP would come and see me a few times. He was the main negotiator, and we came to an agreement on a price of £1.9m. I would still have the haulage based in the Truck Inn and George Holiday would run that. I met a few times with my solicitor, Donald Livingstone, and my accountant Michael Bland to plan out what were my best options regarding my tax matters.

They came up with the advice that if I left the UK at the end of March 1987 I would reduce my tax bill substantially, so I had to give this considerable thought. Over time I decided I would take this option. I asked myself "Well, why not, challenges were my life. I had a house in Nerja in southern Spain, near Malaga, so this is where I would go to. BP and my solicitors had not got all the papers sorted by the time I was getting ready to leave, so I had to give power of attorney to my accountant Michael Bland.

I advertised my Rolls in *The Times* newspaper and a man from Penzance called, asked about the condition of the Rolls and all the details. I gave all of this to him and said

*I also have a Mercedes E Class Diesel, and a Ford diesel Sierra.*
I gave him all the particulars. He said
*I will come back to you in a couple of days.*
He came back to me and said
*OK I will offer you £47,000 for the three of them.*
*No, not enough, give me £50,000 and it's a deal.*
*OK, I will collect them when you have them ready.*
*Will you inspect them and pay me before you collect?*
*No, I will post you a banker's draft for the £50,000.*
*You have not inspected them.*
*I have spoken to Walter Clark at Glencaple, Dumfries, and he said if you're buying these from Geoff Bell they will be in tip-top condition.*

The cheque arrived, into the bank no problem, and they were collected a few days before I left for Spain.

I had bought a new E Class Mercedes diesel left-hand drive to take to Spain. So I booked the ferry from Southampton to Santander in Spain for Monday 30 March 1987. I drove down to Southampton on Sunday 29. I had the car loaded up with clothes and all kinds of bits and pieces to take to the house. I stayed in a hotel for the night in Southampton. One of my pals Ray Wright, who drove a tanker truck for BP Oil London Depot, delivering oil to the Glasgow area every week, came into the Truck Inn from the very first day we opened to the day I left. He would stay for the night on the way up and on the way back down. Ray was also a very good singer and he came armed with a country shirt and cowboy hat and earned the name of the Truck Inn Cowboy. He was a fan of Franky Lane. He came over from London to Southampton for the night to see me off. We had dinner together and a few drinks and of course plenty of reminiscing and a lot of laughing.

Monday morning I was up early. Ray and I had breakfast together then we said our goodbyes and I drove down to the dockside and loaded onto the ferry. Two nights on the ferry was quite a nice journey with plenty of time to do my thinking – how had I done all this starting with nothing? Would I be able to settle anywhere after spending 47 years in the UK and I'd be on my own. My wife Lorraine was living with her mother. I did ask her if she wanted to come with me but she did not want to leave the UK. We divorced.

My son Chris was running the Truck Inn until BP took over and George was running the transport side. Chris was by himself in the house at Dalston but he had plenty of mates. He and his pal Brian Baird were go-cart racing most weekends, which kept him busy. They were doing very well and winning quite a lot of races. They had started when he was about 15 years old, and it was good experience doing all their own repairs and rebuilds.

We sailed into Santander and I drove off the ferry. My idea was to stop about half way down to Nerja, reckoning it was about 600 miles. I stopped at a road-side transport cafe and got chicken and chips and a big plate of bread thrown in, very crispy nice bread. Then I was back on the road and it was almost impossible to pass. When it was possible to overtake, you could not see for the smoke coming from the trucks ahead. The trucks in Spain were very old and obsolete compared to the UK. It was more or less 'follow the leader' most of the time. I pulled up at a hotel and I had done just over 300 miles. I got a bed for the night and a meal and also a few San Miguels.

I was up and had the English type breakfast, then on the road for 8am. It was the same old thing – follow the leader through all the diesel smoke for about another 150 miles. I dropped into a road-side cafe for coffee and a few Spanish tapas and again a lovely basket of crispy bread. Next stop Nerja. I dropped my things in the house and went into the bar restaurant at the Capistrano resort. I knew quite a few people in Nerja because I had been there quite a few times and met a lot of people. In the Capistrano resort there were a lot of English people. My friend from Carlisle, Ian Benson, and I used to go there for one-week holidays and let our hair down – great weeks. We would hire a Panda car at Malaga airport and drive up to Nerja. It was a very narrow winding road then and took quite a long time, now it is all motorway and takes less than half an hour. We would be down in Nerja little town every night until the early hours; there was an abundance of small good bars and plenty of good restaurants.

The first couple of weeks were like a good rest for me. I think I was tired out. I would get up late, drop in at the restaurant at Capistrano and have late breakfast and there was always someone in there for the crack. After late breakfast, or you could call it early lunch, I would drop in at the tennis club and see who was about. There were quite a lot retired people in the Capistrano area and many used the tennis club, even if they didn't play tennis. There were some rare characters in there and they were all full of fun and laughter, but many of them would be drinking most of the day. That's one thing I never did – drink through the day. I had the bar at the Truck Inn for 10 years and never drank through the day. The only exception was when George Cleasby the DAF sales manager took me out for lunch on occasions, and we had the afternoon off with no work to attend to. George would have other hauliers that would join us we would be there until five or six o'clock having a good laugh. George was a character and a very clever salesman. He liked the Drambuie and even got me on it. But he was very good at spending DAF's money; it didn't seem to matter what they spent on entertainment. When I was running the Volvo trucks it was difficult to get a cup of coffee from Volvo.

After a couple of weeks I got myself a tennis racquet and decided that, with not doing any work, I needed to keep myself in trim. I had brought my squash racquet with me as I used to be in the squash league in Dalston. I had met a chap and his wife some years before in the Capistrano bar when I was on an inspection trip to see the show houses when I decided to buy there. He was Ron Wright and his wife. He was the head designer for tennis racquets for Gowdey, which was taken over by British Tyre & Rubber Co. He would design these racquets go over to China and get them made there for £1 each, but they would get strung back in the UK; the same with the squash racquets. Ron said he had quite a lot of shares in the company and he was planning to sell them and retire to Nerja, so he was buying a house in Capistrano. He was a top-class player at squash and tennis.

So would you believe, Ron had retired and was living there. I met him in the tennis club and he put me through my paces on the tennis court. We became best of mates and would go out mostly every night together. We started going down to La Herradura to play squash. I was not in his league, but he would teach me a lot on the court and we enjoyed it. There was a squash league in Andalucia and Ron would put us both in; it was played just down the road at Rincon de la Victoria. I was knocked out in the second round, but big Ron was knocking his young opponents out round after round. Then came the final, Ron against a young fit Spanish lad of about 21 years old. I was sitting with Ron's wife and after 15 minutes Ron was sweating heavily and I said to his wife "Ron is tiring" and she said "no, he is just getting warmed up, he has not started yet". Well was she right. I had never seen a man at that age have so much stamina, unbelievable. He went on and on against last year's fit young Andalucia champion and won the match. Big Ron was now Andalucia squash champion, and he did it again the next year.

Ron was a tall well built good-looking chap, always well dressed in white jacket and white shoes, well-tanned – a real jack the lad. He got to seeing this young woman Marcia who was very nice, but then his wife got to know and all hell broke loose. He eased off for a while, but then he and I were out one night to get a few drinks; we were in a few bars and who did we bump into but Marcia. So they were all over each other and you know the rest. Things between Ron and his wife deteriorated and Ron started living with Marcia.

We all used to meet at the tennis club in the mornings and have a game with various people. Ron used to have most of us running around the court; there were some good players but most were average, just like I finished up.

I met a lady called Judy playing tennis, who was an American from Long Island New York. She had a house in Capistrano and we played tennis quite a lot together; she was a very good player. We would have a coffee after in the tennis club with the other people and be chatting away. She was mentioning about going up to Geneva to see her sister in a few weeks, and I was thinking that I wanted to travel and had heard it was a very nice place and worth seeing. Playing tennis with Judy a couple of days later I said

*How are you going to travel to Geneva?*

*By car.*

*I wouldn't mind driving up there to see Geneva.*

*You are quite welcome to come with me, my sister and husband would welcome you.*

Well, I thought why not? We made plans with the dates and Judy was in touch with her sister Mary.

We got all organised and had an early start and planned to stay at certain places on the way up. Judy had driven up before and she knew France very well and also spoke French. Our first night stop was near Barcelona and we had done about 560 miles. We found a nice little hotel for the night, got dinner and a few drinks. We were up sharp in the morning, had breakfast and hit the road and decided to head straight to Geneva. We had a couple of stops, for coffee and a snack, then we had a stop for late lunch. Our next stop was Geneva. We went through passport control from France into Switzerland without problem then into Geneva. Judy's sister lived up on the right-hand side of the lake past the Geyser. We arrived at the house in a very nice area.

I was introduced to Judy's sister Mary and husband John and their daughter. They invited us into the house and showed us to our rooms; it was a lovely large house with big bedrooms and plenty of bathrooms. It was like a big bungalow with garages underneath the house; actually the garages and storage under the house was the same size as the house. It also had a nice-sized garden, mostly lawns with beds of roses. Mary made a very nice dinner for us all and I soon got settled in and was made very welcome. John and Mary McCarthy were American. John was a head hunter and was away a lot of the time on business all over. Mary looked after John's daughter. This was their second marriage each. John had two sons in America and the one daughter at home here. Mary had two daughters, one in London, married, and the other in Geneva. During the next couple of days we went all around Geneva and I found it a very nice place; we would go out at nights to have dinner and a few drinks. I would go into Geneva each morning for the paper, get coffee, relax and read, then have a wander around the shops. John and Mary had a large chalet up at Villars, the skiing area. They would go up there some weekends and we would follow them up. It was a very popular place and very nice, with good restaurants and hotels. Mary was a very good cook and Judy would help with the cooking. They did a lot of dinner parties in the house, inviting business people. John was also an ambassador for George Bush Senior, the American President. He would get a lot of calls and be meeting people all of the time.

John McCarthy's mother Mary was twice married and John had a half brother; they had both been left trust funds. John McCarthy's grandparents had invented a mouth wash called Listerine and were very wealthy; his grandmother and mother lived next door to the Johnson & Johnson family in Pennsylvania USA. We stayed in Geneva for four-or five weeks and were made very welcome. I did enjoy the change and staying with the family. Then we made an enjoyable one week trip back to Nerja, staying at a few places in France along the way, having a good look around.

Back in Nerja playing tennis again and meeting up with big Ron, I would be out every night for my dinner and meeting up with someone to have a drink; there was always entertainment on somewhere so I would finish up there. A fellow from Southampton Tony Harris and his family lived in Capistrano and he always had a band going. Linda, a girl from Carlisle, did a fire-eating act and her husband Carlos, a Portuguese lad, was a singer and keyboard player; they were a very good act and often played separate venues. There was a very good drag act called Sapphire with his own bar who put on very a good show with plenty of adlib and laughter.

Judy was telling me she was heading back home to Long Island very shortly, and I said it was my intention to travel and visit America. She said

*Why don't you come with me and I will show you around New York? My father died some years ago and my mother just died recently and the house on Long Island is empty; only my mother's nurse in still living there.*

I thought how could I refuse that? This seemed to have been planned for me, so I said to Judy

*Are you sure about this?*

*Of course. My mother's nurse in staying there until she finds another job. We are preparing it for sale. I have two brothers and my sister Mary and they don't want the house.*

So we booked two one-way tickets to New York from Malaga. I had been to Florida a couple of times but never ventured out of Orange County.

Judy had an apartment in New York, so when we landed we stayed in her apartment for a while. I would go around sight-seeing, and at nights we would go out for a meal; then Judy would go back to the apartment. I, of course, was looking for entertainment and found a comedy club or two. There were many of them around and I enjoyed them and had a few drinks.

In the mornings I normally started at Trump Tower, the 58-storey skyscraper that Donald Trump constructed in Manhattan. I would have a coffee and sandwich while reading the *Daily Mail,* and then off again sight-seeing around the place.

*Judy Otto from Long Island, New York.*

We eventually went over to Judy's house at Chicken Valley Road, Long Island. We were using Judy's mother's car so we could get about looking all around long Island, it was a very lovely place in Judy's area where it was two-acre zoning but in other areas it was five-acre zoning. We used to go and play tennis regularly in the local club and pass by John McEnroe's house. There were a lot of New York business people living on Long Island.

\* \* \*

I was in regular contact with my son Chris who was still running the Truck Inn. BP had not taken over yet and were still sorting the paperwork out with my solicitors. Chris said BP had sent a man to work with him to take over as manager so BP would be paying me the following week, and had asked him to stay on for two weeks to show this new man the ropes. I was also in regular contact with George who was running the haulage side. I called my accountant Michael Bland and he said he had signed all the papers in my solicitor's office and BP had paid the money over and he had put it into my bank account.

Chris stayed a couple of weeks to assist the new BP Truck Inn manager, then he went over to the haulage business; he wanted to drive the HGV vehicles. Chris chose Eddie Boyd, one of our drivers, to teach him to drive the trucks. Chris was very capable as he had been shunting around in the trucks on the Truck Inn lorry park for a few years (it was 10 acres). Eddie was riding shotgun and Chris was always driving; he really was enjoying it and took to the job. He passed the test for the HGV and started driving full time, and he always says, even now, that they were the best years of his life.

* * *

In New York I met a very nice man, Shelby Coats, who was an accountant. I told him that I had sold my business and was looking for an investment; he asked what line of business I was looking for. I said I had two or three fruit machines in my place at Carlisle and they were taking lots of money and this had led me to thinking of a small casino. He said he might have the ideal place for me down in Atlantic City where there was a small casino in liquidation and the accountant had a government man looking after it. The casino was closed but the hotel was open. He said

*Why don't I take you down there, have a free week or 10 days in the hotel and I will come and pick you up when you finished?*

Off I went, all excited, arrived at the hotel in Atlantic

City, where he introduced me to the man in charge of the hotel and sorted me a first-class room. I had a coffee with them both, then Shelby said he'd head back to New York and to give him a call when I was ready to return and he would collect me.

I couldn't wait to see Trump Plaza Hotel & Casino; on the way to the casino, buses were parked on every spare piece of land – hundreds of them. I was thinking "where can all these people be?"

To enter Trump casino you went up a wide escalator and, when I arrived at the top, I could not believe my eyes. The idea of owning a casino had suddenly completely disappeared from my head. As far I could see were rows and rows of slot machines, and into another part was a massive area with roulette tables and all kinds of gambling tables with thousands of people all around. The hotel had 614 rooms, seven restaurants and a 750-seat showroom; every day and night there was entertainment on, with bands and comedians in the bars. I had my dinner there in Trump Plaza – very reasonable and good food. In the gaming areas there were bunny girls giving away free drinks and food, which was also very nice. I stayed in there all night to see the entertainment and had a few drinks. I left about midnight and the place was still booming. I walked back to my hotel and the caretaker was still there. We had a drink at the bar and then I retired to bed, with all ideas of owning a casino completely gone.

I stayed in Atlantic City for about a week and had a good look around all the casinos. There was a half- built casino called the Taj Mahal, intended to be the biggest one in Atlantic City; 500 million dollars had been spent and it was still not completed. It was owned by Resorts and was in liquidation. Trump wanted to buy it and so did Mervin Griffin a TV host. He bought it for one day, then resold it to Donald Trump who completed the job; he called it

Trump Taj Mahal and opened it in 1990.

I called Shelby Coats in New York to see if he could collect me and he said okay and collected me the next day. I told him what I thought and that it was out of my league, and he said

*Look, I have two families in Puerto Rico that have a small hotel and casino, who are looking for a partner; why don't you go down there and have a look and talk to them?*

I wanted to travel and see this part of the world so I thought I had nothing to lose. He gave me all the particulars, I booked an eight-day return flight from New York to Puerto Rico, landed okay, hired a car and drove to the hotel casino. It was up in a nice country area. I arrived at the hotel and they were expecting me. I met with the two owners and their wives, who seemed very nice; they were two sisters and their husbands showed me to my room, very comfortable and clean. I went down and they showed me around the casino, which was not like the massive casinos in Atlantic City but was small and compact and it was a nice-sized hotel. The complex had been built and owned by the Teamsters union as a holiday complex for its members; but this was not now allowed by the law, so I don't know if they were forced to sell or it was taken from them, but these two American families had bought it.

It got quite busy at nights and the family showed me how to play the gambling games. I had no interest at all in gambling but liked the buzz, and a drink in the busy bar and the chats. The hotel was doing a nice trade and the family were so nice but I could not work out why they would want a partner. Through the day I would explore Puerto Rico in the rented car, keep stopping for a coffee and read a daily paper, have lunch somewhere different every day. It was a very relaxed place to be; everyone spoke English. I went back to the hotel late afternoon for a swim and chat with the owners. The nights passed quickly with people all around in the casino and in the bar and I was having a few beers and chatting with various people. Then when it was time to go, all four owners were having a good chat with me and were offering various deals; they wanted me to be with them in this venture but I still did not now why. But I had already made my mind up that I did not want to live in Puerto Rico; it was a small island and would not suit me. I flew back to New York and Judy picked me up.

I wanted to go to Florida. I had heard Fort Myers was a very nice place, so I phoned George Davidson, a chap down there who was from Carlisle. He had owned a few businesses in Carlisle. I phoned him and said I was coming down to Fort Myers and he said to call him when I got there and he would meet me. I flew into Fort Myers – nice new airport -and hired a car. I had already looked at hotel brochures on the flight down and had got my eye on The Robert E Lee Hotel. I drove into Fort Myers, found the hotel, looked around; it was spot on so I booked in for one week; it was a nice big room with two king-sized double beds, large en-suite, bath and shower, overlooking the water front. The other side was all restaurants. I went out at night to a restaurant called Steakhouse, ordered a steak, and there was a help-yourself salad bar with everything on, water for free on the table – a plentiful, lovely meal. I returned to the hotel and had a couple of beers in the bar.

Next morning I was up and showered, phoned George Davidson, had a chat and said I would meet him at Shoney's for breakfast. It was a help-yourself breakfast, as much as you want; there were pancakes, bacon, eggs, cheese, fried bread, fruit, jelly, ice cream, coffee, tea. We talked away about Carlisle and spoke about what he was doing in Fort Myers; , we finished breakfast and I followed him up to the business he was running. It was a lovely large warehouse-type building with offices upstairs. He had a few people employed and his daughter's husband's father was the manager and was doing building work and doing a lot of aluminium work. George also had quite a few building plots on Cape Corral to erect houses. He took me to various jobs they were doing and where the building plots were.

I was impressed with the depot building but it seemed to be wasted by harbouring a lot of rubbish that would rarely be moved. George said he would like a partner in the business and would I be interested? I said I would have to think about it. In the next few days I looked all around Fort Myers and Cape Corral and really liked the area; the day before I was leaving for New York I spoke with George and he asked me if I was interested in going into the business with him. I said I was still thinking about it, and I would give him a call from New York.

A few days went past and I was thinking about Fort Myers. New York was a big city but not my cup of tea, but Fort Myers was like being in the country and more my style. I had the idea I could make something of that lovely building in Fort Myers. So I called George Davidson from New York and made a deal with him, and said I would come down in the next week or so. Could he give me any idea where I could stay when I came down? He said

*I have a small new bungalow on Cape Corral you can use that for the time being until you get sorted out.*

I told Judy I had made a deal with George Davidson in Fort Myers and would she fancy going down, and she said

*Yes, we can take my car. We can call and see Bill and Abbey on the way down at Philadelphia.*

We got a good start. Judy was driving and she knew New York like the back of her hand, so we were soon out of New York and on the turnpike heading south. It was about 100 miles to Philadelphia so we were there by 11am. Bill and Abbey had coffee and snacks for us; they had a house in Capistrano Spain and knew Judy from there; I had also met them there. They were a lot of fun but Bill would take a bit too much drink some nights and could get very awkward, so we would all disappear from him. We stayed just over the hour and then hit the road again.

Our idea was to do about 400 miles per day and we would have two night stops on the road and be in Fort Myers on the third night. It was about 1,200 miles in total. After we had gone about 150 miles from Philadelphia, we had a stop for fuel and a something to eat. Driving in the US was a problem because of keeping to the speed limit of 60 mph. If the police stopped you, there were no excuses and you were just fined on the spot. If you disagreed with the traffic cop, it was "follow me to the station", so you soon paid up. We set off again and I was driving to give Judy a rest; we were getting on fine and soon we had the 400 miles behind us. We decided to go another few miles as we had changed drivers and I was still quite fresh. After about 70 miles we started looking for a place for the night. These road-side places in the US are very large and have a few hotels together and the restaurants are all separate and not attached to the hotels. They are very good actually and more or less are all the same all over the US. We found a place and pulled in, got booked in for the night, wandered out and got dinner and a couple of beers.

The next morning we got up and wandered out for breakfast. I was having the pancakes, eggs and bacon with tea; Judy was going more for the fruit and coffee. So we were filled up and back on the road, Judy at the wheel. I was taking in the scenery and all the different types of trucks, which were so different from the English ones. All had long bonnets and big cabs. English people who are not in the transport business think that these trucks have far more power than the English trucks, but this is not the case. In the UK the trucks are governed by the law that stipulates the maximum length a vehicle can be; the maximum was 13 metres so an articulated truck, to have a 40-foot trailer on to carry a 40 foot container, can be no longer then 13 metres. So the artic unit is designed with a flat front and engine under the cab. In the US the length does not seem to come into it.

After a couple more stops to eat and fuel up and to change drivers, we were doing well and had done some 460 miles in the day; so we thought we would try and get the 1,000 behind us before pulling up for the night, which would leave us about 250 miles the following day. At just under the 1,000 miles we started looking for a service area with the hotel and restaurant complex, pulled in, checked the car over for oil and water and fuelled up; we then booked into one of the hotels, looked around at the restaurants, chose a one, popped in for dinner – all very nice and we took our time – then finished off into the hotel bar for a couple of beers.

The next morning we breakfasted and were back on the road again, Judy at the wheel. It was all dual carriageway all the way from New York down to Fort Myers, no turn offs, just the same I-95 road. So in 250 miles we should be there or somewhere near; after about 170 miles we decided to stop to refuel, have some food and I took over the driving.

Back on the road I started thinking about staying at the Robert Lee Hotel that night in Fort Myers; we should be there just after lunch, book in and then have some lunch in the restaurant beside the hotel. We could then go over and see George Davidson about the house we could use, go and have a look at it with the intention of moving in the following day. His business was just up the road from the hotel and his house was in the same area. All went to plan; we booked in, had a bit of lunch and then around to see George.

I had phoned George before we set out from New York to give him an idea when we would arrive. I called in to the warehouse but he was not in there; they said he would be around at the house. We drove around to the house and met George and his wife. I introduced Judy to them. George then took us over to Cape Corral to show us a bungalow he had built but not sold. It was about three-quarter furnished, a very nice place. He said

*You can stay here until I sell it; that will give you time to have a look around.*

*This will do fine, we will move in tomorrow.*

George showed us around a few places and ideas he had about the future. We left George and headed back to the hotel, got showered and went out for a drive, then some dinner. We drove into Bell Tower, a large shopping area and had a good look around, and had dinner in TGI Fridays – a very nice restaurant and very busy; we enjoyed it very much and went back to the hotel ready for a good sleep.

Next morning we were up sharpish, showered and went into the diner next door. I was back to try the pancakes, bacon, eggs, and ice tea, , Judy was on the fruit and coffee. We checked out of the hotel and moved into the bungalow in Cape Corral. Judy dropped me off at George's warehouse and picked me up at about 5pm. I saw what the business was doing and what I had let myself into. George introduced me to most of the workers; his manager was the father of his daughter's husband, and he worked in the business. There were two men in the warehouse making up aluminium frames to cover swimming pools, and some workers out building a couple of houses on Cape Corral. George took me around to see these houses being built; there were some very lovely houses on Cape Corral, but there was plenty of competition because lots of people were building there. Cape Corral was a massive area with thousands of building sites.

In 1957 it started to be developed from 103 square acres of

swamp into building sites. They had hundreds of men and diggers that were dredging, making canals and building the land up with the dirt that was coming from the canals. On each side of the canals were building sites, with access to the canals for boating. Some had direct access to the Gulf of Mexico. There were 400 miles of canals and it was going to be the biggest city between Miami and Tampa.

We had bought some building land in Pine Island, just further on from Cape Corral. It was 120 acres; 10 acres on the road side was for commercial and the rest was for houses. It was planned in wheels and was four blocks of two houses, being eight houses per wheel, and the site was for 20 wheels – 160 houses in total. The deal we got was that we bought three wheels now and had to buy one wheel per year thereafter. Within a couple of weeks, I came to the conclusion that George was not like me and was not a hands-on man but left it to his manager to sort the work out. His manager was a very nice guy but not a man I would have put in charge with the expectation of making any money. George said I was to be over him, but I told him that would not work.

The big warehouse was really making nothing and there was no time limit on any job they were doing. It was going to be impossible for me to sort this out; there was too much of a family tie-up because the manager and his son worked there and George's daughter did part-time work.

I got very friendly with Jim Woodring and his wife; they had a large shop called "Price Cutter" which was doing very well. He would go over to Miami early in the mornings twice a week with his big van, and would buy bankrupt stock for a few cents in the dollar. I spoke to Jim

Would you fancy doing a shop in our warehouse?

It would be an ideal site for that, right on the busy roadside and with ample parking.

So I spoke with George and he agreed to have a meeting

with us, so we all met up – Jim, George and myself – and we soon agreed that this would work. All we had to do now was to work out the money side. Jim said he had no capital to put in, but would run the shop, buy all the supplies from Miami, but we would have to pay for all the stock. So George and I would pay for all the stock and use our warehouse. We agreed to share the profit three ways. George and I stumped up the money for Jim to go to Miami for stock, we had the warehouse all cleaned out ready for Jim to fill up.

Within a couple of weeks he had the place filled with all kinds, all racked out; and what a site it was, an ideal place for a shop, with lots of lovely clothes for all sizes and all ages. This building was very big and was made for this kind of job. Jim arranged the sales ladies with no problem and we were going to be open seven days a week. We had the opening day well advertised and the place took off from the very first day. We made money from the first week and had a share out every week.

Judy and I moved from the bungalow in Cape Corral to a house George had near to our shop because he had got a buyer for the bungalow.

We were planning to start the building on Pine Island; we needed a road built and also the main drains. We had talked to various architects and also drainage contractors, and they came up with different ideas. It was more difficult in Florida than in England to build because the water table is only about one to two feet down. On Pine Island, being near to the sea and lower lying, the water table is one foot down. So when you are putting the main drains in, you have to have pumping machines to extract the water permanently until that particular job is completed. After long consideration I was in favour of putting a large septic tank in to accommodate our first wheels of 24 houses. George was going for the full site to be fully fitted with the drainage system at a rough estimate by the drainage contractor of over $300,000, With my idea, we could have put in a septic tank and built quite a few houses for that money and could start selling houses.

I could see that our partnership was going to be difficult. George would not try to overcome the problems of the project we were doing but rather wanted to move on to something else. Before we had got started building on Pine Island, George was dragging me off to see the site next door for a golf course, wasting my time since I was not the slightest bit interested. Certainly not until we had got selling houses on our own site. Now I knew how I had succeeded in the UK, by having no-one to hold me back.

I could see things were not going to work out with George. Fort Myers was a very nice place and I liked it there; it was quite big but more like a village. So I started looking for a house of my own. The real estate lady we were using took us around quite a few places. After a few days we would go back around some of the areas we had been with the real estate lady. I got my eye on a place that had been empty for a couple of years. It was a bungalow with four bedrooms all ensuite, big kitchen, big lounge, double garage, air conditioning, and the swimming pool was at the back of the house in front of the kitchen window; it was all lovely caged in with aluminium which had just been renewed. You could walk out of the kitchen and have your food at a big dining table beside the pool; it also had a tennis court. It was a two-acre site with a curved drive in from the road, all lawned. It was not fenced around; the site was just all open on to the road. The area was all open planning with no walls or fences around the houses; all bungalows had two acre sites. It was also on a no-through road which made it very private.

I met with the real estate lady and said I was interested, it was priced at 350,000 dollars, so I started using my buyer's experience, going through all the problems the house had, which I was expanding on. So I said I would offer 200,000 dollars; she said they would not accept that. But she told me the law in Florida was that if anyone made an offer it had to be passed to the owner. The sales lady came back to me and said the owner and his wife would like to meet with us, so we arranged a meeting. We met the owners – a Mr and Mrs McNew – and we got on very well; he was in the road building business and I was in the transport business so we hit it off. They accepted the offer and within a few days the house was mine. At that particular time the pound was buying two dollars so I was really paying £100,000 – a very good buy.

Within a few days we had moved in. It was a lovely area, 7123, S. Brentwood Road, Cypress Lake Drive, Fort Myers, just down from Bell Tower shopping mall and an abundance of very good diners. All the houses around us were very well-kept, with immaculate lawns, all with sit-on mowers flying around at the weekends.

George had got his mind fully fixed on putting the complete drainage system into Pine Island for the approximate price of 300,000 dollars. I said I was not going this way but wanted to put in the septic tank system and get started with building. He would not hear of it, so I said I was not putting my money into his system; so he could buy me out. We came to a settlement with the big shopping warehouse we had set up with Jim Woodring, which was going well. George paid me out of that part of the business but he still had to settle with me for the building project; he said he would sort that out very shortly.

We were back in New York for a visit early in November 1988 and there was a message on Judy's phone for me to call my accountants Dodd's in Carlisle. I called them and asked to speak to Michael Bland. They put me through to his secretary and she said he had gone to Portugal to look at an investment project that could be of interest to me. I said I would be back in Carlisle in two weeks and I would call him then.

* * *

Angela my daughter had come back into the haulage business in about December 1987, and was working with George Holiday, my partner, in the office in Carlisle. I spoke to her and Chris on a regular basis. In February 1988 I spoke to Angela and she said George had taken a week's holiday. She had been told by one or two of our customers that George had been to see them to ask for work as he was starting a haulage firm of his own. I then spoke with my accountant Michael Bland and we agreed he should be dismissed instantly. We agreed it best if my accountant dismissed George, which would keep my son and daughter out of it. On the Monday my accountant went up to our transport office and spoke to George and told him he would have to go. George had no capital in the business so he only had the week's pay to come.

The haulage company was changed back into my own name Geoff Bell, from Bell Holiday. We installed one of the senior drivers to organise the transport, a Rodger Weeden; also Angela was in the office. My son Chris passed his HGV test in May 1988 and started driving full time.

* * *

I arrived back in the UK in mid November 1988 and met with my accountant Michael Bland. He filled me in on this investment in the Algarve, Portugal, which he had been to inspect a couple of weeks previously. He was very impressed and was, he said, a very good investment. It was 27 acres with planning for 100 building sites. The price was £2 million, and needed two investors with £1m each. We arranged to go for about a week. I wanted to have a good look around the area. I had never been to Portugal so I needed to get myself familiarised with the area, and get the value of other projects that were on offer. Michael Bland booked our flight for Sunday 20 November 1988 to Faro Portugal for one week; he also had us booked into Trust House Forte's hotel in Quinta do Lago, plus we had one week's car hire from Faro airport.

We arrived at Faro, collected the hire car, went over to the hotel, booked in and then started to have a drive around. We drove into Vale Do Lobo resort which was founded by Sir Richard Costain in 1962 and was helped when Faro international airport opened in 1965. The Dona Filipa Hotel was opened in 1968; it was a five-star luxury hotel named in the honour of Queen Philippa, a noblewoman of English birth, who married King Joao of Portugal in 1386. Their union is widely considered to have cemented the English-Portuguese relationship for many years. In 1971 the first house was built and then many more followed.

In 1977 a Dutch man Sander Van Gelder bought the resort and expanded the site by buying more land totalling 400 hectares (900 acres). What a place: beautiful big houses and well-manicured golf courses, a shopping centre with restaurants, bars and coffee bars. Ayrton Senna had a house there in Senna Avenue; he was a top- class Formula One driver who got killed on 1 May 1994 at the San Marino Grand Prix when he came off the track and hit a concrete bollard. Many more stars had mansions there. We then headed to the project that was for sale, maybe a mile from where we had seen all these lovely houses. There was a big sign up: For Sale "The Village" 11 hectares 100 sites with planning permission. It was a nice piece of land, all pine trees. I got to thinking what a lovely area it was and how people were buying judging by the project I had just seen in Vale De Lobo. By the time we we'd been all around Vale De Lobo and this site, we were looking for a place to have our dinner. We soon found one and had a nice meal. Mike and I thought the same: it was very nice area and many people were coming to the Algarve for holidays and buying retirement homes. We went back to the hotel and had a few beers in the bar and retired for the night.

We were up sharp, had a good breakfast and then onto the road to have a look at other projects. There were quite a few developments going on in the surrounding area and I wanted to know what they were building and what were their selling prices. All these projects had Portakabin type sales offices on site, so I had to pretend we were potential buyers, not just picking their brains. I collected all the sales brochures and most were very well done, not just photocopy on cheap material. I also wanted to look further afield and see what else Portugal had to offer. We kept stopping for a coffee or tea and a bit to eat. I found the food very good and the Portuguese liked us English. Almancil was the local village, a very nice little place with banks, restaurants, coffee bars, shops, car sales – all the amenities you would want.

When we had our coffee stops, I would be weighing up the brochures I had picked up at the various sales offices. The were offering two options: firstly, just buy the site and get your own builder to erect your house, secondly, they would give you a price for the completed house including the site; they had many types of houses so you could choose what you wanted and the price was already in the brochure. Equivalent building sites were selling for between £60,000 and £100,000 each as against a proposed cost of approximately £20,000 per building site we were looking at, based on a purchase price of £2 million for the whole development, divided by 100 potential building sites. On the basis of what Mr Bland said, I decided that this was a good development opportunity.

During the course of the visit to Portugal Mr Bland introduced me to Martin Corlett, who was a builder and showed me the plans of the site. He had a construction company and if the investment went ahead he would put all the infrastructure in and ready the sites for sale; he would take his part of the profits and his costs when the sites were being sold. He could also build the houses if required. Mr Bland explained to me I could take part in the construction, or make a loan and receive interest.

We looked around the area for a few days, getting as much information as possible to help me with my decision. Mr Bland said the other investor would be a client of Dodd's, his partnership accountancy practice in Carlisle. I really liked the site and knew money could be made and with Michael Bland, my trusted accountant, to look after the job, how could it go wrong?

We were meeting the owners on the Friday and I had made my mind up to invest half of the money, but I had questions to ask the owners before I would hand any money over. The idea that day was if I was to go ahead, I was to put a deposit down. We met the owners in the Trust House Fortes Hotel at La Quinta Golf and I got all the information I required and could see no obstacles. Michael Bland wrote two of my cheques out, one for each owner for £100,000 each. Mr Bland wrote out a receipt on the hotel typewriter and both owners signed it. The owners took us to a small bar and treated us to a nice late afternoon snack. Michael Bland and I returned home to Carlisle on the Sunday.

On the Monday I called into Dodd's office and spoke with Michael Bland and went through all the details, and how the job would progress; he was very keen on this project and he said this was what he wanted to get more into. By the end of June 1989 I had invested £1,240,035 into the Portugal project.

The investment terms were the full capital to be paid back in one year and 50% interest to be paid back six months later. In 1989 Mr Bland briefed with me that he had an excellent investment in Campillos Spain for a golf course, hotel, and housing project, around a lake, which I was not interested in. He insisted I go with him to have a look at the project. It was a lovely setting but I did not want to be involved. Mr Bland said it needed a £400,000 loan and would pay interest of 65% in one year. I was still not interested. After a couple of weeks he came back to me and said he had another client with Dodd's that would put £200,000 in if I would do the same. He said that it was a very short-term loan and I would be silly to miss the opportunity. I gave in against my good judgement and said yes.

In March 1989 £200,000 was paid into this investment along with a Mr Armstrong, one of Dodd's clients from Carlisle, who also put in £200,000. The conditions were: full amount and 65% interest paid back in one year.

In early 1989 Judy and I set off on a trip heading for the California area just to see more of the USA. I had my Mercedes shipped over from UK. The first night we stayed at Pensacola, and the next day moved on. I asked one American guy before we set off what advice he could give me. He said to make sure we kept your fuel topped up wherever possible because it might be many miles between fuel stations. After Pensacola we stopped for two nights in New Orleans; we picked up a hotel advert on the roadside and headed into the hotel covered car park and got booked in – very nice hotel. We wanted to see all the night life we had heard about over the years. We had a couple of nights to look around and it was great fun and we fully enjoyed it all.

On the long road the next morning heading for San Antonio – about 550 miles and all straight roads as far as the eye can see – we kept stopping for snacks and fuel top-ups. We stopped at a small hotel for the night, and found dinner and breakfast OK. We were back on the road the next morning on to Monterrey, California. There were many nice hotels there and we got one sorted out. The next day we were going on the 17-mile Pebble Beach Drive. Noted for its scenic attractions, famous golf courses and mansions, we also visited Carmel and we had a nice meal there. From Monterrey we headed for El Paso on more long straight roads. We stopped a couple of times for snacks, coffee and fuelling up. After a long day, we just pulled up at a nice-looking hotel for the night. Next day we would head for San Diego through Tucson. It was a long old drive with more coffee breaks and snacks and fuel-ups. We arrived in San Diego and booked into a very nice hotel for two nights. We wanted a good nose around. We left San Diego and now headed for Palm Springs. What a nice place! We decided to stop for the night and have a good look around – really enjoyable.

On the road again, next stop was Los Angeles for three nights in another lovely hotel. There was plenty to see and good night-life entertainment and comedy clubs. Next port of call was Las Vegas for a three-night stop. We booked into a hotel and went into the casinos at nights, watching the top-class shows. I had no interest in the gambling side. We would go out in the car each day touring around to see what was about.

Next we wanted to see the Grand Canyon, about 259 miles away; but on the way I wanted to see the Hoover dam. You drive over a narrow bridge on the Hoover Dam which was very narrow one-way traffic. The dam was built from 1931 and finished in 1936 and is 726 feet deep from the foundation to the roadway, and weighs 6,600,000 tons. It took 4,360,000 cubic yards of concrete. It supplies water to Nevada, California, Arizona, Los Angeles, Phoenix, San Diego and the farmers – it supports 18 million people in total.

After seeing the dam, we carried on to Williams and stayed in a hotel there; it was actually very cold. We had dinner and a few beers. We had an early start and had breakfast; we went outside to find everything was all frosted up. The car was all iced up but luckily I had some de-icer left in from the UK. We got in the car and I was wondering if she was going to start; it was diesel so they take more starting than the petrol cars. I gave it two or three times on the heater plugs and up she fires, no problem. We were then on to see the Grand Canyon, which was very interesting and worthwhile calling in. Our next destination was Dallas, which was more than 1,000 miles away, so we would make a stop somewhere about half way. At just under the 500 miles, we started looking for a hotel, spotted a hotel and services up ahead and pulled in. It looked OK so we booked in for the night, popped next door to a restaurant and had dinner, very good. I found most of the American dinners very good. We had a couple of drinks and called it a day. We were up in the morning, breakfasted, got all fuelled up and were soon out on the road again, next stop Dallas; maybe we'd stop a couple of nights with JR at South Fork, maybe I would be lucky and JR would be out so I would have to spend the night with Su Ellen. We found a nice hotel in Dallas on a Friday night, so we decided to stay for three nights. I found the best way to explore a city was on a Sunday as it was always the quietest day and there was very little traffic. I liked Dallas.

Dallas was a tiny trading post and frontier town which became a major centre for the cotton, railroad, merchandise, oil, and financial industries. We had a very enjoyable time in Dallas, but time to move on.

Our next destination was Memphis Tennessee, about 450 miles away and the home of Elvis. We found another good hotel and booked in for two nights. We would probably spend the biggest part of a day in Graceland. While Nashville is known for country music, Memphis is known for its famous blues and rock and roll. On the next day we went into Graceland and I found it very interesting. Elvis purchased the 14-acre Graceland in 1957. People come from all over the world to see the legend's treasures; his trophies tell the story of Elvis's personal life with memorable things like Priscilla's wedding dress, numerous flashy suits once worn by the singer on stage, also toys from Lisa Marie's childhood. We saw the office of Elvis's father Vernon where the star's personal business was conducted. A separate building contains a collection of his favourite cars: a 1955 pink Cadillac, a 1956 purple

Cadillac convertible, a red MG, and also Elvis's two aeroplanes; you can step aboard his lavish Convair 880 to admire the gold seat belts and leather-covered tables. We thoroughly enjoyed Elvis's place. We also visited the Memphis music hall of fame with its many memories. There were plenty of nice restaurants all around where you could sit and have a coffee and watch all the people going by.

Next stop was Nashville, the place I was really looking forward to, with me being a country fan. During the 10 years I booked bands in the Truck Inn, they were 95% country-based. It was just over 200 miles from Memphis to Nashville so we were there quite early and we searched for a place that would be handy for the Grand Ole Opera, and near to the night life where the live country music was being played. We settled on an area, found a nice hotel, booked in for three nights with an option to stay longer if we required.

Nashville was founded in 1779 and is now the capital of country music as evidenced by such attractions as the Country Music Hall of Fame, and the city's famous music country district, and The Grand Ole Opry. The first night we found quite a large pub with very good country music on all night; we had a few drinks and really enjoyed the crowd, stayed there the full night with no reason to leave. The next morning we wandered out for breakfast at one of many diners to choose from, all help your self and as much as you want. We then drove around to get our bearings and see the area and we planned to visit the Grand Ole Opry that night. We visited the Opryland Hotel which is a beautiful hotel and I wish we had booked in at this unbelievable place. What an experience in the Grand Ole Opry for the night with all kinds of top-class country singers and musicians on stage. They all joined in with each other. We came out at the end of the show and found another venue to have a few drinks and more country music. The next night we found another country music venue, had a few drinks and enjoyed all the different acts. Next morning, it time to head for Fort Myers. It's about 830 miles so we would have a one-night stop – don't forget the speed limit is 60 mph. So we fuelled up, got breakfast and went back on the road home.

* * *

In May 1989 my son Chris and my sister Amy came over to Florida for a couple of weeks. They flew into Tampa, hired a car and drove down to Fort Myers. We had a very good couple of weeks with them and showed them all around.

Also in 1989 my friends Malcolm Wright and Davina came to visit me in Fort Myers. Malcolm had sold his hotel in Carlisle and decided to have some time off; he had bought a camper van and towed a little car behind. They wanted to travel around the US and explore the places. He stayed with us quite a few days and then moved on.

* * *

In November 1990, the four of us set off from Heathrow airport on a world tour, Malcolm, Davina, Judy and I. Our first stop was Singapore. We had made no hotel booking ahead so when we landed we just called an hotel from the airport advert board; we chose Holiday Inn, booked in, got a taxi to the hotel checked in, no problem. We liked Singapore which was a very lovely nice clean place. The way this round the world trip worked was that, when you wanted to move on, you just phoned the airline you were allotted to and told them where you wanted to go next and when; they then told you what was available and you chose the flight that suited you. The only thing you had to remember was that you had to keep going forward, with no going back. You could take as much time as you wanted in any particular place, so there was no time limit on your trip.

We stayed in Singapore for three or four days and our next destination was Bangkok. We arrived in Bangkok airport, checked the advert boards, chose Bangkok Palace hotel, got booked in, taxi to the hotel, all checked in for four nights, could be extended if required. We went out into Bangkok and there was a big difference from Singapore, with narrow packed streets, people making food on the side of the streets, people living very poorly. Malcolm's son joined us with his wife Angela. John was a bit more outgoing than his dad and like me wanted to experience a bit of the night life that we had heard about. In the hotel there were quite a few tailors making up suits in just a couple of days, at very reasonable prices, so we all had to get a couple.

I had visited Bangkok before with an American group from Nerja; on that trip we did Hong Kong. It was a laugh landing there because there was washing hanging out each side of the runway from apartments; we all thought the aeroplane was going to take the washing on its wings. We also had a day trip into China. I never forget that we stopped in China for a buffet type lunch; we all sat around a big round table that turned round, and just got what we wanted. After lunch one of the guys said to me "how did you enjoy your lunch?" I said "okay, " then he said, "so you like dog do you?" I could not believe him. Well the next stop on the bus was an open market and what was hanging up? Dogs, all butchered and dressed up for sale and lots of different types. One night I said to this tut-tut taxi "can you take us to a nice restaurant?" "Yes yes I take you to my family restaurant it very nice." He dropped us off at this place and we went in. Where was the restaurant? It was a strip joint. I said "let's take a look for a laugh." It was more of a sex show. What an eye-opener – never seen anything like it, and unexplainable in words.

I said to my friends that we must go to the bridge over the river Kwai. I had been before on my previous trip. We hired two cars and off we went. It was a slow drive because they were building a new road and there were trucks everywhere and many diversions, but we got there eventually. We went on the train ride to get the full picture of what went on. Last time I had been to the museum and got a lot of the story, heart-breaking and unbelievable.

It all happened in World War II when the Japanese occupied Thailand and used allied prisoners to build the bridge joining Burma to China. The Japanese used all kinds of brutal methods to get the workers to work, with next to no food and the men were whipped with bamboo canes to work until their knees were showing through their skin.

During the construction of the bridge approximately 13,000 prisoners were buried alongside the railway, and an estimated 80,000 to 100,000 civilians died in the course of the project. Cheap forced labour was brought in from Malaya and Dutch East Indies or conscripted in Siam (Thailand) and Burma.

Next door to the Bangkok Palace Hotel was a travel agency and we were looking to visit Phuket for a week or so; we got sorted out with flights and booked the Diamond Cliff Hotel. The flight took about one and a half hours. We landed at Phuket, got a taxi to the hotel, and got booked in to what was a lovely place. We were out at nights, down to a restaurant, then the bar area; all the bars were together and there was always something going on, such as Thai wrestling or kick boxing, and the crack was good. There were plenty of English people about and we met two lads from Birmingham who were characters and good company.

Malcolm's son John was walking down on the beach one day and he came across this very smart young lady with her bathing suit on, all tanned and very attractive. She was selling massages so he booked in for the next day at 2pm. John came back from the appointment and I asked him how it had gone. He burst out laughing, saying the old mother was doing the massages. We had a very enjoyable time in Phuket, but soon it was back to Bangkok and next we were off to Pattaya, another Island not far from Bangkok. We all enjoyed this very much, a nice place with plenty of holiday-makers and plenty of fun.

Back in Bangkok, it time to move on, next stop Perth, Australia. When we landed in Perth, Davina recommended the Burswood Casino Hotel because she knew some friends from Shap near Penrith Cumbria and they were regulars in Perth and said it was a good hotel. We called the Burswood, got booked in with no problem, again a lovely hotel. Actually we were travelling a good time and all the hotels were very reasonable, maybe because the Gulf War was on and the Americans were not holidaying. We hired cars and got to see lots of different places, I really liked Perth. There were two tennis courts so Judy and I played quite a lot of tennis. We were there for Christmas and it was a very nice place to be. We moved up to Observation City Hotel, the project Alan Bond built, on Scarborough beach Perth – another beautiful hotel and lovely beaches.

Alan Bond was born in London and the family emigrated to Fremantle Perth when Alan was only very young and still at school. The family were very poor and when Alan left school he got a job as a sign writer. He was a very cocky young fellow, and soon started his own business painting and sign writing; he undercut all his competition by cutting corners. He started quite a few men and as one of the men was quoted saying "we went one weekend about 70 miles up north to paint a hotel, we took a 45 gallon drum of paint and spent the two days to finish the job, we came back with about 20 gallons of paint in the drum Bond kept watering it down". He actually started with nothing, built a multibillion dollar empire, all with borrowed money and always had more borrowed than his empire was worth. In the year up to June 1989 Bond Corporation has made a loss of $980 million, by far the biggest in Australian corporate history, but it was revealed and resulted in a doubling of his annual Interest bill to around $1000 million. Which was to say that if all his assets were sold off there would be a short fall of $100 million. His empire finished up bankrupt and he finished up in jail. He had won the Americas Cup in 1983 which the Americans had commandeered for many years.

Malcolm's son John and Angela flew from Perth back home to Carlisle. We spent about six weeks in Perth. Then Judy and I moved to Sydney and went to see the tennis tournament in Melbourne, normally played in the last two weeks of January. Malcolm and Davina stayed in the Perth area to attend a golfing competition they wanted to see and they would join us in Sydney later. We found a good hotel overlooking the Opera House, near to famous Bondi beach and overlooking the famous Sydney Harbour bridge, which is an icon opened in 1932. It's the largest steel bridge in the world and nick-named The Coathanger. The building contract was awarded to Dorman Long & Co in England big steel producers in those days. All the Steel was made in Middlesbrough and shipped to Perth. When I was truck driving from 17 years old, I used to go to Dorman Long's Steel works for basic slag; they had steel making plants all over the UK.

We hired a car and travelled to the tennis most days in Melbourne, where John McEnroe won but was disqualified and Ivan Lendl was crowned the winner for 1990.

Malcolm and Davina arrived from Perth and they also hired a car and we set off to go to New Zealand. We arrived at the ferry but could not take our cars over but we had to hire cars when we got over into New Zealand. We were having a good drive around New Zealand and then we decided we had better get an hotel booked for a few nights. We tried a few but there were no vacancies; apparently there was a bicycle rally on and the hotels were booked up. There were a lot of bicycles on the road but we thought this was normal. So we decided to split up and each of us try and find a vacancy. Judy and I found a hotel, but we had lost Malcolm and Davina. We met up on the next morning and they had also got a hotel for three nights. New Zealand was a very nice clean place and you could even see to the bottom of the lakes. The people were so friendly.

Next we were over to Tasmania for a couple of nights. It was much larger than I had anticipated. It covers 16,902 acres, which is 98 times larger than Singapore and two thirds the size of England. We were trying to get a glimpse of the Tasmanian devils, but in general it was a very nice experience with good food and very nice people.

When back in Sydney, Judy and I decided to drive up the coast to Cairns. Malcolm and Davina would have a few more days in Sydney as they had been later coming from Perth, and they would follow in a few days and meet in Cairns. They told us in Sydney that each year the roads up to Cairns could be flooded up until the end of February, but luckily they were all cleared by the time we drove up. We had a couple of stops on the way up. There were some very poor areas and people living in tin huts, but also there were some nice houses and expensive areas. They call this the Gold Coast. We stayed in Brisbane for one night, a very lovely city.

We arrived in Cairns, stayed for three nights and had a

good look around. Malcolm and Davina turned up after taking a flight up. Our next destination was Hawaii. We called in at a travel shop and the staff showed us brochures on hotels in Hawaii and advised on one which looked the part. So we arranged the flight, landed in Hawaii, took the taxi to the hotel, good choice. We hired two Jeep type cars and had good runs around the island. The place was all very nice with good nightlife, including comedy and good bands in the hotels. Hawaii is a big US military base with Pearl Harbor. At that time there was a parade and celebrations because a lot of solders were coming back from the Gulf War.

We had a tour round Pearl Harbor and saw all navy war ships and submarines. We were enjoying the place so much we decided to have another week in Hawaii, so we approached the hotel reception and spoke to the lady and said we would like to stay one more week. It was no problem but the price she quoted was far in excess to what we had paid the travel agency in Cairns, so I said to the lady that we'd think about it. Then I telephoned the travel agency in Cairns, asked if he could book us in for another week and within minutes he had us booked for one more week at the same price as before. I gave him our card numbers, job done. I went back to reception and it had been confirmed from Cairns. We were in for one more week. I still think it was one of the best places I have been on holiday to.

Our next stop was Los Angeles. We checked the advert boards at the airport, got a taxi to the hotel, booked in and hired a couple of cars to go around all the sights by day and entertainment each night. We had a guided bus tour all around the Hollywood houses, well I mean 'palaces'.

Judy and I booked our next flight to Fort Myers. Malcolm and Davina booked their flight back to Heathrow UK. We had enjoyed what you might call a very successful world tour.

So back in Fort Myers to the house and everything was in order. I had two brothers, garden contractors and very good lads, who looked after the garden each week. I stayed there a while and then I returned to Carlisle to see my son and daughter.

I was still doing quite a bit of travelling from the US to the UK and also Spain. It was very reasonable flying in those days.

* * *

When Judy and I were in New York and Mrs McCarthy invited us up to Martha's Vineyard for a couple of weeks. There were quite a lot of her family going to her house there so Mrs McCarthy booked us a hotel for the two weeks so we accepted. So off we went, driving from New York to Martha's Vineyard, approximately 266 miles up through Newhaven, Providence, then onto the ferry. We had a couple of coffee stops and snacks on the way up. We were booked into the beautiful Harbor View Hotel, Edgartown, with stunning views and also overlooking the famous lighthouse. Many celebrities visited here every year with their families, including the Kennedys. The big disaster for them was in 1969 when Teddy Kennedy's car went off the bridge at Chappaquiddick into the water and Mary Jo Kopechne, aged 28, drowned in the submerged car. The Kennedy insurance paid out $141,000 to Jo's family.

We had a fantastic time with the McCarthys and all dined together at night, mostly in restaurants, sometimes in Mrs McCarthy's house. The women would all get together and prepare the odd dinner for about 12 or us. The restaurants were top-class and also the coffee bars to snack in and chat. We played tennis quite a lot and Mrs McCarthy would insist she booked me in for a tennis lesson. I was in her company some years later and she said "Have you kept your tennis lessons up? I said "No, I have not mastered what the man was trying to teach me in Martha's Vineyard." I liked Mrs McCarthy and the visit was an excellent two weeks.

Mrs McCarthy also invited us to her house at Vermont for a family get-together. We arrived at the house and it was more like a mansion, and all the houses around were massive lovely homes. Next door was the Johnson's and Johnson's family home – what a house that was. There were quite a lot of us – must have been 20 at least – and we were all in the sitting room and the waiter was serving pre-lunch drinks. Mrs McCarthy's mother was in a wheelchair and had a carer looking after her permanently. They also had a butler and a chef and two maids. After pre-dinner drinks the butler appeared with a tea towel on his arm and said "dinner is served madam". We all followed Mrs McCarthy senior into the dining room. It was like being treated as royalty.

After lunch we spread about into different areas. I was out on the terrace talking to John McCarthy's half brother Peter, not the quiet type like John but full of chat and laughs. About 3pm unsuspectingly some doors opened and about 30 dogs ran and jumped into the swimming pool. I had never seen anything like it. I think they were Labradors and they swam around until they got tired, then got out and thoroughly shook themselves to get dry. Around the house was a very large area with lots of buildings and horse boxes, but there were no horses in at that time. We had a memorable day with the McCarthy family and Mrs McCarthy invited us down to Palm Beach Country Club for four weeks later and we said we would love to come and join them there.

We drove over to Palm Beach and found a lovely hotel for three nights. Judy spoke on the phone with Mrs McCarthy and got details of where we would meet the next day. We were looking forward to the lunch at Palm Beach Country Club, a strictly members only club. We met the next day at 12 noon outside the club and got signed in. It had a beautiful restaurant and surroundings. There were about 10 of us and nobody I knew except Mrs McCarthy. We had a lovely lunch and everyone chatted away, all of them asking me questions about England and the royal family. We were there all afternoon finishing off with coffee and brandy.

This Palm Beach Country club was very strict on who could join and Donald Trump was rejected. In 1985 Trump decided that Mar-a-Lago would be his personal castle. The original owner willed it to the government to be used as a winter White House for American presidents. But presidents didn't use it and the federal government grew weary of paying for the $1 million a year it took to maintain it. Eager to unload the Florida mansion, the government agreed to a $10 million sale to Trump, who was a hotshot 39-year-old New York real estate developer in a contract that required Trump to put down only $2,812 of his own money.

When the Mar-a-Lago investment was in doubt, Trump had launched another local real estate venture across the Intracoastal Waterway in West Palm Beach, an ailing 33-storey, twin-tower complex that a Palm Beach developer had lost in foreclosure. Trump bought the property in 1986 for $40 million cash, $3.2 million less than the Bank of New York paid to reclaim the property at a public foreclosure auction. Trump renamed the West Palm Beach condo project after himself and he spent millions to spruce up the public areas of the Trump Plaza of the Palm Beaches and to advertise the sale of its luxury condos in North-eastern newspapers. But after four years of heavy promoting, fewer than half of the units had been sold, and Trump had borrowed $60 million from Marine

Midland Bank of New York to pay for the project, money he couldn't repay.

In 1991, two months before he would file for corporate bankruptcy on his Trump Taj Mahal casino in Atlantic City, Trump turned over Trump Plaza of the Palm Beaches to Marine Midland Bank, in exchange for the bank agreeing to forgive Trump for his $14 million personal guarantee on the loan.

We had three splendid days in Palm Beach and I was very grateful again to Mrs McCarthy.

*The Bell family: Lorraine, Geoff,
Christopher and Angela*

*Opening night of the Carlisle Truck Inn. From right to left: Vic Essex, Geoff, Lorraine and Vic's wife. They are from Derby. Vic became a very good friend when I was buying trailers from him. We met regularly at the Harrogate tipper convention each year, and had some very happy, memorable times.*

*From left to right: my brother Reg, my father Harold, my mother Hannah and me.*

*From left to right: me, Gib Baird, Fred Abbot. I met Gib when I was about 15 years old and we have been friends ever since. He is an absolute born gentleman. Gib is an entrepreneur like myself. I revolutionized truck drivers' accommodation, Gib revolutionized dairy farming by milking a few hundred cows; the norm on the dairy farms then was milking about 50–60 cows. Gib started from scratch and finished up with three large farms. My wife Celene and I meet up with Gib and his lovely wife Dolly every time we are in the area and really enjoy their company.*

In 1989 when I was back in the UK, Angela was in the transport office and Chris was driving, . Rodger the man we had put into the transport office to run the trucks was not up to the job. Chris and I went over to the Truck Inn and we were having our lunch and we talked about the problem with our man running the trucks and I said

*Chris, I have a new man to go in the office.*

*Have you, who is he?*

*You, you know the job now, and you have Angela in the office.*

So I spoke with Rodger the man we had taken off the trucks to run the office and I told him that I didn't think things were going so well for him and that Chris would come in the office. I asked him if he would go back on the road on the truck Chris was driving and he said that it was no problem. I think he was quite relieved because it is a very stressful job running a transport business.

In 1990 I spoke with Angela and Chris and said that I was away a lot and why don't they take over the transport business which I didn't need. We had a good talk about things and we decided that they would still run it for me for one year, see what the profits were, then decide.

After the year was up in 1991, we had a good talk and Angela said she did not want to be in the haulage business; Chris said he was not over the moon to be in the transport business either. Angela said she was going to open a restaurant. I said to Chris

*So are you going to drive for some other transport firm? I think you are making a big mistake, I have run transport for many years and done very well out of it. Listen I will stay with you for a few weeks. Also why don't we cut down from 12 trucks*

*to eight and sell four off and make it easier?*

So we took four off and they were sitting in the yard. I was having a snack with my pal Mark Winter in the Truck Inn and Chris came over and said he need another couple of trucks on because it is very busy. So he finished up with 10 trucks on the road. He took over the truck business and I was free from trucks. I stayed with Chris for quite a while and went with him to see various customers.

In September 1991 BP still owed me £30,000. I had called Keith Cripwell at BP many times and he kept saying he had instructed their solicitor to settle this, but during the last call I made to Keith he told me to get my solicitor to write to them. I spoke with one of my solicitors, Donald Livingstone, in the early part of the year and said I thought I would order £30,000 worth of diesel to settle the £30,000 BP owed me. He said "why not?" So I did order the diesel.

After a few months, BP was on to me asking me to pay for the diesel. I said that we were all-square now since they already owed me this amount of money. My son Chris had taken over the truck business from me, and early one Sunday morning Chris rang me and said all the trucks had a no movement order issued by the courts on the instructions from BP. The order was on Geoff Bell Ltd, but Chris's company was Geoff Bell (Uk) Ltd. So I told Chris to go down to the police station and take all his paperwork with him to prove that he owned the trucks not me. After he passed all the papers to the police for inspection, everything was removed from the trucks which were then all clear to go.

I got my solicitor Patricia Hall, a very good solicitor, and a judge, to sort this out with BP. Patricia got it all settled by November 1991, BP offsetting the £30,000, and then paying me £6,800 for the four-year's delay in paying me, plus all solicitor's fees.

* * *

In the summer of 1991 Judy and I were invited up to her sister's place in Geneva as she and her husband John normally went to the US for six weeks. They knew I would take care of the house and do any jobs around the place, do the gardening and cut the lawns. We took up their offer and I mentioned this to Malcolm and Davina who by now had finished touring the US and had returned to Europe with the camper van. They were touring Europe so they said they would call in. I also mentioned it to our other friends Tony and Kath Armstrong, the chap that had made the investment with me in the golf course project in Spain. So they all came to Geneva we had a great time. Geneva is a lovely place with plenty of nice restaurants and coffee shops to sit and pass the time away.

The investment in Portugal that my accountant Michael Bland was looking after had not been re-paid. Even after constant phonecalls and requests to Mr Bland, I had received nothing. Also the investment that Mr Bland took me into in the Campillos golf resort in Spain had not been paid back. In about October 1991 my pal Ian Benson, a certified bailiff and private investigator and process server in Carlisle, was asking me the whereabouts of Michael Bland. I told him that Mr Bland was at his home in Welton, Dalston. He said he had instructions from a London solicitor to serve a writ on Michael Bland for a sum of £1.2 million issued on behalf of First National Bank. I acquired a copy of this writ and I could not believe it. Mr Bland had told me the other investor was a client of Dodd's my accountants, where Bland was a partner. I tracked down the other investor in the Campillos Golf project in Spain and he had not received his investment back either; he was a Tony Armstrong from Carlisle, whom I got to know very well.

It was a revelation. Michael Bland had turned out to be a professional fraudster. The investment in Portugal was not paid back and the Spanish investment had not been paid back either, so I was having to invest in something that I never thought I would have to do, that is a lawyer. Choosing a solicitor is one of the most difficult things to do. You meet with them and explain the problem to them and before you finish they have won the case. It is the only job I know that when they give you advice and it is completely wrong, they still want to be paid. I find with nearly all solicitors, barristers, and judges that they do not read up on the full case you are providing to them. When I started these cases against Michael Bland I had Dickinson Dee from Newcastle and I was getting on well with one of the partners, but within a few weeks they moved me to another solicitor with no explanation, so I had to explain the case all over again. I spoke to Dodd's accountants and they advised me to go and see a John Whitehead at Granger King and Hynes in Penrith. I had a meeting with him and he seemed OK so I moved all my paperwork to him and we got started. We had various court cases but nothing like getting my money returned. We had various barristers but none we were really happy with, except a Mr Leaming, who was also a QC. We were getting on well with Mr Leaming but we were unlucky again because he had a heart attack and was off work for a long time.

One day John Whitehead called me and said

*I think I have found a barrister that will suit you.*

*How did you find him?*

*I had a case in Manchester today and he worked rings around me.*

*What's his name?*

*Mark Cawson.*

So John Whitehead and I met with Mark Cawson in his office in Manchester and I took to Mark instantly; he had a different approach, wanting to know all and not winning the case before we got out of his office. His statements were fully detailed and showed a complete picture that you wanted the judge to see. Michael Bland was all into offshore companies so we were having cases in Jersey also. I needed a lawyer in Portugal and used a one in Largos, an Artur Rego. We did court cases in Jersey and won, but no money back. I was doing court case after court case but getting nowhere, and got to thinking that this Michael Bland was a really professional fraudster.

In Fort Myers George Davidson had not paid me back for my half share in the construction project, so I had to employ a lawyer there. After having no confidence in the first two lawyers in Fort Myers, I was advised to go to Henderson & Franklin. This law firm had about 100 partners and after explaining my case to the receptionist she then introduced me to the one she thought would be best for my job, but he was full up and could not take me. I moved on to the second choice, same again too busy, and on it went. Then she said that they had a new lawyer who has just started from law school and she would introduce me to him. He was Doug Szabo. I explained what my problem was and he said he would be happy to work on this for me. Like with Mark Cawson, 1 took to him and could see he was a thorough man and was absorbing everything. Over the years I would never have to re-tell him anything. Once he had all the paperwork, he rarely bothered me.

* * *

In 1992 we were back in Spain. I had let the house in Fort Myers to an American retired couple I had met in Spain. They were a very nice couple and he was a real character; he had worked with the English a lot in the forces. Judy was heading from Spain back to New York for a while and it was decided that from then we would go our separate ways. That was the end of our relationship.

So I was back in Nerja again by myself, like a new start. I was down to the tennis courts to see who was there. I thought that big Ron wouldn't be far away and he was, and we had a good old chat. His wife had put in for a divorce and she had gone back to the UK. He said he had no chance of defending the divorce as he had two sons, both educated to be solicitors. He had a bar now with his girlfriend's mother and he asked me to call down any night as he was always there to open the bar.

I started playing tennis with various different players most mornings, then headed down to the Plaza Cavana Hotel for coffee and my midday snack and daily paper. It was a good meeting point and there were always a few regulars around. Ron and I started playing squash again and was joined by another fellow called Frank; we had a lot of fun together.

I used to get showered at night and headed down to Ron's bar which got very busy later on. Ron and I would go downtown after his bar staff had come in and we'd have a meal and then go around a few bars, then sometimes finish off back at Ron's bar. Nerja had lots of good restaurants and one of our favourites was the Round Bar. After dinner we would go to one of the many places of entertainment and have a few beers. The company was good and there was plenty of crack and banter. One night we were out and we got in the company of some holidaymakers from Newcastle. I got talking to one of the girls called Joanne Le Blond and we had a drink or two together and I asked her out for dinner the next night and she accepted. I met Joanne the next night and we went to the Round Bar restaurant and had a very good meal. We then met up with the others and went to a bar for the crack and a few drinks – a very

160

good night. I quite liked Joanne so I asked her out the next night and we were out together every night until her holiday was over. I told Joanne I would be coming back to Carlisle very shortly, and asked if I could give her a call and meet up. She said yes, and that she lived with her mother in Gosforth, where they had three bedrooms so I could come over and stay for a couple of nights.

A few weeks later I was back in Carlisle and after a few days I phoned up Joanne and she asked me over for a few nights, which I accepted. I met her mother and we all got on well together. There were plenty of restaurants and bars to go around in Newcastle. In the next two or three weeks I was going back to Spain and asked Joanne if she would like to come with me. She said yes and so I booked return flights for three weeks from Newcastle to Nerja.

In Nerja we would be around the tennis courts in the mornings for the chat with the lads and then down to the Plaza Cavana Hotel for coffee and banter with the regulars. We often went out for dinner with Joe and Isobel who I had met at the Plaza Cavana Hotel having coffee some time ago; they often went there for coffee because it was the place to meet people. We went to various restaurants like Frigiliana, one or two places in Torrox, all good restaurants; they also liked the Round Bar.

We returned to Newcastle and I started work on a job I took on to refurbish an apartment there in Montague Court. It was a three bedroom all en-suite with a veranda overlooking the town moor. The moor is 1,000 acres, larger than Hyde Park and Hampstead Heath combined, also larger than New York City's Central Park which is 843 acres. I soon got the apartment all sorted and it turned out to be a lovely place. I had never stayed in an apartment so it was all very different to me. It was a penthouse on the top floor and had a lift up from the two-car garage. But I was always used to houses from which I could walk right out into the garden.

I was there a while but never got used to it. I was truly a house man. I took Joanne to Fort Myers for a few weeks which she enjoyed very much. We returned to Newcastle and within a couple of weeks I needed to go back to Nerja. Joanne didn't want all the travelling so she did not come. That was the end of that relationship. I just went alone, no problem. I liked Nerja and I had plenty of company there, so I was back playing tennis in the mornings and meeting the lads at night.

After tennis we would have coffee and plenty of banter in the club and laughs. There were quite a few lady players and some very good players. I started playing with a Spanish girl who worked in reception at the Plaza Cavana Hotel. She was a nice girl we played quite often together.

I had met a lovely couple, Joe and Isobel, in Nerja at the Plaza Cavana Hotel in the centre of Nerja. I used to go for dinner with them on occasion with various friends. They often dropped in for a coffee in the mornings and I got to know them quite well; they were from Ireland and had been over in Nerja for a few years. They were importing pool tables to distribute all over Spain. Joe and I would start talking about business and one thing led to another and we started doing a job together in Malaga. We would meet at the Plaza Cavana, have our coffee and I would have a snack and read the paper. Then we would set off for Malaga, but on the way to Malaga we could not get past Torre del Mar, where there was the best coffee and cake cafe you ever saw. Every time we were down that way we always had to stop. We would work until about 8pm then head back to Nerja and I would drop Joe off at his home. I would go home, have a shower and head down to the Fontainebleau Hotel in Nerja to meet the lads, then we would have a drink and go to one of the restaurants for dinner.

I was still in regular contact with my solicitors and trying to recoup my investments, but no luck yet. I was back to the UK quite regularly, stopping with my son Chris, and seeing my solicitor John Whitehead and also meeting Mark Cawson, my barrister in Manchester. When I was in Spain it was quite easy getting from Malaga to Manchester for court hearings. We took most of my cases against Michael Band in Manchester.

In 1993 back in Nerja, Joe and I were still working down in Malaga but I would be playing tennis on Saturdays and Sundays. My car was in the UK so in May I decided to go back to Carlisle, see my family and drive my car back to Spain. I drove from Carlisle down to the ferry and over to Santander, then down to Nerja. I arrived in Nerja on the Friday night and on the Saturday morning I phoned Joe and said I was back. He said he'd see me in the Plaza Cavana Hotel for coffee. So I went down for coffee. Malcolm and Davina were there, Joe, Isobel and also their daughter Celene. She was on holiday from Ireland and we were all introduced to her. She looked a very nice young lady, with long blond hair and a good figure. I was thinking "what a catch this would be". So I was eating my salad and thinking what line could I use in the situation. I know her mother and father so I would have to be careful. I thought I would start with a joke so I said to her "where are you taking me tonight?" Davina told Celene "don't listen to a word he says", and we all laughed. But I had planted the seed. Nothing more was mentioned.

Joe and I went off to Malaga and on the way back at night I said

*Joe, if Celene would like to join us tonight I am meeting Malcolm and Davina in the Fountainbleu Hotel, then we are going to the Round Bar for dinner.*

163

*So I am making your dates now, am I?*

Nothing more was mentioned and I dropped Joe off at his home and I went home and had a shower; then the phone rang and Joe said

*I have a young lady here waiting for you.*

I was a bit knocked back, because I thought Joe was a bit offended for asking him if Celene would go out. I said I would be there in about 15 minutes. My thinking and system had worked. I now had a beautiful young lady to take out tonight, which would surprise Malcolm and Davina. We arrived at the Fountainbleu, and they were both gob-smacked. We had a drink there and then went to the Round Bar restaurant for a nice meal, then met up with some more friends and went to another place of entertainment. We all had a very good night. I enjoyed Celene's company and we decided we would meet up the next night as we were going out with her mother and father and their friends for dinner.

Celene was on one week's holiday from Ireland so we were out every night together, and we got on very very well. On the last night I said

*Do you have to go back to Ireland? I would like you to stay here.*

I had really fallen in love with her and desperately did not want her to go back. Celene spoke with her mother and told her that I wanted her to stay. Her mother said she had better speak with her father; they had a talk and asked me to come up in the morning and speak with them. I went to the house and spoke with them. We both said we had fallen for each other and I told her father that I had asked her to stay in Nerja.

Joe said

*If you want to stay, you stay, you are always welcome here with us. Geoff is a good man and a good hard worker.*

Celene did stay. We were later married and have been

together for more than 27 years. Celene has been by my side through all these court cases as I've tried to recoup my investments from the fraudulent Michael Bland.

In January 1994 Celene and I flew from Malaga to Newcastle and stayed in the apartment at Montagu Court for two nights; then we went over to Carlisle to see my family, stayed with them for two nights and then went back over to Newcastle and got a flight to Orlando

*Celene and I signing on our wedding day with Chris & Angela.*

\* \* \*

We hired a car in Orlando and drove down to Fort Myers to a court case there against George Davidson for the return of my investment in Pine Island. We stayed in the Robert E Lee Hotel as the house there was rented out. We arrived in Fort Myers Court House with my lawyer Doug Szabo, and spent the day in court but without much achievement for me. More paperwork needed to be done and George Davidson's lawyer was just prolonging the case. I was in touch with my solicitor John Whitehead in the UK on a regular basis with faxes and telephone calls.

We made the best of it while we were in Fort Myers and visited Captiva Island, Sannibel Island, and Cape Corral. There are some lovely restaurants on these Islands serving very good food at very reasonable prices. In February we moved over to Palm Beach area where Celene's uncle Philip was living. He was an artist and his paintings were in the Wentworth Gallery. We were looking at various car sales and noticed new cars were very cheap in Florida. We called in at Sherwood Motors who were Honda dealers and we'd got our eye on a little sports car "Honda Del Sol". We had a test drive in it and we liked it; the roof could be taken off quite easily; it was a very compact two-seater, with a large boot so i couldn't fault it. The salesman was very good and he took a liking to us and said to take it for a few days and see if we liked it, and to come back in three days and pay him if we wanted it. So off we drove – couldn't believe he was letting some strangers out with a new car without paying. Anyhow we loved the car, returned in the three days and paid up. At the end of the trip we would ship it to the UK. On 22 February Celene passed her USA driving test and I already had a US licence.

*Celene with Honda car.*

We had a very nice time in Palm Beach playing tennis most days and going to the various shopping centres, going to the beach, eating in different restaurants each night. Celene's uncle would often join us for dinner and show us different places to go, including the Breakers Palm Beach Hotel. The Breakers founder Henry Morrison Flagler was the man who transformed South Florida into a vacation destination for millions. He first visited Florida in March 1878 and he had already accumulated a vast fortune in Cleveland and New York as a long time partner of John D. Rockefeller in the Standard Oil Company. He retired from the company's day-today operations and started buying and building Florida railroads, rapidly extending the lines down the state's east coast. He acquired and constructed resort hotels along the route. Flagler sought to extend the Florida East Coast Railway to Key West, located 128 miles (206 km) beyond the end of the Florida Peninsula.

On 6 March we got the car picked up to be containerised for shipment back to the UK. We hired another and drove down to Key West for two nights and could see some of the old construction from the Flagler railroad. We enjoyed the time in Key West looking around and seeing different things, including the Ernest Hemingway House. We couldn't believe the number of cats at the house, you could smell them everywhere. We had a great time.

We arrived back into Gatwick on 18 March, hired a car and drove into London where Celene's sister Sharon and her two brothers Karl and Joseph were living in Enfield. We stayed with them for two days and then drove back to Newcastle. Early in April we had four days in Dublin to see some of Celene's family, her uncle Oliver and auntie Lolie, Isobel's sister. Oliver was a rare character, a well-known rugby player and golfer, and good company to be with, full of witty jokes and banter. He took us to various restaurants and places for many pints of Guinness, and we have great memories of them.

*Celene and Audrey.*

We also met up with a very good friend of Celene's, Audrey and her husband Des. We went for dinner to Oscar Taylors restaurant in Malahide; always very nice food there. We called in at White Sands Hotel at Portmarnock and had a few drinks; they had entertainment so we had a very good night. Audrey is well known for her Audrey Taylor Boutique in Glenageary, Dublin.

Back from Dublin, we collected the shipped Honda car from Charlton in London. We then drove the Honda from Portsmouth to Bilbao, and down to Nerja.

On 6 July 1994 I was driving my Mercedes back to the UK up through France to Le Havre Port and onto the ferry for Portsmouth. I was back into the UK on the 9th and we headed for Derby to see a few of my old friends, Oscar and Marian Dixon and Vic Essex and his wife. We found a nice hotel for two nights near Derby. We had a nice evening meal and a couple of drinks and an early night, tired out with all that driving. After breakfast we went to see Oscar and Marian; we had plenty to talk about. Oscar, like me, was in the haulage business and we used to meet every year at Harrogate tipper show – a three day event with entertainment and dinners every night. We also did quite a bit of business together. We later met up with Vic Essex and his wife. Vic worked as a salesman for Oscar and his brother Brian, so he also used to meet up with us all at Harrogate.

We had a couple of nice days in the Derby area, then set off for Carlisle to see my family and stayed with my son Chris. We had a good look around Dalston and Celene liked the area very much. I was also thinking of starting up in business again, and we came across a house named Woodsyke, in Unthank, Dalston. Celene thought it needed quite a lot of work done to it, but that it would be a good investment. I told Celene we could do most of the work, also could use the men that worked on the Truck Inn for me. We got all the things ordered that we needed to refurbish the house – new double-glazed PVC windows throughout, new kitchen, all new bathroom fittings, all the light fittings. It was going to take at least two or three weeks to get all these goods delivered, so we flew back to Spain, then drove the little Honda back to Carlisle via the Santander to Portsmouth ferry. These ferry journeys were like little cruises.

*Woodsyke.*

We stayed with my son Chris on our return to Dalston which was very handy for the house we were refurbishing. In the middle of September we had received all of the goods delivered to refurbish the house, so we got a few lads gathered together and by the end of November we were all finished. We now had a fabulous house. Celene chose all the colours, curtains carpets and chandeliers.

We found some wonderful friends in Unthank, Alison and Johnny Faulder, who had three daughters. They farmed just over the road and looked after the house when we were away. We had some very good get-togethers in the house and they loved coming over for Celene's sandwiches and going out for bar meals.

On 22 December 1994 we went over to Spain to spend the Christmas and New Year with Celene's family and had a very nice time. We were out for entertainment and a few drinks, played tennis and had plenty of banter in the tennis club. On 9 January 1995 we were back in the UK at the house in Woodsyke, and then we went down to Manchester with John Whitehead my solicitor for a meeting with Mark Cawson my barrister to discuss the fraud case against Michael Bland. This case was never ending and Mr Bland was like Houdini and could wriggle out of anything.

*Left to right: Chris my son, me, Celene, Sandra (Ian Benson's wife (Ian is taking the photo), Eddie Stobart's wife Silvia Stobart, and Eddie.*

On 15 February 1995 we flew into Dublin because Celene's grandmother was dying. We stayed in the excellent Old Sheiling Hotel. Sadly her grandmother died on 21 February. We stayed in Ireland quite a while. All the family came over and it was a great family get-together.

In March we went back to Woodsyke, and on 7 March flew over to Jersey for a court case. I had a very good solicitor over there but Michael Bland kept moving assets from offshore companies to other offshore companies, then moving assets to other jurisdictions, like the Isle of Man, the Cayman Islands, and many other offshore centres. I won the court case in Jersey but we still had a long way to go. Michael Bland had formed a web so you can imagine what it is like for us trying to unravel that web. It was Celene's birthday in Jersey so it was a good present to win that court case. On 12 March we flew from Jersey back to Spain via the UK, to surprise Celene's mother and father.

On 2 April 1995 Joe, Celene's father, suffered a massive heart attack and on 4 April took another bad turn; then got a hospital infection and was in intensive care. With the help of all the doctors' treatment, he remained stable. On 19 April Joe started breathing by himself without the oxygen. On 3 May Joe was discharged from hospital back home to Nerja.

On the 7th we came back to the UK for more meetings with my solicitors. On 11 June we went back to Spain to see how Joe was doing and then back again to the UK on 25. June. My ex wife Lorraine died the day of our return; she was 52 and this was a great shame. We had many good years together and brought up two children; she was a very good mother and kept them immaculate until they began looking after themselves.

On 13 July 1995 I had a court hearing in Manchester just another of the many that was to come over the years. On 6 September Doug Szabo, my lawyer in Fort Myers, had a court case regarding George Davidson to repay me my half investment back. I was awarded $680,000 dollars to be paid within six months; it was never paid so more court cases were to come. We drove down to London on 15 September to surprise Celene's mother and father. Joe had a business in London and his two sons were also there. We always had great times with Joe, Isobel and the lads. We were back to Woodsyke on the 17th and then there were more meetings with my solicitor John Whitehead regarding my court actions against Michael Bland.

On 11 November we went over to Spain, then in December 1996 drove to Portugal to see my lawyer. We were trying to put a lien on the land that I had invested in at Almancil on the Algarve. I drove back into Spain on 9 December and flew from Spain to Manchester on the 14th for two days for meetings with my QC, Mr Leeming, discussing the way forward to get my investment back from the fraudster Michael Bland. We stayed in Nerja for the Christmas and New Year. Joe, Celene's father, had to go for tests to the Malaga hospital and they recommended a heart by-pass. On 7 January he had a double heart by-pass, then in recovery he had a cardiac arrest and died. We were all devastated. We were waiting in a cafe in Malaga next to the hospital for him to wake up. This was a terrible time for Joe's wife Isobel and all the family; he was only 54 years old, and to me he didn't seem to have any problem with his health. We worked together for quite a while and he was a very strong hard-working man. I was very fond of him and we were big friends.

Joe's funeral was on 9 January. He was cremated. All

173

his brothers came, so too Joe's two sons Karl and Joseph, and his daughter Sharon with her boyfriend Raul, and of course Celene, also Isobel and her sister Lolie. It was a very sad day. On the 15th Joe's two sons returned to London.

On 26 February we were out having dinner with Isobel, Sharon, and Raul as it was Sharon's 30th birthday. Celene's brother Karl in London had not heard from his brother Joseph all day and he could not find him. Next day I was playing tennis with Celene, then having a coffee in the tennis club, when Celene's mother rang me and told me Joseph had been found and that he had committed suicide. I didn't tell this to Celene; I didn't know how. We just drove up to her mother's house and her mother explained what had happened to Joseph. It was so hard for them; they were devastated all over again – it had only been seven weeks since they had lost Joe Senior.

On the 29th we all flew to London for Joseph's funeral. Joseph's uncles and their wives were all there and it was another very sad day for the family. Joseph was a single, very smart, tall, slim, good-looking fellow; why he did this we will never know.

My friends Oscar and Marion came to Nerja to buy a house; they had sold their transport company, 50 Volvo artic tippers, to one of my friends Alan Sherwood. I actually brokered the deal for them because Oscar and Alan could never see eye to eye. Oscar wanted me to buy a house for them in Nerja, but I said he would have to choose his own home. I said that Celene and I would get them a nice suite in a good hotel and then they could look around and get a house of their choice.

On 7 May 1996 our friends Tony and Kath Armstrong came over to Puerto Banus for a holiday. We joined them for a couple of days and we stayed in a hotel down there. We would have dinner in the port then go for drinks and entertainment to Joy's Bar. The piano player and singer was Andy Anderson who use to play in the Truck Inn for me. His brother Billy Anderson had a band and young Andy started playing with him. They were from Annan. Later that May we were back in the UK seeing my solicitor John Whitehead for an update on the progress of my fraud case against Michael Bland.

We collected the car from Mercedes and then drove down to Southampton to meet one of our customers we did the haulage work for. My son Chris and his partner Susan came down in their own car. We were meeting Jim Rodgers and his wife; he was the transport manager for Enichem in the Southampton factory, and we did quite a lot of work for them. We had dinner in a lovely area in the Black Forest and a thoroughly good night. We stayed a couple of days in Southampton – very enjoyable.

*Top of table is my son Chris and his partner Susan. I have six grandchildren; Chris has three children and my daughter Angela has three.*

Back in September 1995 my son had received an email from a Mike Duffell which he passed on to me.

From Mr Michael John Duffell, White House, Chywoone Hill, Newlyn West, Penzance, Cornwall TR18 5AR.

24/9/95

Dear Mr Bell,

I understand that you have been having trouble with Mr Michael J. Bland, in relation to his duping you out of Companies which you owned. You have my sympathy in this respect, as he has done the same to me.

In the Spring of 1993, we were having taxation problems and our Auditor retired through ill-health. Our insurance Broker, Robert Bacon Ltd, recommended Bland to us and he became our Auditor & tax advisor.

Among other dishonest and fraudulent acts, which I will not go into detail in this letter, he duped my family and that of my colleague Mr Michael Belcher, out of their shares in a Company called Hampshire Cosmetic Laboratories Ltd. In this respect, I own an extract from an affidavit sworn by my solicitor.

I sincerely wish you every success in any litigation you have against Bland, as he must be stopped from feeding off other peoples' trust and taking advantage of his professional standing. Yours sincerely, Mike Duffell.

176

**BLAND & CO.**
Chartered Accountants

Tel: 0228 5٠5298
Fax: 0228 595301

,Dispensary
٠pel Street
٠lisle
٠umbria CA1 1JA

FAX MR G BELL     14·03·2000

Jorcan & Son (Guloralco) Lm
Suite 2A
Ensuite Building
1 camar Eo
Gubralar

*MR BLAND HAS SAID THAT
THE MONEY TO BUY THE
SHARES IN HAMPSHIRE COSMETIC
WAS COMING FROM THE SALE
OF A PLOT OF LAND IN
PORTUGAL OWNED BY MARTIN
COLETT AND HIMSELF.*

17th May 1998

Dear Sir

ALDEBURGH ENTERPRISES LIMITED

I write in connection with the above company's intended
purchase of shares in Hampshire cosmetics Laboratory,
Lumbert and Topsy Hair cosmetics Limited and can
confirm the following :-

1. The source of funds to be used for the purchase of
the shares is from the sale of plot of land in
Portugal and which was owned by Martin Colett and
myself, the funds being used being my half share one
of which £10٠٠٠٠ is currently held on my client
account.

2. I will effect the funds payment and will be
covered by drawing Bank Drafts from my client
account and these will be handed over on the
signing by the Vendor. I will hold sufficient
Aldeburgh sufficient funds to cover the future
payment to be made, and will hold these funds one
the source of these funds being my half share in the
future issue of plot of land in Portugal.

③

A list of Partners is available at the above address.
London office: Suite 401, 302 Regent Street, London, W1R 5AL

177

Brcher e Co.

. Evans (Gibraltar) Law
May 1995.

the Land in portugal comprises 21 Acres of Land
divided into 109 units for sale

① My (M.P. Belcher) contact No 01392-210846
② My Solicitor Timini Bland to Cross (in May)
Mr. McCaughey, Leeds - Tel 01532 606232
contact - Roger Horton.

MR BLAND DUPED US
OUT OF OUR SHARES
IN HAMPSHIRE COSMETICS
& I BELIEVE HE WAS
USING THE MONEY TO
BUY THE SHARES FROM
THE SALE OF THE LAND
YOUR FATHER OWNED.
I WOULD LIKE TO PROVE
THAT THIS IS THE CASE.
AS YOU WILL SEE I OBTAINED
A COURT ORDER FOR THE
AFFAIRS OF ONE OF BLANDS
COMPANIES — HE WAS HIDING
BEHIND, TO BE INVESTIGATED
& THIS IS HOW I CAME TO
FIND OUT ABOUT THE LAND
IN PORTUGAL. M.P. BELCHER.
④

178

On 24 September 1995 I received a fax from Mike Duffell, who was one of the owners of Hampshire Cosmetics Ltd. He had started this company a few years previously with three partners – himself, Mike Belcher and a manager that was a very experienced cosmetics producer that would run the cosmetic business, Paul Younger.

The two Mikes put all the money up to build a brand new factory and the shares were split three ways. The factory was at Brambles House, Waterberry Drive, Waterlooville, UK. It was a purpose-built factory and a fantastic building. They employed some 220 people in the factory producing goods for various clients and supplying all The Body Shop outlets. It was a very thriving business, making very big profits and the company was valued at around £8-10m.

Mike Duffell and Mike Belcher had many other businesses. Later on in this book you will see how Michael Bland manipulated my investments from me and he did the exact same to Hampshire Cosmetics.

Like me, the two Mikes had been through many court cases trying to regain control of their company Hampshire Cosmetics, but Michael Bland was changing offshore companies so frequently that the courts could not handle such a manipulation.

The two Mikes finished up with an offer of only £750,000; they had had enough of all the costs and all the court cases, so they came to the conclusion that it was impossible to get justice.

10.   Other companies of which Mr Bland was a director during the same period as he was a director of Epiette are the following:   → MAIN ONE

Rainy Day Holdings Ltd (Turks and Caicos Islands);

Atlantic House Holdings Limited (Turks and Caicos Islands);

Atlantic House Limited (Gibraltar);

Iberian Development Corporation Limited (Gibraltar);

Waburn Investments Limited (Gibraltar);

Sandwell Properties Limited (Isle of Man);

Holgate Corporation (USA); and

Aldeia das Ferrarias (Portugal) (again see paragraph 29 of his eleventh witness statement).

11.   A number of other companies feature in the evidence:

Aldeburgh Enterprises Limited (Gibraltar), a company which it is said the court in Gibraltar has found to have been owned by Mr Bland (1/3/52) but about which I know very little;

Hampshire Cosmetics Limited, a UK company the shares of which are owned by Wystan Holdings Inc (Turks and Caicos)

(1/3/53) which the trustees suspect Mr Bland owns or controls but in which Mr Bland says he has no interest (1/4/60);

New Capital Management Limited, a company which Mr Bland was able to sign for but in which he says he has no interest (1/3/53; 1/4/60; 1/4/57);

Rosewood Associates Limited, about which again I know little;

Rosewood Consultants Limited, which Mr Bland says is/was his business through which he provided accountancy services (1/13/1948, 1958);

Aston International Limited (Isle of Man), a management company from which the trustees have recently obtained some 10,000 pages of documents and with which Mr Bland has had extensive dealings; and

Blenheim Trust BVI, which was intended to take over from Aston (it may in fact have done so) and which, like Aston, provides what might be described as corporate services.

## Some of Michael Bland's Offshore Companies

IN THE CIRCUIT COURT OF THE TWENTIETH JUDICIAL CIRCUIT IN AND FOR
LEE COUNTY, FLORIDA                                    CIVIL ACTION

BARAKOT, LTD. and I. GEOFFREY          )
BELL,                                  )
                                       )
            Plaintiffs,                )
                                       )
v.                                     )     CASE NO. 93-1442-CA-LGJ
                                       )
ALLENDALE, LTD., GEORGE                )
DAVIDSON, CUMBRIA DEVELOPMENT          )
CORPORATION, and HAMPTON               )
INTERNATIONAL, INC.,                   )
                                       )
            Defendants.                )
_____)

## MOTION FOR FINAL JUDGMENT AGAINST ALLENDALE, LTD., CUMBRIA DEVELOPMENT CORPORATION, AND HAMPTON INTERNATIONAL, INC.

COMES NOW the Plaintiffs, BARAKOT, LTD. and I. GEOFFREY BELL, by and through their undersigned attorneys, and hereby move for the entry of a Final Judgment against ALLENDALE, LTD., CUMBRIA DEVELOPMENT CORPORATION, and HAMPTON INTERNATIONAL, INC., on the grounds that none of these Defendants have filed a response to the Amended Complaint. Plaintiff has submitted a Default against HAMPTON INTERNATIONAL, INC. The facts and circumstances surrounding the relief sought by the Plaintiffs are within the knowledge of this court since the Settlement Agreement had previously been approved by the court.

WHEREFORE, Plaintiffs would request that this court enter a Final Judgment against the Defendants and allow Plaintiffs the relief sought in the Amended Complaint in having the deed to the property released as well as the stock ownership interest in CUMBRIA DEVELOPMENT CORPORATION, as well as finding that HAMPTON INTERNATIONAL, INC.'s interest in the real property described in

HENDERSON, FRANKLIN, STARNES & HOLT, P.A.   P.O. BOX 280   FORT MYERS, FLORIDA 33902-0280
Telephone: 941-334-4121

181

the Amended Complaint, if any, is subordinate and inferior to the interests of the Plaintiffs.

### CERTIFICATE OF SERVICE

I HEREBY CERTIFY that a true and correct copy of the above and foregoing has been furnished by facsimile and regular United States Mail to GEORGE DAVIDSON and ALLENDALE, LTD., c/o County Hotel, 9 Botchergate, Carlisle, Cumbria CA1 1QS, and by regular United States Mail to HAMPTON INTERNATIONAL, INC., c/o Registered Agent ASTON CORPORATE TRUSTEES LTD., 25 Greystone Manor, Lewes, Delaware 19958, this _____ day of September, 1997.

HENDERSON, FRANKLIN, STARNES & HOLT
Attorneys for Plaintiffs
Post Office Box 280
Fort Myers, FL  33902
(941) 334-4121

By: _____
Douglas B. Szabo
Florida Bar No. 710733

*Above: Judgement in Florida awarding me the land in Pine Island.*

At last I got a judgement in Florida, I was awarded the land on Pine island.

I was still fighting court cases in Manchester to try and recoup my investments but Michael Bland was clever and manipulating, but we kept fighting although it was costing lots of money.

In September1996 we went down to Spain and then back to the UK. In October I had to go to Portugal for a court hearing so we flew to Spain then drove over to Portugal. In November 1996 I had an appeal hearing in the courts in Manchester. I had broken my ankle so I was crutches.

In January and February 1997 we were in Nerja with our friends Oska and Marion, Davina and Malcolm. We dined together most nights, very good company.

*Sister Amy with Geoff.*

In April I got a call from my sister-in-law to say my sister Amy had been diagnosed with a brain tumour and was receiving treatment. In May 1997 Amy was given just a few weeks to live. Celene and I stayed with her three days and nights each week and my other family stayed two days each. My sister Amy was more like a mother to me with her being 17 years older. We were always very close and loved each other very much. It was very sad to see someone deteriorate away each day. The Marie Curie nurses came every day and were first class.

*My sister Amy and Celene.*

My brother Reg was 14 months older than me and a different type. He was married with a family, and the children were very nice. They lived in Wigton, Cumbria. Reg left school like me and went to work on the farms and he moved to quite a few very good farms. He was a very good man and demanded a top wage. He was very good with animals and started in the hound dog racing; he could get the best out of them and won a lot of races, but like in all those gambling sports, not all things were above board.

My brother Tom was 12 years older than me. He was in the army and when he came out, he drove a truck delivering farm machinery for a local Carlisle agricultural firm Rickerby's. He saw how I had built a truck business and decided to get a truck too, a Leyland Comet tipper. But he was not like me and didn't have the 'go and get it' style to bring in the customers. You have to have a certain approach to get customers; each customer has different ways and you have to work out while talking to them which way will get you his business.

Tom's wife Joyce was a top-class sister-in-law; she took her two-day shift to look after Amy. They were very close over the years. My other sister Molly was 19 years older than me and was quite different from Amy and me. She had been a nursing sister in the hospital most of her life and she was one of the really tough ones you would see on TV. Molly was like a Sergeant Major type and carried this into her normal life back home. She tried to take control at Amy's house when we were looking after her, but I put a stop to that. I wanted Amy to have a peaceful and calm time. Celene was very good with Amy, feeding and washing her and making her as comfortable as possible; they loved each other.

On 6 June 1997 my sister Amy died. Celene and I were by her side. The Marie Curie nurse said to talk to Amy, which we did. Celene noticed a tear flow from one of Amy's eyes down her cheek and Celene gently wiped it away. Just then, at that moment, we heard a gentle gasp of Amy's last breath; she was gone. We made all the arrangements for the funeral and said our farewells to a very loving sister.

My father had a tough time during the last few years of his life after he got TB from all the fumes from the oven coke he was using in the furnace in his blacksmith's shop. He had to go to Blencathra TB hospital which was beside Keswick, high on the mountain. This was the only cure in those days – to get plenty of fresh air from high altitude. He was in hospital for quite a long time and when he came home he was never the same man and he died in 1997.

My mother was still in Little Bampton as was my brother Tom and his wife Joyce. Joyce was very good with my mother and looked after her very well. My mother had a stroke and went into hospital but although she made a recovery, she wasn't back to normal. She got a lovely pensioner's bungalow in Wigton and was made very comfortable. My mother died in 1998.

My brother Tom was retired and put his time in with one of his neighbours, a farmer John Millican, whose nickname was mousey. He was a real character. I knew him all my life and we used to meet when we were out in our younger days. He got too much into gambling but my brother Tom would not have had one bet in his life.

In 1998 we were back and forward between the UK and Spain, spending lots of time on court cases and meetings in Manchester with my barrister Mark Cawson and my new solicitor Richard Price from Pannone's. On 12 June Celene's grandmother died in Ireland. Celene her sister Sharon and their mother Isobel went to the funeral in Dublin. In July Celene and I decided to spend more time in Spain so the house in the UK was sold. I was still spending large amounts of time with my solicitors in Portugal and Manchester trying to recoup my investments.

In December we moved from Nerja to a house in Torrequebrada, Benalmadena, Malaga. It needed refurbishing and Celene's and my idea was to do it all and resell. We were very good at refurbishing, so why not keep doing it?

*The house we were refurbishing in Torrequebrada, Spain.*

In November 2000 we had an ongoing court case that was being heard in Liverpool, against Dodd's accountants and Michael Bland who was a partner, for wrongful advice on my investment. The judge ruled that the case was out of time for Dodd's but left us to go ahead with the case against Michael Bland. The solicitor I was using at the time was Granger King and Hynes Penrith, so I now had a case against them, which a solicitor Mark Whittell would take on. It was never ending.

The investment advice I received from Michael Bland as a partner of Dodd & Co was in Dodd's office in Carlisle, but Dodd's never gave me any help to recover this investment, but instead turned a blind eye on the problem. Dodd's came to a settlement agreement with Tony Armstrong, the other investor that invested in the Spanish golf course project, but there was a confidentiality agreement. They did not offer me the same deal.

Getting a solicitor is no problem; getting a perfect one is very difficult and Michael Bland knew this and was up to working the system.

*Celene's Del Sol Honda.*

In December the little Honda Del Sol we brought back from Florida was stolen in Spain. We reported it to the police and they phoned us later to say they had found the car just outside Malaga in an old used quarry and that it had been set on fire. If we called in at the police station, they would take us up and show us the car. Well, it was burned out completely. Celene had just filled up with petrol the day before so that would not have helped. The aluminium wheels were even melted. What a shame – we really liked that car.

* * *

I now had to restart on Michael Bland so I got a new solicitor at Linder Myers in Manchester, Anthony Robinson. I went through my case with him and he was keen to take the job on. I gave him lots of files but my previous solicitors Richard Price had a lot of my files which we needed. So I had all the files delivered to Linder Myers. Anthony Robinson called me and said all the files had been delivered, but the papers were all loose and had been taken from the box files, and he would not know what went where. He said

*There are stacks of them, impossible to sort out*

*Look Anthony I will come to Manchester for a week and sort them all out into box files I know the case like the back of my hand.*

*All our files are in the cellar and it's also the boiler room with all the heating equipment in; it is very hot down there so it is up to you.*

*I will bring my shorts with me.*

So I went off to Manchester for the week into offices of Linder Myers. I met up with Anthony and while we were talking he said

*Look, I am going to hand you over to another junior solicitor.*

189

*No I don't want a learner, I need you on the job with me.*

*I charge a senior top rate. David Pouts, a junior, is going to save you a lot.*

So I had to go along with that. Well, I knew all about the case and would have all the papers when we had them all sorted. So I started. What a mess they were – papers all just thrown into big boxes; but at least there were plenty of empty box files around. It was warm and I had my shorts on and shirt off. I used to start about 8.30am and stop for one hour at 12 midday. I'd go down to Arndale Shopping centre for my lunch. I would knock off about 5.30pm or 6.00pm.

I was staying at the Gardens Hotel; they had a buffet breakfast which was very good. Next door was a Wetherspoon pub so I would get my dinner in there and have a couple of pints of John Smiths. I wanted Mark Cawson, my barrister now a QC, to do the case for me, so I needed to introduce Anthony Robinson and David Pouts to him; they had never met Mark. I made an appointment and we met him in his office. Mark knew all about what Michael Bland had been up to so went through what was to be done. Our plan was that David and I would make all the statements up and attach all the papers and Mark would go through them and rehash them as needed. By the end of the week, I had all the files sorted out and it ended up better than we thought it would.

So David and I got started the following week. Mark Cawson gave us what was to be done first. David and I were then back and forward with emails with the statements, and also – very important – all the enclosures that I had restored into the binders. These enclosures were the papers that were produced at the time recording any transactions that took place, letters that I had received from Michael Bland over the years when he was investing on my behalf, and also all correspondence from solicitors.

Theses papers were all important to prove to the judge what had really happened, and we had to have the paperwork to back it up.

David sent the finished statement to Mark, who rehashed it or let us know what adjustments to make. Bland was being very awkward and claimed he had lost all his paperwork and asked for certain papers which he thought we had not got. But we always delivered what he requested. He tried all kinds of tricks to stop the case. His first try was a 'strike out case' to stop us going on but he failed; next was 'out of time' – he was claiming that this matter happened some 20 years ago and people's memory would not be good enough. He tried all kinds, but the judge was adamant that this case would be heard. At last we got a date for the trial: 27 April 2009.

We were seven days in court and I got a judgement on Michael James Bland for £6.2 million. The judgement is in Appendix 1.

*Michael James Bland the architect of manipulation of my down fall and quite a few others.*

I now had a judgement on Michael Bland for approximately £6.2 million; then he made himself bankrupt. I was advised by council to put a freezing order on his assets, which we did, meaning lots more court appearances. Michael Bland also defrauded me out of the company pension fund, total of £240,000; the tax was £100,000 and Bland got the remainder of £140,161.01

Michael Bland's Trustee was Kevin Mawer, a partner at KPMG. Mawer worked with solicitor Mark Whittell, a partner at Cobbett's Manchester. They did a large number of court cases in the UK and many offshore places where Bland was, and is, hibernating his money. They were being backed by Harbour Finance for up to £300,000, which was for court expenses and other out-of-town solicitors, not for Kevin Mawer or Mark Whittell.

The Trustee Kevin Mawer found out that a Thomas Waite was acting as the front man for Bland, as you can read in all the Judge's findings.

The Trustee put a figure of what Bland had filtered away, in the region of £10 million, with £5 million from the Portugal project and at least £5 million, from Hampshire Cosmetics. I agree fully with the Trustee Kevin Mawer's assessment.

Kevin Mawer and Mark Whittell worked from 2009 until 2013 on this case. They proved many times, which you will have read in the documents, that Thomas Waite was the front man hiding Bland's assets. In 2013 Cobbett's went into liquidation. Kevin Mawer had disagreements with his partners at KPMG and resigned. A new Trustee was assigned to Michael Bland and the whole thing was aborted. I got a letter from this new Trustee at KPMG and he let Michael Bland completely off the hook. In all the correspondence, it is well-documented that Bland has in the region of £10 million.

* * *

On Sunday 7 June 2009 I was trimming a Yucca tree from the top balcony and I had a rope around the slim tree pulling in to me so I could reach it with the hand saw. I had my hand around the slim tree and started sawing. The rope came adrift and the tree pulled me over the railings, so I was in mid-air and fell to the ground onto the hard ceramic tiled floor. I came about three floors down but I was very lucky that I did not fall on my head.

I collected my thoughts and hauled myself over to the pool; my ankle was paining me so my idea was the pool would cool it down and maybe cure me. I cleaned all the cuttings up as I did not want to tell Celene what had happened; we had planned to go to play tennis when she returned from church.

But when Celene came home the ankle was no better and I said I would not be able to play tennis because I had hurt my ankle in the garden. Celene took me to the hospital to get checked over. The doctor could not do much so he said to come back when the swelling had gone down. We went to the hospital on 9 June and got an x-ray. After the doctor had inspected the x-ray, he called me in and said

*You have broken your ankle and foot; it has split so it will need to be pinned.*

*Can you not just put it in plaster?*

*No no, I will have to operate and put a pin in.*

*When can you operate?*

*Have you had breakfast?*

*No.*

*Then I can do it today.*

So I was shown into a lovely clean bedroom and they got me all ready for the operation, took me to the operating theatre and put me to sleep. The next thing I knew was that I woke up in a nice comfortable bed and Celene was sitting there, by my side as always.

They looked after me very well and gave me nice food. Celene stayed with me the two nights in the hospital. They did not plaster the ankle, I had to put this boot on, which was fine.

On 14 July I still had the boot on to support the broken ankle. Celene and I were watching television when we received a call from Michael Wright in Ireland, a very good friend of Celene's brother Karl. Michael had bad news for us: Celene's brother Karl had committed suicide in the same manner that her brother Joseph had. He had left his mother Isobel, and his sisters Sharon and Celene devastated, and something that they will never get over – impossible to come to terms with. The three men in their family were gone. So, there was another funeral to arrange. This one was in Dublin.

\* \* \*

Michael Bland's new trustee was a Chris Nutting. All his communication with Bland must have been behind closed doors, because I was never kept in the picture regarding this unbelievable settlement. The settlement says 'confidentiality agreement', which makes a complete mockery of our court system. Michael Bland flashes about always in a top of the range Mercedes, and gets it serviced at Mercedes in Carlisle.

The Judgment I was awarded of £6.2 million has not been collected. Michael James Bland has put the money out of reach into offshore companies.

It is estimated that Mr Bland has in the region of £11 million salted away, with the help of Thomas Waite who resides in the Turks and Caicos Islands.

Mr Bland uses Thomas Waite as his front man and uses offshore companies for banking, in and around The Turks and Caicos Islands, Bahamas, BVI, Cayman Islands, Belarus, Barbados, etc.

You can see in the appendices many of the offshore companies Mr Bland is involved in.

Mr Bland lives a life of luxury in the best of houses and always in a top of the range Mercedes Benz, all with my money.

Anyone who can lead me to the collection of this money will be rewarded with a substantial percentage of the funds.

# Appendix 1

The Confidentiality Agreement

**KPMG LLP**
**Restructuring**
Dukes Keep
Marsh Lane
Southampton
SO14 3EX
United Kingdom

Tel +44 (0) 23 8020 2000
Fax +44 (0) 23 8020 2003
DX 154200 Southampton 49

Mr IG Bell

by email:
geoffbell670@hotmail.com

Contact    Chris Nuttiing
023 80202114

2 September 2014

Dear Mr Bell

**Michael James Bland - in Bankruptcy**
**High Court of Justice No. 4711 of 2009**
**Bell-v-Bland 1MA30300**

I refer to your email dated 25 June 2014 and apologise for the delay in responding.

Please find enclosed a copy of a letter sent by my solicitors to Manchester District Registry in connection with the above claim, the contents of which are self explanatory.

Yours sincerely

CJ Nutting
*Joint Trustee in the Bankruptcy of Michael James Bland*

Christopher John Nutting and Kevin Roy Mawer are authorised to act as insolvency practitioners by the Insolvency Practitioners Association

Enclosure

# OLSWANG

Manchester District Registry
Chancery Division
1 Bridge Street West
Manchester
M60 9DJ

22 July 2014

**Email**    Louise.Bell@olswang.com
**Direct Line**    +44 20 7067 3051

**Our Ref**    LGB\SQW\15369-6
**Your Ref**

Dear Sirs

**Ian Geoffrey Bell v Michael James Bland and between (1) Hampshire Cosmetics Limited (2) Wystan Holdings Inc (the Applicants) -and- Ian Geoffrey Bell (the Respondent) Claim No. 1MA30300 (previously 1994 B No. 10474) ("Proceedings")**

We act for the joint trustees in bankruptcy ("Trustees") of Michael James Bland ("the bankrupt").

On 12 June 2009, prior to the date of the bankruptcy order, Ian Geoffrey Bell ("Mr Bell") obtained a post judgment freezing injunction in the Proceedings against the Bankrupt. This was subsequently varied in or about February 2010 ("the freezing order").

In addition to the bankrupt, the injuncted parties under the freezing order included a number of companies owned or part owned by a Mr Thomas Waite ("Mr Waite").

The Trustees have now settled all claims in the bankruptcy against Mr Waite and all of the companies referred to in the attached schedule ("the scheduled companies"). The terms of that settlement are confidential. However, we can confirm that the terms of settlement:

1.    provide for no payment of money or transfer of property by Mr Waite and/or the scheduled companies to the Trustees or any third party; and

2.    do not restrict the rights of Mr Waite and/or the scheduled companies in relation to the freezing order including their ability to apply to set aside the freezing order, enforce any undertakings as to damages given in respect of the freezing order, or seek costs of or

90 High Holborn      T +44 (0) 20 7067 3000
London WC1V 6XX      F +44 (0) 20 7067 3999
www.olswang.com      DX 57972 Kingsway      Olswang LLP is authorised and regulated by the Solicitors Regulation Authority.

Berlin | Brussels | London | Madrid | Munich | Paris | Singapore | Thames Valley

17850555-1

198

**OLSWANG**

relating to the freezing order against Mr Bell or any third party who could properly be made liable for those costs, with the exception of the Trustees.

We are writing this letter immediately on reaching settlement so that the position is clear without contravening the confidentiality of the settlement, and so that the Trustees can conclude any involvement in relation to those proceedings.

Yours faithfully

*Olswang LLP*

**OLSWANG LLP**

## SCHEDULE (THE SCHEDULED PARTIES)

1.  Brambles House Investments Limited (formerly Hampshire Cosmetics Limited), a company registered in England & Wales under Company Number 02873670, New Kings Court Toligate, Chandler's Ford, Eastleigh, Hampshire, SO53 3LG

2.  Brambles House Facilities Limited (formerly Hampshire Cosmetics Laboratories Limited), a company registered in England & Wales under Company Number 05171123, 57 St Ives Park, Ashley Heath, Ringwood, Hampshire, BH24 2JX and dissolved on 10th December 2013

3.  Wystan Holdings Inc. (Wystan Holdings Inc a company incorporated in the Turks & Caicos Islands under Company Number E29228, Hibernian House, Leeward Highway, Providenciales, Turks and Caicos Islands, BWI)

4.  New Capital Management Limited a company incorporated in the British Virgin Islands under Company Number 169447, R.G. Hodge Plaza, 3rd Floor, Wickhams Cay 1, Road Town, Tortola, British Virgin Islands

5.  Epiette Limited, a company registered in Jersey under Company Number 42870, Garfield-Bennett Trust Company Limited, CTV House, La Pouquelaye, St Helier, Jersey, St Helier, JE2 3TP and dissolved on 1st October 2013

# Appendix 2

On the following pages is the Judgement against Michael James Bland.

No 2 amended.

Case No: 1994 B No. 10474

**IN THE HIGH COURT OF JUSTICE**
**CHANCERY DIVISION**
**MANCHESTER DISTRICT REGISTRY**

Manchester Civil Justice Centre
1 Bridge Street West
Manchester M60 9DJ

Date: 27th April 2009

Before:

**HIS HONOUR JUDGE PELLING QC**
**(Sitting as a Judge of the High Court)**
- - - - - - - - - - - - - - - - - - - -
Between:

|  |  |
|---|---|
| **IAN GEOFFREY BELL** | **Claimant** |
| - and - |  |
| **MICHAEL JAMES BLAND** | **Defendant** |

- - - - - - - - - - - - - - - - - - - -
- - - - - - - - - - - - - - - - - - - -

**Mr Mark Cawson QC** (instructed by Linder Myers) for the Claimant
The Defendant appeared in person.
Hearing dates: 30th March to 3rd April and 6 to 8th April 2009
- - - - - - - - - - - - - - - - - - - -

# Approved Judgment

I direct that pursuant to CPR PD 39A para 6.1 no official shorthand note shall be taken of this
Judgment and that copies of this version as handed down may be treated as authentic.

............................

202

**His Honour Judge Pelling QC**:

**Introduction**

1.    In these proceedings, the Claimant claims restitution alternatively equitable compensation or damages from, alternatively an account of profits made by, the Defendant in consequence of what is alleged by the Claimant to have been a breach of fiduciary duty on the part of the Defendant in relation to two property developments – one relating to some land at Farrarias in Portugal ("the Portuguese development") and the other at Las Pilillas in Spain ("the Spanish development").

2.    In essence the Claimant's case is that he was at the material time (now some 20 odd years ago) a recently retired businessman who had operated mainly in the road haulage business but who had operated a lorry driver's motel known as the Truck Inn. He says that although successful he was essentially a practical businessman of no great commercial sophistication who was almost wholly dependent on his accountants (first a Mr Dodd then the Defendant) for commercial and investment advice. He says the circumstances were such that the Defendant owed him fiduciary duties in relation to each of the investments I have referred to and that the Defendant acted in breach of those fiduciary duties by failing to make full disclosure of the interest that the Defendant had in the investments concerned and/ or by preferring his own interests or those of others with whom he was connected over the interests of the Claimant. In consequence it is alleged that the Claimant was induced to invest a total of £1,250,035 in the Portuguese development and £200,000 in the Spanish development when he would not have done so had the Defendant fully and frankly disclosed the nature of his involvement in each of the projects concerned. The whole of the sums invested (which in each case was in the form of unsecured loans) were lost and the Claimant seeks to recover the sums invested together with interest as his primary remedy either in restitution or as equitable compensation or damages for breach of fiduciary duty. In relation to the Portuguese development, one of the witnesses called on behalf of the Claimant alleged that he had paid the sum of £1.3 million odd to the Defendant on the assumption that he was acting for the Claimant. If this allegation is true, the sum paid over to the Defendant has not been paid to the Claimant and it is on the basis of that allegation that the Claimant seeks an account of profits in the alternative to his primary claim in relation to the Portuguese development.

3.    The Defendant denies that he owed the Claimant fiduciary duties as alleged because he asserts that however reliant the Claimant was on Mr Dodd, the position was different as between the Claimant and Defendant. The Defendant denies that he was in any sense acting for the Claimant in relation to the Claimant's investments in either of the projects and that his sole role was to act as an introducer. The Defendant maintains that the decisions to invest were taken by the Claimant without any advice or encouragement from him and in any event the full nature of his involvement was properly disclosed.

4.    The trial took place between 30th March to 3rd April and 6 to 8th April 2009. I heard oral evidence from the Claimant, Mr Corlett, Mr Armstrong, Mr Dodd, Ms Young (nee Fisher), Mr Szabo (by telephone from the United States of America) and the Defendant. Mr Dyer was due to give evidence but was unable to do so apparently as the result of ill health and his statement was admitted under the Civil Evidence Act and a statement from Mr Walsh Deceased made in other proceedings was also read.

5.    As I have already said, the events with which I am concerned took place some 20 years ago. These proceedings were started over 14 years ago on 28th October 1994. For a significant period following the commencement of these proceedings, the Claimant was bankrupt as the

result of a failure by him to pay a costs bill in relation to some other connected proceedings and the litigation was carried on by his trustee. Following the Claimant's discharge, the cause of action and right to continue these proceedings was assigned by the trustee to the Claimant. Last year there was an application by the Defendant (who was then represented by solicitors and leading counsel) for an Order that these proceedings be dismissed for want of prosecution. That application was heard by me and was dismissed. There has been no appeal from that decision. In his opening, during the course of his evidence and in his closing submissions, the Defendant repeatedly claimed that his ability to defend himself was handicapped by the absence of documentation which he asserted was the inevitable result of the passage of time to which I have referred. He also claimed that he was unable to recall critical events when asked specific questions. In relation to documents, this complaint must be viewed in context. Disclosure took place in these proceedings in excess of 8 years ago in 2000 some 12 odd years after the events with which I am concerned. Neither party applied for specific disclosure from the other nor were any third party disclosure applications made by either party at that stage or, indeed, thereafter. There is a substantial amount of contemporaneous material that has contributed significantly to the size of the trial bundle (19 lever arch files). In relation to Mr Bland's assertion that he was unable to remember critical events, it will be necessary for me to decide whether this was a genuine assertion of a loss of memory or whether this was a convenient strategem for avoiding answering difficult questions. That assessment depends on an assessment of the other evidence as a whole and so I postpone expressing a concluded view on this issue until later in this judgment. However, I record at this stage that the Defendant was younger than most of the other witnesses with the possible exception of Ms Young and Mr Szabo. None of the other witnesses appeared to have any difficulty in recalling the critical events though obviously some struggled with specific dates. However, in this case it is not the exact date of particular events that is material but rather their sequence that is important to the issues that I have to decide.

**The Legal Framework**

6.    In essence:

i)      A fiduciary is someone who owes fiduciary duties to another – see _Bristol & West Building Society v. Mothew_ [1998] Ch.1 _per_ Millett LJ at 18 and _Arklow Investments Limited v. MacClean_ [2000] 1 WLR 594 _per_ Henry J at 600;

ii)     Fiduciary duties are owed by one to another where someone undertakes to act for another in circumstances which give rise to a relationship of trust and confidence – see _Mothew_ _per_ Millett LJ at 18 – or where the relationship between the people concerned is such as to give rise to a legitimate expectation that the person alleged to owe the fiduciary duty will  not use his or her position in a manner adverse to the interests of the other person concerned – see _Arklow_ _per_ Henry J at 598;

iii)    As to the duties owed, each has as its founding characteristic a duty of single minded loyalty and fidelity owed by the fiduciary to the other party to the relationship which in turn leads to obligations:

a)      To act in good faith;

b)      Not to profit from his trust;

c)      Not to place himself in a situation where his duty and his own interest are in conflict;

d)    Not to act for his own benefit or the benefit of a third party without the informed consent of the principal;

e)    In dealings with the principal, whether by the fiduciary on his own behalf or on behalf of a third party, to prove that the transaction is a fair one and that he has made full disclosure of all facts material to the transaction;

-   see *Mothew per* Millett LJ at 18; and

f)    not to exploit or take advantage of the position of fiduciary at the expense of the principal – see *Arklow per* Henry J at 598;

iv)   A principal is entitled to equitable compensation for loss caused by breach of fiduciary duty – see *Mothew per* Millett LJ at 17;

v)   In relation to a claim for equitable compensation for breach of fiduciary duty, the onus is on the Claimant principal to show that but for the breach the principal would not have acted in the way that caused his loss but once that has been established the principal is entitled to be placed in the position he was in before the breach occurred unless there is evidence from it can be inferred that some other outcome would have occurred had there been no breach – see *Nationwide Building Society v. Balmore Radmore* [1999] PNLR 606 *per* Blackburn J at 671G-672A and *Gwembe Valley Development Co Ltd v. Koshy per* Mummery LJ (giving the judgment of the Court) at Paragraph 144; and

vi)   The fiduciary's obligation to account for any profit made is strict - it depends on the mere fact of profit made – see *Nationwide per* Blackburn J at 638.

The onus clearly rests on the Claimant to prove both that the Defendant owed him the duties relied on and that those duties have been breached as well as satisfying the "but for" test to which I have referred in relation to the claim to be entitled to equitable compensation. In advancing a case based on breach of fiduciary duty there is no necessity to allege dishonesty although in fact dishonesty on the part of the Defendant is alleged here. Because dishonesty is alleged (and arguably even if it was not, given the nature of the factual allegations made against the Defendant and the effect findings in favour of the Claimant might have on the Defendant's professional status as a chartered accountant) it is right that I should remind myself that as was noted by Richards LJ in *R(N) v. Mental Health Review Tribunal* [2006] QB 468:

> " … *Although there is a single civil standard of proof on the balance of probabilities, it is flexible in its application. In particular, the more serious the allegation or the more serious the consequences if the allegation is proved, the stronger must be the evidence before a court will find the allegation proved on the balance of probabilities.*

7.   There is one further preliminary matter that I need to mention at this stage. As I have already said, the events with which I am concerned occurred some 20 odd years ago. As will become apparent from my factual findings set out below, there have been a number of claims made both other entities connected to the Claimant and/or Defendant in relation to the matters in dispute before me. In particular on 5th December 2000 a judgment was delivered by HH Judge Tetlow sitting as a Judge of the High Court in *Barakot Limited v. Epiette Limited.* The Defendant was keen to rely on various findings made by Judge Tetlow in that and a later judgment given by him in those proceedings as in some way determinative or at any rate persuasive as to the conclusions that I should reach on certain factual matters in issue in

these proceedings. This was misconceived. Those judgments do not give rise to any form of estoppel as between the parties before me, as was accepted on the application to dismiss these proceedings to which I have referred above, and in dismissing that application, I rejected submissions based on the failure to bring the claim now before me as part of the earlier proceedings – see Paragraph 1 of my Order made on 30th October 2008 (A/146). Thus in my judgment my duty is to arrive at my findings exclusively by reference to the evidence that I have heard and the documents that were put in evidence before me. I would add that aside from the position in principle, it is clear that evidence has been adduced before me that was not before Judge Tetlow. This is an additional reason why I ought to approach the factual issues before me exclusively by reference to the material before me. It is of course open to either party to point to conclusions other judges have reached in other cases concerning the reliability of particular witnesses. Where that was done I have taken that into account.

## This Judgment

8.    It is necessary that I now say something about the structure of this judgment. Not unnaturally, the way in which evidence has been adduced has not in all cases been strictly chronological. Clearly it is necessary to consider whether fiduciary duties were owed by the Defendant to the Claimant in relation to each of the projects. That issue is to be determined in relation to the Portuguese project primarily by reference to the facts down to 25th November 1988 which is when it is alleged that the first breach relevant to that project occurred. The advances in relation to the Spanish project were made in February and March 1989. Thus it is possible that events occurred between 25th November 2008 and February 1989 that affect the duty issue in relation to the Spanish project. Events occurred thereafter which are relevant to the Portuguese project but not to the Spanish project loan. In these circumstances, I have found it more convenient to consider the facts and where necessary to resolve the factual disputes between the parties broadly in chronological order (although it has been necessary on occasion to depart from this principle in order to maintain coherency) before then turning specifically to the questions (a) whether duties were owed and (b) if they were, whether those duties were breached in relation to (i) the Portuguese project and (ii) the Spanish project. I turn to remedies at the end if and to the extent that it is necessary to do so. I record that I have been significantly hampered in this approach by the absence of a properly particularised and cross referenced chronology.

## The Witnesses

9.    Before turning to the facts of this dispute, I must mention the witnesses before me. There are fundamental differences between the Claimant and Defendant. Each have at various stages said different things about or have emphasised different aspects of the events with which I am concerned in affidavits and witness statements sworn or provided on other litigation both here and abroad. Each submits that I need to approach the evidence of the other with caution. This I have done by seeking to test what each says in relation to the relevant events by reference to either contemporaneous documents and/or by reference to the oral evidence of witnesses whose evidence I have concluded I can safely accept before deciding whether the evidence of the Claimant or Defendant is to be preferred.

10.   I have concluded that I can safely accept without qualification the evidence of Mr Szabo and Mrs. Young. I have concluded that I can also safely rely on the evidence of Mr. Dodd who I am satisfied was an entirely truthful witness. There were differences between some of his evidence and some of Mrs. Young's evidence which were the result of mis-recollection of some dates (but not the sequence of events) and by the different roles they had at the relevant time in the firm of Dodd & Co, a firm of chartered accountants founded by Mr

Dodd and in which both the Defendant and Mrs. Young became partners. Similar considerations apply to Mr Couzens. None of these witnesses had any reason to mislead me and I conclude that they were honest witnesses whose evidence as I say I could safely rely on.

11. Mr Armstrong had a well developed dislike of the Defendant who he regarded as having dishonestly induced him to invest in the Spanish project. Nonetheless it is clear that any litigation with which Mr Armstrong was involved concerning this issue has long since been resolved. Whilst I cannot ignore the possibility that Mr Armstrong might want to give false evidence against the Defendant in order to harm him, I consider that I can rule that out as a possibility because (a) it was not suggested to him (b) there is no material basis on which he could benefit from giving false evidence and (c) I am satisfied having seen him give evidence that what he told me was what he believed to be true. I accept his evidence.

12. Mr Corlett is in my judgment someone about whose evidence it is necessary to be rather more circumspect about. He appears now to have a well established dislike of the Defendant which borders on the contemptuous. However, the evidence establishes that on any view he was for a period in close commercial collaboration with the Defendant. He was for most of the time prior to the trial of this claim regarded by the Claimant as hostile to him and his interests. Mr Corlett told me that he has initiated both civil and criminal proceedings against the Defendant that are pending in Portugal. The Claimant's case (which was not disputed) was that Mr Corlett approached him out of the blue to provide evidence to assist the Claimant. This approach came after Mr. Corlett had commenced proceedings against the Defendant in Portugal. However, as against that, the evidence that he gave orally was consistent with what was contained in his statement in these proceedings. That statement consists for the most part of a lengthy commentary by him on a statement prepared by the Defendant for use in some earlier proceedings. Mr Cawson submitted that these comments were provided unprompted by Mr Corlett and without there being any evidence that he was aware of the significance of the points so far as Mr Bell was concerned. There is some evidence that Mr Corlett was a reluctant witness. Having heard him give evidence and be cross examined by the Defendant I am bound to say that whilst he did not bother to hide his dislike for the Defendant, he did not give me the impression of giving misleading evidence. Notwithstanding that this is so, in my view I ought to be cautious before accepting the evidence of Mr Corlett save where it is corroborated by either evidence from a witness who I have concluded can safely be relied on or by the contents of contemporaneous documentation.

13. Finally before turning to the facts, I should note that the Defendant appeared in person. The Defendant is in my judgment both highly articulate and highly intelligent. His cross examination of the witnesses would have done credit to a junior barrister of some years call. Thus I am satisfied that at a factual level all of the witnesses called on behalf of the Claimant were fully tested in the evidence that they gave.

**The Facts**

14. Mr Dodd was obviously in his day a highly competent chartered accountant with (as Mrs. Young and the Defendant both acknowledged) well developed entrepreneurial skills which ultimately led him to leave private practice and the firm he had formed to take up a position as the CEO of a trading company with, at its height while he was in post, about 600 employees. It is clear that while he was in practice, Mr Dodd's interests lay in the realm of special projects of a commercial nature rather than the every day activities of a chartered accountant in Carlisle.

15. Mr Dodd founded Dodd & Co in 1981 and he remained the senior partner at that firm until he formally ceased to be a partner in March 1987. Mr Dodd told me and I accept that the Claimant became a client of the firm in 1982 when Dodd & Co acquired the client base of another Carlisle based accountant, Mr Nixon. Mr Dodd said that his first impression was that the Claimant was not astute at any rate outside his chosen field of road haulage. Outside the four corners of his business his affairs were a mess. He described the Claimant as having an "… *aversion to paying tax*". He explained this in cross examination as meaning that he thought the function of his accountant was to eliminate the need to pay tax but that his relationship was one in which he gradually introduced the Claimant to the concept of tax planning. Mr Dodd told me that it was not a question of persuading him to pay tax but rather of planning and that there was never a situation where the Claimant had income and Mr Dodd had to tell him to pay tax which he was refusing to pay. I accept that evidence. The correspondence that there is supports this approach. Thus the letter to HMIT dated 3rd December 1986 (S/5380) shows that (a) an offshore account had been disclosed and (b) a new source of untaxed income from abroad was disclosed. A letter of 4th December 1986 (apparently signed by Mr Dodd since it bears his reference) shows that this was to be taxed at 60%. Overall in my judgment the nature of the relationship between Mr Dodd and the Claimant is in essence as described by Mr Dodd – the Claimant was left to get on with what he did well which was trading his businesses as a road haulier and operating the Truck Inn while Mr Dodd was left to handle all other matters of a commercial, investment, administrative, or fiscal nature. However, I accept that the Claimant was capable of embarking on business projects outside his main areas of commercial activity without consultation and that he had done so at least once in relation to a property transaction in Spain in respect of which he took no advice. However, the size and circumstances of that transaction were wholly different from those with which I am concerned and does not necessarily negative the existence of a fiduciary duty being owed to him where he was persuaded to enter into a transaction because he was recommended to do so by someone in whom he reposed trust and confidence.

16. I turn next to the introduction of Mr Bland into the relationship with the Claimant. The Defendant's case is that Mr Dodd did not leave the firm until the end of March 1987 and that prior to that he retained responsibility for the affairs of the Claimant and his various companies. Mr Dodd says in his witness statement that the Defendant was groomed from March 1986 to take over the client relationship with the Claimant and by September 1986 was so heavily involved in his affairs that really all that Mr Dodd was doing was meeting the Claimant informally and only occasionally as opposed to the one day a week that he had been devoting to the affairs of the Claimant. Whilst I think that in essence what Mr Dodd says is correct, I think that his timing might be a little out. He told me and I accept that by the end of 1986, he was spending much of his time in the USA. I accept that evidence although as I have noted above, in early December 1986, Mr Dodd was signing letters to the Inland Revenue on behalf of the Claimant. Thus I think he is correct in saying that by the end of that year at the latest in practice much of the work that had in the past been done by Mr Dodd for the Claimant and the companies he controlled was being done by the Defendant. Whilst it may well be correct that Mr Dodd remained nominally the client partner until shortly before his notice to the firm expired in 1987 that was formal only. In practice the work had increasingly been handled by the Defendant and the Defendant had increasingly become the Claimant's point of contact with the firm.

17. Whilst Mrs. Young said that she first became aware that Mr Dodd was leaving at the end of 1986 that is not in any way inconsistent with the position being as I have described it. Mr Dodd's other interests, particularly those which caused him to spend time abroad, of necessity meant that the work he would otherwise have done would have to be done by others.

18. Some reliance was placed by the Defendant on the minutes of a meeting of the partnership that took place on 13th February 1987 as supporting his case that there was no sort of transfer of the sort alleged by the Claimant and Mr Dodd. However, the section of that document relied on (Paragraph 4) relates to the minutes of an earlier meeting which is likely to have occurred either in late December 1986 or early January 1987. The notes record in passing the Claimant as having said it was all over. Quite the context and timing of that comment is unclear. However it is not inconsistent with the concept of the relationship gradually changing from one involving the Claimant and Mr Dodd to one involving the Claimant and the Defendant and is likely to be attributable to Mr Bell receiving the letter referred to earlier in the minutes which informed clients of the departure from the practice of Mr Dodd. Thus I do not see this document as contradicting in essence the evidence of Mr Dodd as to how things developed on the ground during the latter part of 1986. At page 4 of the minute there is a reference to the Defendant being involved "... *in detail on major clients of the firm who had previously been dealt with by ...*" Mr Dodd. I do not read this as supporting the suggestion that the Defendant was to become involved from a date after the date of the minute. Rather, it is concerned with how his role would work with that of the new senior partner. It is not inconsistent with the position being as Mr Dodd describes it.

19. The analysis set out above is consistent with what the Defendant said in a witness statement signed by him in proceedings commenced by Mr Armstrong against Dodd & Co and the Defendant in relation to his investment in the Spanish project. At paragraph 3 he says that he became a partner in July 1986 and in Paragraph 4 that from that time Mr Dodd became increasingly involved in a company called Lilliput Lane Limited and that he would have an increased role is the commercial department in order to cover Mr Dodd's absences from the office. It is also consistent with the Claimant's oral evidence that although Mr Dodd may have formally left the firm in March 1987, he and the Defendant were working together in 1986.

20. As I have mentioned already, it is common ground that the Claimant was successful in his chosen areas of business activity at an operational level. However that was not directly the source of the wealth he acquired which funded the loans with which I am concerned. The Claimant was nominally the leasehold owner of some property leased from the City of Carlisle District Council from which the Truck Inn business operated. In the early 1980s, a decision was taken to transfer the Truck Inn business to a limited company which was wholly owned as I understand it by another company called Geoff Bell Limited of which the Claimant was the majority shareholder and his then wife the minority shareholder. The company was incorporated on 19th October 1983. It was intended that the Claimant would be allotted 826,804 shares in the company in return for the transfer by him to the company of the leasehold interests to which I have referred. In fact the shares were allotted but the leasehold interests were not transferred although the accounts for the company in subsequent years showed the leasehold interests as being the property of the company. Why there was no formal transfer at the time is not clear. Although the Claimant maintains that it was never the intention that he should transfer the leasehold interests to the company, I am not convinced that such was the case. However, this issue is collateral to the issues that arise in relation to this claim and have not been investigated in the course of the trial; before me. That being so, all that can be said is that it is at least arguable that the Claimant held the leasehold interests on resulting trust, and any proceeds of sale of those interests on resulting or constructive trust, for the company.

21. In 1986 BP Oil Limited became interested in acquiring the leasehold interests for redevelopment purposes. Ultimately by a contract in writing dated 28th July 1987, the Claimant purported to sell the leasehold interests to BP for a total consideration of £1,845,400. It was the net proceeds of this sale that were used to fund the loans that are the

subject matter of the present dispute. Clearly an issue which arose was whether the company owned the leasehold interests or the Claimant. As I have said already, on the facts as they are known to me, a conventional legal analysis would probably lead to the conclusion that the company was the beneficial owner of the leasehold interests which were held by the Claimant on resulting trust for the company. Thus either (a) the bare legal title ought to have been transferred to the company and the shares in the company then sold to BP or (b) the Claimant could sell as trustee in which event the interest of the company in the leasehold interests would be overreached by the sale but the proceeds of sale would be held by the Claimant on trust for the company. Mr Cawson submits that if course (a) had been adopted at a time when the Claimant was non resident for tax purposes no question of CGT would have arisen. He submitted that such was the advice that ought to have been given, had it been concluded that the Claimant held the leasehold interests on trust for the company. Again this issue was not investigated in the trial before me and I make no finding in relation to it. That issue is at least potentially for another court on another day.

22.   However that is not how things proceeded. On 6th March 1987, the Defendant wrote to Mr Livingstone, the Claimant's then solicitor who was a partner in Messrs Burnetts. The Claimant told me and I accept that Mr Livingstone was the person he regarded as "his" solicitor at that time. Although the Defendant maintained that this was the first letter he wrote on behalf of the Claimant and represented the time when he started to become involved in his affairs, that is not how I read that letter. The letter itself refers to an earlier conversation which is in itself inconsistent with the suggestion that this letter represents the point at which a handover had taken place. Secondly, in my judgment the letter suggests a degree of further prior discussion between the writer and the Claimant (who was at that stage involved in divorce proceedings) and finally it displays the sort of involvement by the Defendant in the affairs of the Claimant that Mr Dodd says he had in the affairs of the Claimant. Finally before moving on I should mention that the Defendant maintained that following the departure of Mr Dodd the arrangements within the firm altered with the Defendant having responsibility for companies and others having responsibility for investment and individual tax affairs. I reject that. It is not what Mrs. Young said the position was – indeed her evidence was that one partner remained responsible for particular clients. This letter is consistent with that – this letter relates to the private affairs of the Claimant not one of his companies. No doubt different people within the firm carried out specialist tasks but ultimately one partner was responsible for the affairs of a particular client. In my judgment in relation to the Claimant and his companies that was Mr Dodd but with a  gradual handing over of day to day responsibility to the Defendant which for all practical purposes was complete by the end of 1986 or the beginning of 1987.

23.   The issue with which the letter referred to above was substantively concerned was the subject of a meeting at the offices of Burnetts on 11th March 1987. The attendees were the Claimant, the Defendant, Mr Livingstone and Mr Noctor of Burnetts. It is noteworthy that Mr Dodd did not attend. It is clear from the attendance note that it was the Defendant who was driving the discussion on behalf of the Claimant as is apparent from the third paragraph. It is clear that what was being discussed was the question of CGT tax saving in relation to the sale of the leasehold interests. The note records the Defendant as saying that if the leasehold interests were owned by the Claimant then if the Claimant became non tax resident before 5th April 1987 and the sale took place after that date then the Claimant would not be liable to UK tax. The note records advice from Mr Livingstone to the effect that "… there was no problem in I G Bell selling the land direct to BP as he had not transferred his interest to the company. Having established this we agreed to proceed with BP on a basis of I G Bell selling the land direct to BP and for the sale to be affected post 5th April 1987 when I G Bell would be UK non resident." Whilst this advice may have been incorrect for the reasons already identified (I cannot be certain that this is so because the Claimant disputes

the suggestion that he ever agreed to transfer the leasehold interest to the company, the issue was collateral to the matters that arise in this claim and have not been fully investigated before me), I have no doubt whatsoever that the Claimant would not know that to be so.

24.     On 17<sup>th</sup> March 1987, Mr Noctor (another partner in Burnetts) apparently wrote to Mr Bell enclosing a much longer technical letter concerning the ownership of the leasehold interests that had been sent the same day to the Defendant. It was the Claimant's evidence that he did not receive this letter. Aside from this issue, in my judgment what ostensibly occurred shows both that the solicitor understood that the Claimant would look to the Defendant for guidance on what to do (since otherwise he would not have written the longer substantive letter to the Defendant) and also that by this time at least it was the Defendant not Mr Dodd who as carrying out this function.

25.     Although the shorter letter to the Claimant suggested that advice be taken from counsel and asked the Claimant to contact either Mr Noctor or Mr Livingstone, in my judgment having seen the Claimant there was no realistic prospect of that step being taken otherwise than following a discussion with the Defendant. The Claimant was simply not capable of comprehending the issues canvassed in the longer letter. The Claimant had been guided in relation to all tax matters by Mr Dodd in the past and as this exchange of correspondence shows by this date he was being guided in a similar fashion by the Defendant.

26.     On 23<sup>rd</sup> March 1987, a telephone discussion took place between the Claimant's solicitor and the Defendant concerning a power of attorney to be granted by the Claimant in favour of the Defendant. This was the subject of a letter dated 24<sup>th</sup> March 1987 from Mr Noctor to the Defendant. In that letter, Mr Noctor refers to having prepared a power of attorney *"… which hopefully will enable you to carry out most actions on his behalf, including assignment of the leasehold property"*. The need for a power of attorney could only arguably arise if the Claimant was going to be absent from the country. It was clearly envisaged that the power of attorney would give the Defendant wide ranging powers over the affairs of the Claimant and the power of attorney was entirely general in effect as is clear from the copy at C/708 which was apparently signed by the Claimant before Mr. Noctor on 25<sup>th</sup> March 1987. The next day, 26<sup>th</sup> March 1987, the Claimant executed a statutory declaration (C/710) by which an attempt was made to reverse  or evidence the reverse of the transfer of shares to the Claimant in consideration of the transfer to the company by the Claimant of the leasehold interests.

27.     The Defendant sought to rely on the fact that the power of attorney was signed in the face of the advice contained in the letter of 17<sup>th</sup> March as demonstrating that the Claimant had decided to proceed with the transaction notwithstanding advice to the effect that the position was at best questionable for the purpose of demonstrating that the Claimant was not as dependant on his advisors as he maintained. I do not infer that to be the case. There is no evidence that the Defendant advised the Claimant to accede to the advice of Mr Noctor. This correspondence relates to an issue in respect of which the Claimant was out of his depth and dependent on the advice he received from his advisers, much of which would have been unclear to him. In the course of his evidence, the Claimant told me that he had not a clue how to structure the sale to BP and I accept his evidence in that regard. The fact that the longer letter of 17<sup>th</sup> March was sent to the Defendant rather than the Claimant suggests that in truth that was the view of Mr Noctor as well.

28.     As I have said it was the Claimant's oral evidence that he did not receive the letter of 17<sup>th</sup> March. Given the signature on 25<sup>th</sup> March of the power of attorney I think it probable either that such was the case or that a conversation took place between the Claimant and the Defendant between the date of that letter and 24<sup>th</sup> March at which it was agreed to proceed notwithstanding the contents of the letters of 17<sup>th</sup> March. I accept that the Claimant was

someone who was dependent on advice from his advisors in relation to issues such a tax planning. The contrary is not seriously arguable. Having seen the Claimant give evidence, and even allowing for the fact that he is now 20 years older than he was at the relevant time, I do not accept it as at all likely that he would have proceeded notwithstanding advice not to do so from his solicitors and the Defendant. Thus I conclude that either the 17th March letter was not received by him at all and was not discussed with him by the Defendant or that the Defendant provided him with sufficient comfort that he was encouraged to proceed as had been planned originally.

29. This correspondence suggests as I have said that in the mind of Mr Noctor at least, instructions concerning the affairs of the Claimant were to be obtained from the Defendant. Clearly it came as no surprise to the solicitor that the Defendant was to be given a general power of attorney or indeed appointed as attorney over his children's trust or be delegated to act as director in place of the Claimant of his various companies at least one of which continued to trade after the Claimant's departure abroad.

30. My conclusions from the material so far considered is that in practice the Defendant became increasingly involved in the affairs of the Claimant and the Claimant became more and more dependant on the Defendant during the latter part of 1986, as Mr Dodd became more and more involved with the company that kept him away from the office for substantial periods. It may well be that the Claimant was not told that Mr Dodd was to leave Dodd & Co until December 1986 or January 1987 but that is not to the point. I reject the idea that the Defendant only became involved after Mr Dodd had either announced his intention of leaving Dodd & Co or had formally ceased being a partner on 31st March 1987. The correspondence referred to above of itself demonstrated that the latter was not the case. I also reject the notion that the Defendant's role was limited to advice concerning the companies. On the contrary, the correspondence above shows that his role was much wider than that. Finally in my judgment the material referred to above shows that the Claimant was not himself capable of considering how best to structure the transaction with BP, that he was heavily dependent on his advisers and the adviser on whom he was principally dependent was the Defendant. I would add that the fact that the Claimant was prepared to devolve to the Defendant so much power over his affairs, those of his children's trusts and his companies is consistent only with a very high degree of trust and confidence being placed on the Defendant by the Claimant. There were others he could have chosen – he had a subsisting and substantial relationship with Mr Livingstone, his solicitor, for example. The person he chose however was the Defendant who on the correspondence I have referred to was the principal person advising him in relation to the sale.

31. It is necessary now that I consider certain other events that occurred during 1987 and 1988 prior to the Claimant's agreement to invest in the Portuguese project.

32. First, following the Claimant becoming non UK resident for tax purposes, a bank account was opened for him by the Defendant with the St Helier, Jersey branch of Midland Bank ("the Bell Jersey Account"). Mr Bland became a signatory on that account. On 14th September 1987, the proceeds of sale of the leasehold interest to BP was credited to that account by Dodd & Co who in turn had received the sum concerned (£1,822,547) from Burnetts. The Defendant sought to minimise the significance of him being made a signatory of the Bell Jersey Account. He said that the power of attorney was executed for the convenience of the Claimant and was not a power he would exercise as a matter of discretion but only ever following prior discussion with the Claimant. That was not so in relation to at least one payment I refer to hereafter but in any event misses the point. The power was a wide ranging one that the Claimant trusted the Defendant not to abuse. That shows the existence of a relationship of trust and confidence between the Claimant and

Defendant at the latest by the date when it was signed ($25^{th}$ March 1987). Similar considerations apply to the Defendant becoming a mandated signatory on the Bell Jersey Account. The Defendant said that was of no significance because it was simply a means by which the Claimant could arrange for money to be sent to him while travelling. In fact, subsequently the power was used for much more significant purposes than that. In any event, even if that was correct (and I am not at all sure that it is since there is no evidence that the Claimant did not have access to a fax machine during his travels) it misses the point again - the significance is that it was the Defendant whom the Claimant chose as the person in whom he chose to repose his trust and to do so without imposing any limitation on the Defendant's authority to operate the account.

33. The other issue that arose in 1987 was a business arrangement into which the Claimant entered with a Mr Davidson in Florida. The significance of this stems from the fact that (1) the Defendant alleges that Claimant entered into these business arrangements without consulting the Defendant initially but (2) in any event (as is common ground) the Claimant turned to the Defendant when things had gone wrong for the purpose of attempting to broker a settlement. It is also necessary to consider what happened in Florida because, as will become apparent later in this judgment, there came a time when a written loan agreement came into existence which is alleged by the Clamant to have been sent to him by the Defendant as evidencing the loan that he made in relation to the Portuguese project. The Defendant contends that the document is a sham that was drawn up at the request of the Claimant to provide him with protection in the event that Mr Davidson was able to obtain a judgment against him in the US. The Claimant maintains that this is fabrication. My conclusions on this issue go not merely to substance but will also affect my judgment as to the credibility of the Claimant and Defendant.

34. There is an issue between the parties as to the degree to which if at all the Defendant was involved initially in the Florida transactions. Mr Davidson was another former resident of Carlisle and businessman who had sold his business interests in the UK. The Claimant maintains that before proceeding at all he asked the Defendant whether he could safely do business with Mr Davidson. The Defendant denies that this is so. Ultimately this is one of the issues which depend on the view I have formed of the relative credibility of the Claimant and Defendant. Thus my final conclusion on this point must necessarily be postponed until I have considered the issues that impact on the relative credibility of the Claimant and Defendant. However, given the conclusions I have so far reached concerning the nature of the relationship between the Claimant and the Defendant I consider that it is highly unlikely that the Claimant would embark on a business relationship with someone whom he did not know or know well without making such an enquiry of someone. There are two factors which in my judgment make it more likely that the Claimant is telling the truth in relation to this issue when he says that he consulted the Defendant.

35. First, the business arrangements in Florida were carried into effect by the Claimant using as a corporate vehicle a Jersey registered company called Barakot Limited ("Barakot"). Although the formation documents themselves are not in evidence, there is correspondence from the Defendant to some chartered accountants on Jersey relating to the transfer of the beneficial ownership of Barakot to the Claimant and the establishment of a bank account in the name of Barakot. - see C/760, 761, 763, 764, 771, 772-3 and 775. It is noteworthy that the Defendant was to be a co-signatory on that bank account. The Defendant was a director of Barakot from incorporation until he resigned in November 1991. Given the nature of the relationship between the Claimant and Defendant as I have found it to be, it is in my judgment highly unlikely that the Defendant would be involved in the transfer of the beneficial interest in Barakot to the Claimant and the establishment of the bank account

213

without being also consulted about the first business venture to be undertaken using Barakot as a vehicle to at least the level alleged by the Claimant.

36. The other factor that in my judgment points strongly towards this being the position is a letter to the Defendant from a Ms Norton, an accountant in Florida. That letter (C/769) is dated 2$^{nd}$ June 1988. It sets out the nature of the transaction and asks the Defendant whether he has any questions or suggestions for ownership. This letter could only have been written on the instructions of the Claimant and suggests at least some involvement by the Defendant in the initial stages. This was a letter that the Defendant suggested when asked about it in cross examination that he could not recall receiving.

37. All of this is entirely consistent with the relationship between the Claimant and Defendant being essentially as alleged by the Claimant. Equally consistent with that relationship being as the Claimant alleges is the approach made by the Claimant to the Defendant to broke a settlement when differences arose between Mr. Davidson and the Claimant. In his statement made in the proceedings commenced by Mr Armstrong (signed in August 1997) the Defendant said that *"during September and October 1988 Mr Bell approached me to see if I was prepared to act as arbitrator between the parties in Florida which I agreed to do."*. This proposal could only work on the basis that the Defendant was known to both parties (as was in fact the case) which makes it more likely that the Defendant would have given the sort of initial advice which it is alleged the Claimant sought from him in relation to the project. The approach by the Claimant to the Defendant suggests that the Claimant had trust and confidence in the Defendant.

38. In October 1988 proceedings were commenced in Florida by the Claimant against Mr Davidson. A copy of the originating process is attached to the statement of Mr. Szabo (B/(105)). It was these proceedings that led ultimately to a meeting chaired by the Defendant at which the basic terms of a settlement agreement were agreed (B/391-393). The minutes were sent by the Defendant to Mr Szabo under cover of a letter dated 31$^{st}$ December 1988. Ultimately these terms were incorporated into a formal settlement agreement between the parties to the Florida litigation dated 7$^{th}$ or 9$^{th}$ February 1989 (B/(94)).

39. It will be necessary to refer to subsequent Florida litigation later in this judgment. However, although this is slightly out of chronological sequence, I note at this stage that it was the Defendant's case than the formal loan agreement between Barakot and Epiette Limited to which I refer in detail below was a sham document created at the request of the Claimant in order to protect his assets in the event that a claim in damages was made against him in Florida by Mr Davidson and/or a company controlled by him. This loan agreement is dated 17$^{th}$ April 1989. However, the only allegation of loss being caused to Mr Davidson by Mr Bell is that contained in a letter 2$^{nd}$ September 1988. It pre-dated the settlement agreement to which I have referred above and contained an offer in settlement that was overtaken first by the negotiations in December 1988 chaired by the Defendant and then the formal settlement agreement in February 1989. The only other letter referred to was one sent by Mr Davidson to his own lawyer in Florida (Mr Tripp). That letter post dated the settlement agreement but related to losses that occurred prior to the settlement agreement. There is no evidence that it ever came to the attention of the Claimant. Although there was subsequent litigation in Florida, it was commenced by Barakot not Mr Davidson or a company controlled by him, it was commenced on 12$^{th}$ April 1989 (B/(89)) and it related to the enforcement of the settlement agreement. The loan agreement is dated five days later. There is nothing in the events that occurred prior to that date and after the signing of the settlement agreement that could give rise to a concern on the part of the Claimant that was sufficiently serious to cause him to enter into a sham agreement in an attempt to shelter his assets from Mr Davidson or a company controlled by him. The Defence and Counterclaim was filed on

4<sup>th</sup> May 1989. It did not seek any form of relief other than in effect specific performance of the settlement agreement. No monetary claim was intimated by Mr Davidson as far as I can see and certainly none was ever commenced. As Mr Szabo told me, and I accept, there was no cost risk for the Claimant in relation to the subsequent proceedings because the so called "American Rule" applied. Thus the only costs that the Claimant (or rather Barakot, since it was the claimant in the subsequent proceedings) would have to meet were the fees payable to its own lawyer. Finally, as I have observed, the claimant in the subsequent proceedings was Barakot and it was Barakot that was the respondent to the counterclaim. In these circumstances, it is not clear – and the Defendant was not able coherently to explain – how an allegedly sham agreement between Barakot and Epiette was to have the effect for which he contended it was brought into existence.

40.    I now return to the events I have to consider in their chronological sequence.

41.    According to the Defendant, in early November 1988, an advertisement appeared in the Financial Times by which a Mr Brian Wash sought investors to assist in the development of what turned out to be the Portuguese project. He says that he made contact with Mr Walsh who provided some basic information which showed that Mr Corlett was the developer. He says that following an initial telephone discussion with Mr Corlett and a further discussion with the Claimant it was agreed between the Claimant and Defendant that the Defendant would travel to Portugal, meet Mr Corlett and that he would take with him to Portugal another client of Dodd & Co (Mr Connon) who owned property locally and could assist in the evaluation of the project. That trip took place. The Defendant does not record what Mr Connon's views were. However, he says that he returned to the UK with some brochures plans and a sample design of the houses to be constructed on the land. The Claimant was during this period in Florida. There is to my mind no doubt that if the Defendant approached the Claimant as he alleges, he could have done so only because of the relationship that existed between them and equally if as the Defendant alleges the Claimant acceded to the suggestion that the Defendant travel to Portugal with Mr Connon at his expense (or rather one of his companies) he would have done so only because of the relationship of trust and confidence that existed between them which the facts and matters to which I have so far referred (other, obviously, that the events in and concerning the Claimant's interest in Florida that occurred after 25<sup>th</sup> November 1988) show to have existed at that time.

42.    The Claimant denies that there was any contact between the Claimant and the Defendant concerning the Portuguese project prior to a telephone call that he says he received in November 1988 from the Defendant's secretary informing him that the Defendant was in Portugal investigating an investment opportunity for him with Mr Connon.

43.    It is common ground that the Claimant and Defendant met at the offices of Dodd & Co on or about the 14<sup>th</sup> November 1988 after the Defendant had returned from his first visit to Portugal and while the Claimant was returning to his home in southern Spain via London. The Claimant's case is that the Defendant told him that there was a great deal of money to be made, that he had others who would wish to invest if he did not , that he was going to get involved in the project and that it was essential that he visited Portugal. The Defendant's case is that the Claimant was interested, wanted to visit Portugal and wanted the Defendant to accompany him for the purpose (the Defendant maintains) of introducing him to Mr Corlett. The Defendant maintains that there was no need for him to travel to Portugal, that he told the Claimant that there was no need for him to travel to Portugal and that although he travelled to Portugal, all he did was make the introduction and then left the Claimant and Mr Corlett to discuss matters.

44. The Claimant says that he and the Defendant travelled to Portugal on 22$^{nd}$ November 1988, that they were there about a week and that they shared a hotel room and a hire car. He says that they talked a lot about the project and visited various other sites for comparison purposes at all times together. He says that he was introduced to Mr Corlett by the Defendant and that he spoke to him for about 10 minutes. This accords broadly with what Mr Corlett says happened. The Claimant says his understanding was that he was the builder who would be retained in order to carry out the development work (that is the supply to the plots on the site of the necessary infrastructure to enable a property then to be constructed on the site). He says that the Defendant told him there were two ways of investing, one of which as to lend money to the company being formed to carry out the development. The Claimant maintains that he told the Defendant that all he wanted to do was to lend to the company that was to be formed for the purpose of acquiring the land on the basis of a 50% profit return with the sum to be loaned to be retuned on an agreed future date and the profit return paid on an agreed subsequent date. This business plan was commercially feasible because (as I understand the position) the land would be much more valuable once it had the infrastructure installed upon it and the development company would then be able to sell of individual plots at a profit to those who wished to build houses.

45. The Claimant maintains that since Barakot had been formed or transferred to the beneficial control of the Claimant by the Defendant specifically for investment purposes, the mutual but unspoken understanding was that the funds would be provided by the Claimant from the Bell Jersey Account but channelled through Barakot. He told me that he understood that the Defendant was to be a director and shareholder in the investment vehicle that was to be formed for the purpose of acquiring the land and that the primary purpose of this arrangement was to enable the Defendant to protect the interests of the Claimant and another co-investor who the Defendant told the Claimant was another client of Dodd & Co whom he did not identify. The Claimant understood that the Defendant would expect to make some profit from his shares in the investment vehicle to which the Claimant would be lending but that the primary purpose of him having shares in and being a director of the investment vehicle was so that he could protect the interests of the investors. While in Portugal, the Defendant introduced the Claimant to one of the sellers of the site. The Claimant says he was persuaded to sign two cheques each for £100,000 one payable to each of the two owners of the site as a deposit for the site. He says that receipts were drawn up at the hotel at which the Claimant and Defendant were staying by the Defendant which in essence reflected the substance of the transaction that the Claimant thought he was entering into on the advice of the Defendant.

46. The Defendant maintains that he was not a party to any of the discussions between the Claimant and Mr Corlett and that his understanding of what was agreed was that the Claimant agreed to lend £1.2 million to Mr Corlett and Mr Corlett agreed to repay that sum within 12 months and a profit return of 50% of the value of the loan within a further 6 months thereafter. He says that at some stage it was agreed that the Claimant would pay the owners of the land on which the development was to take place a deposit of £200,000 which was done there and then by two cheques each for £100,000 drawn on the Bell Jersey Account. He maintains that at no stage did he offer any advice as to the merits or otherwise of what was proposed and that *""… Mr Bell seemed to me to be far more experienced in business matters than I was"* – see Paragraph 80 of his statement in these proceedings.

47. The Claimant maintains that following their return to England, there was a further discussion between them about the structure of the transaction. The Claimant says that it was expressly agreed that the Claimant would lend through his offshore vehicle Barakot; that the loan would be to the investment vehicle and that he then returned to his home in

Spain, leaving the Defendant to complete the arrangements and make the necessary payments out of the Bell Jersey Account.

48. As will be appreciated there is a fairly fundamental difference between the parties as to what happened in Portugal. In my judgment, the evidence of the Claimant in relation to what happened, what was said and between whom during this period is to be preferred over that of the Defendant for the following reasons.

49. First, the suggestion by the Defendant that the initial trip was made by him at the instigation or on the instructions of the Claimant is flatly contradicted by the Defendant himself in Paragraph 12 of the witness statement he provided in the proceedings brought against him by Mr Armstrong which as I have said already was signed by the Defendant in August 1997. In that paragraph, the Defendant says in terms that *"… I was unable to contact Mr Bell who was travelling somewhere in Florida. I decided to go to Portugal to see the development and asked Mr Connon , who was a client of Dodd & Co and who owned a property in Vale do Lobo in the Algarve, to join me in order  that he could give me his views as to the viability of the development  I was going to have a look at"*. The only explanation that the Defendant had for this discrepancy was that it was made in a statement where the issue under consideration did not have the importance it does in these proceedings. I do not regard that as in any sense a satisfactory explanation. First, as I have said the Defendant is a highly intelligent individual. The idea that he would say accidentally something in a statement which was so flatly the opposite of what he says actually occurred is to my mind inconceivable. Secondly, these proceedings had been started and on foot for some time prior to the date when he signed the witness statement. I simply cannot accept that he would say something that was wrong by accident in a witness statement in other proceedings that might have a negative impact in these proceedings when there was no reason for doing so. Thirdly, given that the point was not centrally important in the Armstrong proceedings, it is inherently much more likely that what was said on the issue in the statement in those proceedings was true rather than untrue because there was no reason to give untrue evidence in relation to the point. Fourthly, the contrast between what is said in these proceedings and what was said in the Armstrong proceedings cannot be said to be the result of an error. There are two flatly contradictory descriptions of what happened. Finally if and to the extent that the problem is attributed to failing memory (which in fact I do not accept to be the case) then the version of events set out in the statement signed in 1997 is likely to be the one containing the accurate summary of events. My conclusion in relation to this issue is that what the Defendant said in his 1997 statement is the truth. This conclusion not only impacts my assessment of what actually happened in Portugal in November 1988 but also adversely affects my view of the credibility of the Defendant as a witness.

50. The contemporaneous material suggests that the initial meeting went far further than the Defendant now suggests and in a direction that was different from and inconsistent with what he says happened on the second visit when he was accompanied by the Claimant. There is a letter dated 10th November 1988 from Mr Walsh to the Defendant. That letter plainly contemplates a partnership between Mr Walsh and Mr Corlett on the one side and the Defendant (using funds provided by others) on the other. This is readily apparent from the letter read as a whole and also from the references within the letter to *"… you  people are able to invest …"* and to the Defendant being *"…in control of the purse strings …"*. The letter also speaks of borrowing *"… the whole amount from yourselves …"*. This is not in any sense consistent with what the Defendant says happened on his initial visit to Portugal. This analysis is also supported by the fact that on 11th November, Mr Bland obtained a reference concerning Mr Walsh from a Blackpool solicitor. Why would that be the case if what had happened during the initial visit was as described by the Defendant?

217

51. On 13th November the Defendant wrote to Mr Walsh. The copy of this letter at C/789 bears the signature of Mr Bell. The Defendant said, and I am sure he is correct on this point, that he asked Mr Bell to sign the document as confirmation that it reflected his instructions. However, I do not see how that is consistent with the subsequent visit to Portugal with the Claimant being for the limited purpose that the Defendant alleges. The letter is significant also because it refers to a loan of £1 million "... *for the purchase of the land ...*". That is entirely consistent with what the Claimant says he understood to be the proposal and what ultimately he understood he had agreed to do. The Defendant maintains that he showed the Claimant the letter from Mr Walsh of 10th November referred to above. The Claimant denies that this is so. I return to this issue after considering the remaining material relevant to what occurred in Portugal in November 1988.

52. I now move forward to the visit to Portugal. On the Defendant's case there was no useful purpose to be served by him being there. If his sole purpose in going was to introduce the Claimant to Mr Corlett there was no purpose to be achieved in him remaining after that had happened. Again the Defendant had no explanation to give for this other than that he had an interest in the area and what was being built. He was at that time a full equity partner in Dodd & Co. The firm was by all accounts busy and successful. There is no basis upon which a professional could justify remaining in Portugal for four days if the purpose was as limited as the Defendant would have me believe that it was. It is inherently more likely that his role during this period was more extensive than he suggests.

53. As I have said already, it is common ground that the Claimant signed two cheques drawn on the Bell Jersey Account before he and the Defendant left Portugal. As I have said already each was for £100,000 and each was made payable to one of the two vendors of the land. Significantly in my judgment it is common ground that each of the cheques was written out by the Defendant though each was signed by the Claimant. The Claimant had his own cheque book and he was a signatory on the account. The fact that the cheques were written out by the Defendant is more consistent with him having been involved in what was being discussed and indeed on the Claimant relying on the Defendant to guide him through the process than with the Defendant's role being the limited one he suggests.

54. The final and to my mind determinative factor which leads me to accept what Mr Corlett and the Claimant say occurred on the Defendant's second visit to Portugal is the text of the receipt at C/794. There is an issue as to when the receipt was prepared and signed to which I refer below. However it is common ground that it was typed by the Defendant and it is dated 25th November 1988. It is necessary that I set out the text of the receipt in full:

> "we [the vendors] hereby acknowledge receipt of the sum of £200,000 sterling from Ian Geoffrey Bell on the following conditions:
>
> 1. We are the owners of the unencumbered freehold title of the parcel of land of some 11 Hectares located in the parish of Almancil, Council of Loula and known as FERRARIAS.
>
> 2. We have agreed with Ina Geoffrey Bell that we will sell to him, or any other person or company as he directs, the land , complete with full planning permission and Alvera, for the total consideration of 495,000,000 Portuguese Escudos, of which the above mentioned two hundred thousand pounds sterling is considered part payment of. If directed we will additionally sell to Mr Bell or as otherwise directed the Portuguese company we have already formed for the purpose of carrying out the development of this land , this sale to be included in the total consideration as mentioned above.

218

3. *The receipt of this money is on the same conditions and terms as will be agreed between ourselves and Mr Bell and included in the contract for the sale by us to Mr Bell or as otherwise directed.*

4. *If for any reason the sale of the land complete with full planning permission and Alvera by us to Mr Bell or as otherwise directed does not proceed we undertake to refund immediately the money in full.*

Signed ..."

There is as I say a dispute as to when this document was prepared. The Claimant maintains that it was typed at the hotel where they were staying using a typewriter belonging to the hotel. The Defendant maintains that it was prepared after he returned from England in the first week of December 1988 following a query from the bank to him concerning one of the cheques. This dispute has no significance for present purposes other than possibly in relation to credit. What is significant is that (a) the Defendant could not sensibly have prepared a document to this effect if his understanding of what occurred was as he now describes it. Indeed, the owners of the land could not properly have signed such a document if their understanding of what was being agreed was as alleged by the Defendant. The document would have been one signed by Mr Corlett acknowledging the payment to his order by the Claimant of £200,000 to the vendors by a payment of £100,000 to each. Further (b) the Defendant does not allege that he spoke to the Claimant before preparing the document yet he maintains that he was not part of the conversations at which what he says was agreed with Mr Corlett was agreed between him and the Claimant. In those circumstances, it is entirely unclear to me how if what the Defendant says is true the Defendant could possibly have prepared the document, much less have procured its signature by or on behalf of the vendors. More generally, this document is in substance consistent with what the Claimant says was the position namely that he was to invest in a vehicle that was to purchase the land and that he paid the deposit at the instigation of the Defendant before the investment vehicle had been formed.

54. I should say that for what it is worth, I reject the Defendant's case as to how the document came into existence. First, I do not accept that there was any rational reason why the bank should contact the Defendant concerning the cheque or why if the bank did so it would not act on either the oral or written assurances of the Defendant who was a co-signatory on the account. It is inherently more likely that such a document would be written out and required to be signed in return for the cheques. The only points made by the Defendant are that an English language typewriter would not be available in Portugal at any rate in 1988 and that the receipt shows that it was faxed to him because it has his name handwritten on the copy in the bundle. As to the first of these points, there is no evidence that is so. The hotel was a Trust House Forte hotel and it was in the Algarve. I have no reason to suppose that such an hotel would not have an English language typewriter. As to the second point, what is written on the copy in the bundle does not demonstrate that the document was faxed much less when and by whom. Following the delivery in draft of a copy of this judgment, the Defendant supplied me with an e mail dated 21st April 2009 apparently from a Mr Pina. This purports to confirm that in earlier proceedings in Portugal, the Claimant produced a version of the receipt with an automatically generated fax header "*Dec 07 '88 14:29 DODD's Broadacre House 0228401043*". Mr Pina says this document was "*... sent by Mr Viegas to you*" – that is by the vendor who signed the receipt to Mr Bland. However, whether this is so is not proved by what Mr Pina says in his e mail not least because he has no means of knowing how the version of the document he refers to came into existence. This point was not explored at all in the evidence led at trial. It does not assist on the point now under consideration. On my evaluation of the material that was before me I reject the Defendant's

evidence as to the timing of the preparation of the receipt as being not merely wrong but regrettably also untrue. However the timing is not the centrally important point – as I have said already, even if I am wrong on this point and the Defendant is correct, it remains the case in my judgment that the Defendant could not possibly have drafted the receipt in the form it is in if (a) the Defendant is correct in what he says was agreed between the Claimant and Mr Corlett and (b) he could not have drafted it at all (or at any rate not without input from the Claimant) if his role on his second visit to Portugal was as limited as he would have me believe. It is the contents of the receipt rather than its timing that is important.

55.     It is now necessary to consider the events that occurred concerning the loan agreement that was dated 17th April 1989 to which I have already referred in passing. The events relevant to this issue occurred between December 1988 and July 1989. It is necessary to bear in mind that during this period the Defendant was involved on behalf of the Claimant in assisting him to resolve his difficulties with Mr Davidson and that between October 1988 and March 1989 the Claimant became involved in the Spanish development. It is also important to remember that the events leading up to the signature and delivery to the Claimant of the loan agreement were all unknown to the Claimant who is not alleged to have played any part in these arrangements.

56.     The first step in the genesis of the loan agreement appears to have occurred on 10th December 1988 when the Defendant wrote to Dickinson Dees, a firm of solicitors based in Newcastle to which appears to be attached the first page of a draft agreement between Barakot and a company called Iberian Development Corporation (Gibraltar) Limited. This appears to relate to a loan of £1.2 million for the acquisition of the Ferrarias land in Portugal. This company was formed on 9th September 1988. Its shareholders were said to be the Defendant (1 share) and another Gibraltar registered company which held 1999 shares.

57.     According to a company search carried out on 13th March 1997 (E/1373), Iberian's directors were Mr Walsh (appointed 27th September 1988), Mr Corlett (appointed 27th September 1988) and Mr Bland who is recorded as having been appointed on 5th December 1988 that is 5 days prior to the date of his letter of instruction to Dickinson Dees and 2 days prior to the date when the first £100,000 payment was debited from the Bell Jersey Account, which he claims was the trigger for the preparation of the receipt. Thus, if the Defendant was correct in what he said about the receipt, the position would be that he was drawing up a receipt on one basis having instructed solicitors to draw up a loan agreement on a wholly different basis two days before. The explanation the Defendant gave for this was that the recorded date of his appointment as a director of Iberian is wrong and too early and that the purpose of instructing lawyers to draw up an agreement was so that there was something on his file recording the terms of the agreement between Mr Corlett and the Claimant which he said became necessary for the reasons referred to in the following paragraph of this judgment.

58.     The case advanced by the Defendant in cross examination of the Claimant was that Iberian was a vehicle formed by Mr Walsh and Mr Corlett and that following the return to the UK of the Claimant and Defendant each went their separate ways with there being no intention that the Defendant be further involved. The Claimant denied this version of events and I reject it for the reasons already given. There is no evidence other than the uncorroborated oral evidence of the Defendant that the Defendant's appointment as a director of Iberian is wrongly stated in the company search and I reject the suggestion that it was. However, the Defendant's case was that he became a director of Iberian as a nominee of Mr Corlett after the second visit to Portugal and after it had been agreed that the Defendant would have no further involvement on behalf of the Claimant. The Defendant's case is that since he was to become an adviser to Mr Corlett he wanted something on his file which recorded what had actually been agreed. I reject this version of events as well. It is inherently unlikely that such

was the actual intended purpose – if such was the case it could have been achieved by other less expensive and more informal means. Further the existence of such activity at this time and for this ostensible purpose is not consistent with what the Defendant says was the purpose of the loan agreement signed in April 1989 which was the ultimate result of this activity.

59. The one thing that does emerge from this activity is that the initial draft document shows the lender as Barakot and thus that the Claimant is likely to be right when he says that the Defendant and he had always understood and had agreed following their return from Portugal that the loan was to be by Barakot albeit funded from funds credited to the Bell Jersey Account. It was put to the Claimant by the Defendant that a discussion had taken place between them in which the Defendant had explained the approach from Mr Corlett and that the Claimant had acquiesced in the Defendant becoming involved on behalf of Mr Corlett. The Claimant denied this suggestion and I reject it. Had the position been as alleged by the Defendant I have no doubt that the Defendant would have recorded the position in writing to the Claimant. It is not alleged that any such letter was ever sent. In those circumstances, the Defendant's case on this issue depends upon his uncorroborated oral evidence and as I have said I reject it.

60. On or about 12th January 1989, Epiette Limited ("Epiette") was incorporated and its inaugural meeting held on that date. The Defendant and Messrs Walsh and Corbett were appointed directors of that company. The first board meeting of Epiette was held on 13th January 1989 (C/824) and the following day the Defendant wrote to Dickinson Dees referring to a draft loan agreement that inferentially had been prepared in draft by Dickinson Dees and sent to the Defendant. That letter identified the parties to the agreement now as Barakot and Epiette and the address for service for each as the home of the Defendant for Barakot and the offices of Mr Walsh's UK business for Epiette. The letter concludes by saying that the Defendant wanted the agreement signed in January 1989 and that the new version was to be sent to him at his home address. A new version of this agreement was sent back to the Defendant by Dickinson Dees on 19th January 1989.

61. The Claimant was asked by the Defendant in cross examination when he first became aware of Epiette. He said that he first heard the name mentioned by the Defendant in early 1989 as being the vehicle formed to carry the venture into effect. The loan agreement is dated 17th April 1989 but the Claimant maintains that the first time he saw it was when it was sent to him by the defendant by under cover of a fax dated 4th July 1989 (D/992).

62. As I have said, it was alleged by the Defendant that the final version of the loan agreement was a sham signed only in order to protect the Claimant's assets from attack from Mr Davidson. Aside from one letter that I will come to in a moment there is no documentation that supports that analysis. There is a letter dated 18th June 1989 apparently from the Defendant to Mr Walsh. In it, the Defendant asks Mr Walsh to sign it "… as I wish to make sure that Geoff has a copy should anything happen to me". This is of course entirely inconsistent with either of the reasons he now gives for preparing the document. The agreement was sent to the Claimant by the Defendant under cover of a fax dated 4th July 1989. That is a significant factor because I have already explained that there was nothing about the litigation in the US that could reasonably have given rise to the sort of concern that the Defendant maintains was the driving force for the preparation of the loan document. Further, by the time the document came to be sent to the Claimant the position was even clearer because the Defence and Counterclaim had been served on behalf of Mr Davidson and his company and it was clear that no monetary remedy was being sought from the Claimant.

63. There is, as I have said, only one document that apparently supports the allegation that the loan agreement was and was known to be a sham by all the parties to it. This document is apparently signed by Mr Walsh, and apparently supports the suggestion that the loan agreement is a sham. The letter suggests that Mr Walsh signed the agreement under financial pressure from Mr Corlett to do so. It was submitted by Mr Cawson that I should reject this document as anything other than a fabrication. There are it seems to me a number of difficulties about the document. First, it is dated as I have said 27th June 1989. It includes the statement that Mr Walsh has signed the agreement and has enclosed it with the letter. However the loan agreement is dated 17th April. Further although the letter from Mr Walsh is apparently written in response to the letter of 18th June, nothing in that letter supports the suggestion that even inferentially the agreement was a sham. Mr Walsh prepared his witness statement in the Barakot proceedings before this letter came to light. There is no mention anywhere within it of the loan agreement being a sham. The Defendant's explanation as to how the letter came to light was given in the Barakot action as being that it had been identified to him by Mr Corlett in the course of a telephone conversation. This was not supported by Mr Corlett's oral evidence before me.

64. There is another difficulty about the sham argument. At no stage in any of the various statements made and affidavits sworn in other proceedings by the Defendant was the suggestion that the loan agreement was a sham made until a very late amendment was made to the Defendant in the Barakot v. Epiette litigation. I remind myself that the legal burden of proving this claim rests on the Claimant and of the strictures that apply in this sort of case identified by Richards LJ quoted in Paragraph 6 above. However it is the Defendant who bears the evidential burden of establishing what he alleges namely that the loan agreement was a sham. The weight of the evidence adduced before me all points in one direction save for the single letter from Mr Walsh referred to above. I have concluded that the allegation that the loan agreement was a sham has not been made out on the evidence before me.

65. Taking a step back from the evidence I have so far considered, I am entirely satisfied and I find that following the visit to Portugal ending on 25th November 1988 and the discussions that took place in Carlisle immediately following their return between the Claimant and the Defendant, the Claimant's understanding of what was to happen was that he was to invest £1 million in a joint venture vehicle which was also to be funded by another client of Dodd & Co which vehicle was then going to acquire the Portuguese site, engage builders to carry out the infrastructure work and then sell on at a profit sufficient to pay the investors their loan and profit and provide some incidental modest profit for the Defendant. He did not think he was lending to Mr Corlett – indeed I accept his evidence that he thought Mr Corlett was a builder who would simply make his money by doing the development work for the joint venture. I do not think that he had any real idea of the role that was to be played by Mr Walsh if any other than that he was going to sell the plots on behalf of the investment vehicle. Further I am entirely satisfied that the mutual understanding of the Claimant and the Defendant at the latest following their return to the UK from Portugal was that Barakot would be used as the Claimant's investment vehicle. Indeed the receipt prepared by the Defendant, which I find was in fact prepared by him in Portugal before he and the Claimant returned to the UK, expressly contemplated such an arrangement although the entity to be used was not identified by name. I am also entirely satisfied that the Claimant thought that Epiette was the investment vehicle.

66. It is now necessary that I consider what in fact was happening as between the Defendant, Mr Walsh, Mr Corlett and Epiette concerning the Portuguese project. As is apparent from the minutes of the inaugural meeting of Epiette held on 12th January 1989, the three founding shareholders held respectively 1500 250 and 250 shares in the company. The inaugural meeting of the board of Epiette was held as I have mentioned on 13th January 1989. That

meeting (apparently attended by the Defendant, Mr Corlett and Mr Walsh) ratified the allotment of these shares to the founding shareholders. On a date which is not apparent from the face of the documents but is likely to have been at or around the time when the inaugural board meeting was held, various declarations of trust were executed by the registered shareholders. Mr Killminster declared himself to be the holder of the 1500 shares registered in his name on trust for the Defendant (L/3212-3214), Ms Richardson declared herself to be the holder of 250 shares registered in her name on trust for Mr Walsh (L/3218- 3220) and Ms Le Gresley declared herself to be the holder of 250 shares registered in her name on trust for Mr Corlett (L/3225-7). Further shares were issued to the registered shareholders in July 1989 which brought holdings of the registered shareholder respectively to 7,500, 1250 and 1250. Further declarations of trust were executed by each of the registered shareholders which mirrored the first declarations. If and to the extent that the initial declarations of trust had not been executed by the time when the inaugural board meeting took place, I have no doubt that it took place in the belief that the declarations either had been or imminently were about to be executed. In the result, as at 13$^{th}$ January 1989 Epiette had 2000 shares of which 75% were held on trust for the Defendant absolutely and the remaining shares were held as to 12½ % on trust for Mr Corlett and 12½ % for Mr Walsh. The reality is that Epiette was controlled by the Defendant from no later than January 1989. The issue of the additional shares in July 1989 did not alter this situation.

67.   There is within the papers a Project presentation (F/1454). It is clear that one if not the sole purpose for which it was prepared was for presentation to First National Commercial Bank Plc ("FNC"). FNC was the institution that was approached by the Defendant on behalf of Epiette for the balance of the funding needed to complete the Portuguese project. This approach was not disclosed to the Claimant who I have found was told by the Defendant that the balance of the funding was to be provided by another client of Dodd & Co. When the document was prepared is not clear because it is undated. However it is clear that it must have been prepared before 31$^{st}$ March 1989, because that is the date when FNC acknowledged receipt of it in a letter of that date addressed to Mr Bland at Iberian Development Corporation (C/899). That report disclosed that with the benefit of planning permission and with the infrastructure completed, the site had been valued at £7.5 million. After repayment of the sums then contemplated as being borrowed - £1.2 million to the Claimant plus his interest payment of £600,000 and repayment of the bank's loan of £1 million and interest thereon and payment of the cost of doing the infrastructure works assuming that this was £500,000 (as estimated in the Project Presentation – F/1463), the result would broadly be that a profit would be made by Epiette of in excess of £4 million of which, assuming the shareholdings reflected the division of the profit, 75% would go to the Defendant. All this is of course before any tax is levied. No account has been taken of the incidental costs of the project. However, even if they were as high as projected in the Project Presentation, that still leave a gross profit of in excess of £3 million of which 75% (£2.25 million) would accrue to the Defendant (before tax). None of this was explained to the Claimant.

68.   The only basis on which this analysis could be wrong (other than in matters of detail) was if the Defendant was not in truth the beneficial owner of 75% of Epiette. As to that, the Defendant's case was that he held the 75% interest on trust for Mr Corlett. However, if that was so, I would have expected there to be a declaration of trust that showed this to be so made at the same time as the other declarations of trust. None has ever been produced. It was said that the reason for this arrangement was for "tax saving" purposes. However that is inconsistent with the other declarations of trust that have been produced. If Mr Corlett's interest was to be protected by a trustee holding his shares then why would the whole of his alleged interest not be held by the relevant nominee registered shareholder? If that was not sufficient to achieve the tax saving desired, then why was the whole of his shareholding not

held on trust by the registered shareholders for the Defendant and the whole of that shareholding then declared by him to be held on trust for Mr Corlett? None of these points were ever explained.

69. On 11th May 1989, FNC made a formal offer of a loan to cover the balance required. As the covering letter made clear (D/934) the loan was to be to Epiette, Epiette was to be the sole corporate body acquiring the site and the interest of the bank was to be secured by a first legal charge over the land and/or a charge over the shares of the Portuguese company that was to carry out the development work. None of this was revealed to the Claimant at the time or until years after the events occurred.

70. The Defendant's case is that in January 1989 he was approached by Mr Corlett with an offer of employment, that he gave his partners notice of intention to leave the partnership in March 1989 and that he left in June 1989. He claims to have informed the Claimant that this is what he intended to do. The Claimant accepted in the course of his oral evidence that he was informed that the Defendant was going to work full time in Portugal but not that he was going to work for Mr Corlett. In my judgment the suggestion made by the Defendant that he was going to work for Mr Corlett as one of his employees was not made out. Mr Corlett denied it. No contractual documentation of any sort was produced which showed that to be so. I regard it as inherently unlikely that an equity partner in a successful provincial accounting practice would give that up to work in an administrative capacity for Mr Corlett. It is inherently much more likely that the Defendant moved to Portugal in order to manage the affairs of Epiette and that he was motivated to do so by the very substantial rewards that were at that time foreseen by him as likely to be made by him from the Portuguese project as the majority shareholder in Epiette.

71. Thus I have no hesitation in concluding that, contrary to the understanding of the Claimant at the time, he was not lending to an entity that was to be financed by him and another private investor whose profit was for the most part to be used in repaying the investors their respective loans and interest but in which the Defendant was to be a shareholder and director for the purpose or predominate purpose of protecting the interests of the investors. Nor was he lending to Mr Corlett so that he could invest in Epiette by way of directors loan as the Defendant alleges. In truth the Claimant was lending to the Defendant, though he did not know such was the case, so that the Defendant could embark on a highly speculative commercial adventure in which all the risks were to be borne by the Claimant and substantially all of the benefit would accrue to the Defendant – the person who the Claimant believed was involved principally to look after the interests of the Claimant and, he believed, his private co-investor but who in truth was interested on his own behalf. There was thus from the outset an inherent conflict between the interests of the Claimant and those of the Defendant which ought plainly to have led someone in the position of the Defendant to advise someone in the position of the Claimant of the true position and to seek independent advice

72. There is one other event which in my judgment makes this much the more likely analysis and shows how in truth the Defendant had become motivated solely by the desire to earn substantial sums from the project irrespective of the best interests of the Claimant. As will be apparent from what I have said so far, key to the success of the venture was that £1.2 million was paid over by the Claimant to Epiette. It is common ground aside from the £200,000 paid in November 1988, payments were made to Epiette from the Bell Jersey Account as follows:

i) 19th April 1989 - £196,931;

ii)      24<sup>th</sup> April 1989 - £3,104;

iii)     3<sup>rd</sup> June 1989 - £25,000;

iv)      21<sup>st</sup> July 1989 - £25,000;

v)       27<sup>th</sup> July 1989 - £750,000; and

vi)      31<sup>st</sup> July 1989 - £50,000.

The significant date is 21st July for it was then and thereafter that £825,000 of the total to be lent was paid over.

73.    As will be apparent from the earlier part of this judgment, it was questionable whether any legitimate capital tax saving could be achieved on the sale of the leasehold interest by the sale being structured so that the vendor was the Claimant. This issue had been the subject of ongoing correspondence with the Inland Revenue in which the Inland Revenue maintained that the assets were beneficially owned by the Geoff Bell Limited and that it was liable to capital gains tax following the sale. This correspondence was carried on by the Defendant on behalf of the Claimant. However, as was well known to the Defendant, though not to the Claimant, the Defendant had a personal interest in the outcome being favourable to the Claimant for if a charge to capital gains tax was to be raised then the practicalities were that the tax would have to be paid at least in part by the Claimant since whilst the company had some assets they were not sufficient to fund the payment of the tax being demanded. This was potentially a difficulty for the Defendant since by this stage he was the sole director of the company and thus was not able to resign unless he could persuade someone else (in reality the Claimant) to become a director. It was also a difficulty for the Defendant because if the Claimant used part of the funds he had obtained from the sale of the leasehold interests then there would not be sufficient money left to fund the loan that was the basis on which the Defendant had been able to obtain effective control of the Portuguese project.

74.    Sometime prior to the 26<sup>th</sup> May 1989, solicitors were instructed to advise concerning the sale of the leasehold interests. The solicitors instructed were Messrs Cartmell Shepherd. Who instructed that firm, when and in what capacity is not entirely clear. What is clear is that a conference with counsel took place on 26<sup>th</sup> May 1989 and the note of what occurred at that conference was sent to the Defendant at Dodd & Co under cover of a letter dated 2<sup>nd</sup> June 1989 in which the solicitors made clear to the Defendant that they were writing to him in his capacity as a director of the company and that there was a conflict between the company and Dodd & Co, at least potentially. The conference was attended not merely by the Defendant but also Mrs. Young (nee Fisher). It is not apparent whether counsel was aware that the sole beneficial owner of the company at that stage was the Claimant. It is clear however that the Defendant knew that to be so. The effect of the advice was stark – the company was the sole beneficial owner of the leasehold interests, the Claimant was estopped from challenging the claim of the company to be the sole beneficial owner of the leasehold interests, the company was liable to tax in a sum which was not less than £400,000 and the statutory declaration (as to which see paragraph 25 above) had no legal effect. Counsel advised that the company may have claims over against Dodd & Co., Burnetts and the directors at the time including Mr Bell and his estranged wife. If the company was placed in liquidation then there was noted to be the possibility of directors' disqualification proceedings which might have an adverse effect on the professional status of the Defendant.

75.    In such circumstances, it was to be expected that the Defendant would wish to inform the Claimant immediately of the situation and, possibly, to advise him to repatriate sufficient

funds that when combined with what assets the company had in the UK (an entitlement to the return from pension trustees of an overpayment to the pension scheme) would enable the tax bill and any interest and penalties to be met. It might also be expected that having been advised in his capacity as a director of the company of which the Claimant was the sole beneficial owner, the Defendant would have advised the Claimant of possible claims that could be made either by the company and/or the Claimant against either Dodd & Co and/or Burnetts. The Defendant did not do any of these things and indeed does not even claim to have done any of these things. He asserted to me that he did not do so because he was advised not to do so. He did not inform me who gave such advice or when. The only advice concerning who was to be informed that appears on the face of the note of the conference came from counsel who advised that (a) the Inland Revenue ought to be informed of the position without delay and (b) Burnetts should not be informed of the position. The only other note of caution was sounded by the solicitor in the covering letter who warned of the (obvious) potential conflict of interest between Dodd & Co and the company. I can think of no proper basis on which either a solicitor or counsel could have given the advice alleged to have been given to the Defendant.

76.    On the 3rd June 1989, the Defendant used his authority to authorise withdrawals from the Bell Jersey Account to transfer a further £25,000 to Epiette. On the same day he wrote to the Claimant. These events took place the day after the sending to the Defendant of the letter under cover of which the Defendant had been sent a copy of the note of the conference and about a week after the conference had itself taken place. The letter read as follows:

> *"Dear Geoff*
>
> *Just to keep you informed of what is going on.*
>
> *I have today transferred a further £25,000 from your account to the account of Epiette for the Vale del Lobo deal. I have asked Mike [Couzens] to include in the next monthly summary he sends out to you his suggestions as to what to sell. It is likely that the next amount to be drawn will be one lump, ie either £575,000 or £775,000.*
>
> *...*
>
> *PPS*
>
> *I have just remembered that Doug Claxton is one of your executors for your will. You may wish to consider this if he has not been in touch with you*
>
> *...*
>
> *Last PS*
>
> *I also enclose the Mem and Arts of Barakot which I have just received from Jersey this morning."*

This letter is in my judgment significant on a number of different levels. First, the reference to the will issue in the PPS and the enclosure of the Barakot Memorandum and Articles referred to in the Last PS shows very clearly the continuing nature of the relationship between the Claimant and Defendant – as it would have been perceived by the Claimant and was intended to be perceived by the Defendant. Secondly, the letter clearly shows that contrary to what the Defendant told me in his evidence, he did on this occasion at least make a transfer from the Bell Jersey Account without discussing it with the Claimant first. Finally and most significantly it contains not one word about the advice that had been received by the Defendant the previous week.

77. It is now necessary to take a step back from the detail. For the reasons set out above, at this time (June 1989) the Defendant was expecting to make a very substantial personal gain from his 75% shareholding in Epiette. However, critical to him making that gain was that the Claimant continue to loan the sums that had been promised. Since the agreement was not a personal one but rather was a loan from Barakot to Epiette albeit funded by the Claimant, the loan could not be enforced against the Claimant personally. Aside from that if the Claimant had been alerted (as he should have been) to the effect of counsel's advice, it was, to put it no higher, a possibility that he would wish to divert funds to fund the payment of the tax. If that was done then the Claimant would not have the means to make the further payments on which the ability of the Defendant to make a substantial profit depended. In my judgment none of this would have been lost on the Defendant. The Defendant's interest clearly lay in maintaining silence about the events in the UK referred to above. That is how the Defendant proceeded.

78. It is now necessary to refer albeit briefly to how the tax issues finally played out. I do so because it throws light in my judgment on how the relationship between the Claimant and Defendant was conducted so far as the Claimant was concerned and how in reality the Defendant conducted matters. In doing so it is necessary that I move forward in the chronology ahead of the principal events concerning the Spanish project to which I refer hereafter.

79. In November 1990, a tax demand was served on Geoff Bell Limited. The Claimant says and I accept that he was not aware of the terms of the advice that had been received from counsel. However it is to be remembered that the Defendant was the sole director of the company at this time. It is clear that he suggested to the Claimant that he become a director of the company but in a hand written fax from Australia dated 17th December 1990, the Claimant declined to do so. The fax does not suggest that any pressure was being applied to him to take this step and he does not rule out taking this step in the future. However, he expresses the wish to put off doing so until "… *a few of the other things [are] sorted out* …". The other things referred to is the failure to repay either of the loans that he had made which totalled £1.4 million. The implication of the letter is that the Claimant had been told by the Defendant that legal advice had been taken and the other way of sorting matters out was simply to let the company go into liquidation – "*if you and the lawyer decide to liquidate then so be it. The problem has gone on for so long so Mike you mite (sic) decide with Mr Sykes to rap it up then you can forget about the thing*". Aside from supporting the suggestion that the full effect of the advice given by Counsel had not been passed on, this letter illustrates very clearly the nature of the relationship that the Claimant considered that he had with the Defendant.

80. On the following day (18th December 1990) the Defendant replied by fax to the Claimant. In that fax, the Defendant said (E/1156):

> "Thanks for your fax of yesterday. I have obtained the name of the offshore company to be used, this is Olkris Limited. This company was previously used for another transaction and because of this we will not need to pay them anything for the use of it. The shares will just sit in this company until the company is liquidated when they will then be cancelled by the liquidator."

In fact Olkris Limited was a company that was wholly beneficially controlled by the Defendant although that such was the case was not revealed and indeed, the implication is that the company had been acquired for a specific purpose. The letter that was signed by the Claimant and drafted by the Defendant (E/1157) clearly shows that the true nature of the problem had not been explained and equally clearly shows inferentially that the Claimant had been told that these arrangements would make the problem go away. In fact the contrary was the case as the Defendant knew full well not least because of what he had been told by counsel. The consequence of these arrangements was that the Defendant gained control of Geoff Bell Limited (for a notional consideration of £2) and thereafter he authorised the commencement of proceedings against the Claimant to recover the whole of the sum that had been paid to him as a result of the sale of the leasehold interests at a time when he knew that the Claimant did not have the means to pay for the reasons already identified. Those proceedings, as I understand it, never came to trial. The litigation was funded by the surplus in the company pension scheme that was returned to the company and net of tax yielded £143,161. No part of that sum was ever returned to the Claimant.

81.    I turn finally to the Spanish project. The Claimant's case in relation to this project in summary is that the first mention of this project was in October 1988 when the Claimant expressed himself not to be interested. However the project was next mentioned in the course of a meeting between the Claimant and Defendant some time between then and February 1989. His case is that he was told by the Defendant that £400,000 was required by the owner of the land in order to fund the process of obtaining planning consents after which the land could be sold or re-mortgaged so as to enable the borrowings to be repaid together with the profit. He was told that if he invested he would make a return of 65% by May 1990 and that there was another investor (subsequently discovered to be Mr Armstrong) who was prepared to invest £200,000 and that the lenders interest would be secured. The Claimant's case is that he was told that a Jersey registered company was to be formed which would receive the money and in turn enter into an arrangement with Campillos Del Golf SA ("CdG"), the owners of the land. The Jersey registered company that was formed on 6th February 1989 was called Arrowstar Holdings Limited ("Arrowstar"). The money that the Claimant had agreed to lend was transferred by the Defendant from the Bell Jersey Account in two tranches - £100,000 in February 1989 and £100,000 on 28th March 1989. The funds were never returned nor was any of the profit element paid.

82.    The Defendant's case is markedly at odds with this. His case is that in the course of a holiday to Florida in early February 1989, the Claimant told him in the course of a meeting that was mainly concerned with his dispute with Mr Davidson and his companies that he wished to invest more in Europe and that the Defendant provided him with some information about the Spanish project. The Defendant maintains that he made it clear he could not advise him in relation to the project and that if he wished to invest then he should contact CdG direct. He says that the next thing he heard was from a director of CdG (either Mr Dyer or Mr Largo) who said that both Mr Armstrong and the Claimant has been in contact and had agreed to lend CdG the sums required. The Defendant maintains that he then spoke to the Claimant who confirmed this to be the case. He says that Arrowstar was formed on the instructions of the directors of CdG in order to avoid the requirements of Spanish exchange control law. He says he was appointed a director of Arrowstar at the request of CdG and that there was no opportunity for him to profit from the arrangement.

83.    Mr Armstrong's evidence was that in relation to him, the Defendant made clear that it was he (the Defendant) who was seeking the investment, that he  was told that the Defendant had another investor who would meet £200,000 of the required £400,000 and also that the investment was almost risk free. As I have said already, I accept Mr Armstrong's evidence. The Defendant's case is also contradicted by what Mr Dyer says in his witness statement – he says that he was introduced to the Defendant by a mutual acquaintance, that he was told by the Defendant that he had investors who would be interested and that shortly thereafter

he was advised by the Defendant that he had obtained two investors each willing to lend £200,000. He says that he was told that they wished to remain anonymous and that therefore the loan was to be advanced through Arrowstar. He says that there was no reason why the loan could not have been made direct to CdG, that Arrowstar was not incorporated at the request of CdG and that using Arrowstar was entirely the Defendant's idea. Finally he says that the £400,000 was never in fact received by CdG – only approximately £260,000 was received by CdG. He said that it was this that caused problems for CdG, that the property market collapsed and that as he puts it "all was lost". The Defendant in his closing submissions said that I ought in effect to ignore this evidence since it was not tested in cross examination.

84. The Defendant's case on this issue is to be rejected for the following reasons. First, in July 1991, Mr Armstrong was becoming concerned about the failure to return his money. Not surprisingly, given what he says was the origin of his involvement in the arrangements, he turned to Dodd & Co. A meeting was convened attended by Mrs. Young, Mr Bloor another partner of Dodd & Co., and the Defendant (who it will be recalled was no longer a partner in the firm having given notice in March 1989 and having departed in June 1989). Mrs. Young verified the notes she took as being an accurate summary of what had been said. The fourth paragraph records that the Defendant had told her and Mr Bloor that he had "... *set up ....* *Arrowstar ... and he himself was a nominee shareholder for the Claimant and Mr* *Armstrong. Arrowstar had then entered into the agreement with* [CdG] *a copy of which is on* *our files. Under this agreement Arrowstar ... purchased a piece of land from* [CdG] *..."* This statement is of course completely at odds with the Defendant's case before me. There is no mention of Arrowstar being set up for CdG, no mention of the Defendant being a nominee director for CdG. What he told Mrs. Young and Mr Bloor is broadly consistent with what Mr Armstrong and the Claimant's understanding save in relation to the arrangements made between Arrowstar and CdG.

85. By a letter of 7th October 1991, Mr Bloor reported to a firm of solicitors that Arrowstar was formed for the purpose of assisting the Claimant who was then non resident for tax purposes. It is not clear to me how that could be right – unless what was meant was in relation to the Spanish tax authorities since that is where the Claimant was resident in 1989. It is certainly not consistent with what the Defendant now maintains is the position. Under cover of a letter dated 14th May 1992, to Dodd & Co., the Defendant produced two declarations of trust, which purported to confirm that the shares that the Defendant held in Arrowstar were held by him on trust for Mr Armstrong and the Claimant. These documents are, of course, wholly inconsistent with what the Defendant now says is the position and are consistent with what he had told Mr Bloor and Mrs Young at the meeting in July 1991. The shares were not registered in the name of the Defendant but in the name of Jersey companies. In the letter the Defendant makes clear that the shares are held by those companies on trust for him and that he, the Defendant, had executed a declaration of trust in turn in favour of the Claimant and Mr Armstrong. On 20th May 1992, Dodd & Co by letter to the Defendant requested the transfer of the shares hold on trust for the Claimant into the name of the Claimant (E/1300). On or about 9th June 1992, stock transfer forms were executed by the Jersey registered nominees in favour of Mr Armstrong and the Claimant (E/ 1301 and 1305). This could only have been on the instructions of the Defendant. Receipt of these transfers was acknowledged by Dodd & Co by letter of 10th June 1992. Extraordinarily in light of this correspondence, by letters of 10th July 1992, the Defendant in his capacity as a director of Arrowstar purported to refuse to register the transfers that he had himself provided.

86. In his evidence before me the Defendant claimed that he had executed the declarations of trust in error. I reject that suggestion as untrue. If it had been true then it must have been

known to him at the time he wrote the covering letter and sent the declarations to Dodd & Co that the documents were executed by him in error but no mention was made of this fact. Similarly, that the declarations had been executed in error must have been known to him at all times thereafter including when, apparently, he instructed the Jersey nominees to execute the transfers. Not a word of the alleged error is mentioned. In the course of his evidence he told me that he had received legal advice to the effect that the declarations were binding even though executed in error. The lawyers giving this advice were not identified. I doubt whether any such advice could have been given but even assuming it was, the refusal to register the transfers was at odds with such advice.

87. On 12th February 1993, Mr McAiety, a partner in Dodd & Co swore an affidavit in proceedings in Jersey brought by the Claimants and Mr Armstrong against Arrowstar and others. At Paragraph 6 he refers to some outline notes that he says had been left on the relevant file by the Defendant prior to him leaving Dodd & Co. This note (P/4581) says:

> "Arrowstar ... (ASH) is a Jersey based company that I formed for the purpose of this transaction.
>
> [The Claimant] and Tony Armstrong have transferred £200,000 to ASH – ie £400,000 in total in contemplation of the contract with CDG. ..."

This note is entirely consistent with the case advanced by the Claimant. It is entirely inconsistent with the Defendant's case before me. Although the Defendant was disposed to dispute the authenticity of this note, I reject that suggestion. Not merely was it verified in an affidavit as I have mentioned but it is entirely consistent with the other contemporaneous documentation that I have referred to.

88. I now return to the evidence of Mr Dyer which I have summarised above. In light of the material extracted from contemporaneous documentation referred to above, I accept the evidence of Mr Dyer even though it was not tested by cross examination. The Defendant was seeking dishonestly to mislead me when he claimed that he formed Arrowstar on the instructions of CdG. He did no such thing. There was no need for him to have used a Jersey registered company for the purpose of advancing the loans by Mr Armstrong and the Claimant to CdG. As Mr Dyer says, the loans could have been advanced direct to CdG. The only funding for Arrowstar came from the Claimant and Mr Armstrong. They were lending money to that entity for the purpose of advancing a loan to CdG and were doing so using this method only because they were advised to do so by the Defendant. The declarations of trust signed by the Defendant by which he declared that he held the shares in Arrowstar on trust for the Claimant and Mr. Armstrong reflected the commercial reality. Thus, while the Claimant considered that he was lending to CdG using a vehicle created for the purpose of enabling that loan to be made, the reality was different. The Claimant was financing Arrowstar (owned by the Defendant) to purchase part of the land with a view to Arrowstar (and, therefore, the Defendant) making a substantial profit. Thus again the Claimant (and Mr Armstrong) were unbeknown to them at the time taking substantially all of the risk whereas the Defendant would be able to take most of the benefit should there be any.

89. As will be apparent from the conclusions that I have reached so far, I consider that the Defendant has sought dishonestly to mislead me as he has sought in the past dishonestly to mislead others about the events with which I am concerned. In summary, he is not a witness who in my judgment can be trusted to tell the truth other than to the extent the truth is perceived by him to assist him in the needs of the moment. Having observed him both a as witness and advocate in his own cause for some 8 days, I have concluded that where and when he claims not be able to recall something, that invariably meant that he could not think

of an answer to the point in issue at that moment. Whilst I accept that to a degree the Claimant found it convenient to exaggerate in relation to some factual issues and was shown to be incorrect on a limited number of matters of detail, I find that his oral evidence was essentially in conformity with the contemporaneous documentation. Where differences occurred between the evidence given by the Claimant and that given by the Defendant which were not capable of being resolved by reference to extraneous evidence, I have been driven to the conclusion that the evidence of the Claimant is to be preferred over that of the Defendant. As to Mr Corlett, clearly he and the Defendant have fallen out and equally clearly to me he did not volunteer his services as a witness for the Claimant other than because of that falling out. My view is that Mr Corlett's evidence needs to be treated with caution but can safely be accepted to the limited extent mentioned above because it is corroborated by other evidence.

### Fiduciary Duties and Breach

**90.** To the extent that it is not already apparent from what I have said above, I accept and find that the Claimant was a practical business man with neither the knowledge, experience or capacity to understand issues such as those that arose in relation to the sale of the leasehold interests or commercial transactions outside the areas he was familiar with. He was someone who came to depend on his professional advisers and in particular Mr Dodd and then the Defendant in his turn to guide him through anything that was not familiar or of which he had no or little knowledge or understanding. In my judgment this was something that became apparent to the Defendant from a very early stage in their relationship. I have no hesitation in accepting that by the end of 1986 at the latest a close working relationship had developed between the Claimant and the Defendant which was simply the result of Mr Dodd not being as available to counsel and comfort the Claimant as he had been in the past. Mr Dodd described his relationship with the Claimant as being in some ways similar to a partnership and I accept that to be so in the sense that the Claimant simply acted without question on the advice of Mr Dodd in relation to areas that he did not understand or had no experience of – that is in a business context everything other than the operational aspects of running a successful haulage business and latterly the Truck Inn. I have no doubt that the relationship between the Claimant and Defendant had come close to that level of confidence by the end of 1986 if only because the Claimant did not have the capacity to deal with the issues on which he depended on the Defendant, Mr Dodd was not able to provide the level of support that he had in the past but Mr Dodd was available in the background as an added source of comfort. It had certainly reached that level when the arrangements for the sale of the leasehold interest came to be considered in March 1987. I accept the Claimant's evidence that he had made it clear to the Defendant that he was looking for investment opportunities following the sale of the leasehold interests and have no doubt that the Claimant would be well disposed to considering any investment introduced to him by the Defendant and would act without question on his advice as to how to proceed if attracted to the idea because of the trust and confidence that the Claimant had developed since they began working together and without any thought that the Defendant might in truth be arranging things for his own benefit. This last thought would simply not have occurred to the Claimant and in my judgment the Defendant knew full well that such was the case. In those circumstances, I have no doubt that the Claimant had a legitimate expectation that the Defendant was advising him to proceed because he had his best interests at heart and that the Claimant would not have proceeded if he had realised the extent to which in reality the Defendant was seeking potentially to benefit himself at the potential expense of the Claimant. In this respect and in relation to the Portuguese project I have no hesitation in accepting that the Defendant told the Claimant that (a) there was a great deal of money to be made by the Claimant out of the Portuguese project, (b) that he strongly advised the Claimant to invest in the project and (c) that he had other investors waiting if he did not act quickly I have therefore no hesitation in concluding that the Defendant owed the Claimant the duties referred to in Paragraph 16 of the Re-Amended Particulars of Claim in relation to the Portuguese project.

91. I have no doubt that the Defendant acted in breach of fiduciary in persuading the Claimant to invest in the project because he foresaw from a very early stage that if he structured the transaction in the manner in which he intended to structure it, he personally would have a substantial amount to gain and that was the basis on which he proceeded from the time he first visited Portugal in relation to the Portuguese project. I have no doubt at all that this was why the Defendant sought dishonestly to mislead me into believing that the loan was a personal one agreed between Mr Corlett and the Claimant in which he had no involvement and gave no advice. I am also sure that this is why the Defendant sought dishonestly to persuade me that he had been approached out of the blue to assist Mr Corlett in forming an offshore company and that he had sought the consent of the Claimant to this course. It was simply not good enough to tell the Claimant that he had a choice whether to lend or seek a share of the profits without also telling him that if he chose to lend, the Defendant would be the principal beneficiary or what the quantum of that anticipated benefit would be. It was equally a breach of duty to represent that the other investor was to be another client of Dodd & Co who by implication would be investing on a similar basis when in fact as the Defendant well knew there was no such investor and the other investor was likely to be a financial institution which was in all likelihood going to lend only on fully secured terms. The reality was fundamentally different from that which the Claimant understood because in reality he was lending to the Defendant to enable him to invest in the acquisition and development of the land not to a third party supervised by the Defendant on behalf of the Claimant who would be acquiring and developing the land and furthermore was doing so on terms that were in effect non recourse terms.

92. In relation to the Spanish project, the position was if anything more stark. The project was one that the Defendant persuaded the Claimant to participate in by exploiting the trust and confidence that the Defendant knew the Claimant reposed in him. The duties pleaded at paragraph 50 of the Re-Amended Particulars of Claim were owed by the Defendant to the Claimant in consequence. The Defendant induced the Claimant to lend by representing to the Claimant that the land was owned by CdG when in fact it was not owned by that entity. He represented that the money was required in order to meet the expenses of obtaining all the relevant planning consents but that was not true either. Finally he told the Claimant that his loan would be protected by a charge when it was not and could not be. These misrepresentations were of themselves breaches of duty. There was as I have concluded no need whatsoever to introduce Arrowstar into the process at all. The only purpose of this was in the end to give the Defendant an interest in the project that he would not otherwise have. It was for that reason that the Defendant sought dishonestly to mislead me in to believing that the loan arrangements were made by the Claimant and the directors of CdG without any invention on his part and that Arrowstar was set up at the request of CdG and its directors and for their benefit when in truth it was for no such purpose. The only possible beneficiary of these arrangements was the Defendant.

**Remedies.**

93. The Claimant is plainly entitled to an account of profits made by the Defendant. If as is alleged by Mr Corlett, he did pay the Claimant £1.3 million in respect of the Portuguese project then that is a profit for which the Defendant is liable to account. However that is not something that can be resolved on the evidence before me and if that route is to be followed then there will have to be a direction for the taking of an

94.

95.

96.

97.

98.

99.

100.

101.

102.

103.

104.

105. account between the parties.

106. The primary remedy that is sought is equitable compensation being a payment by the Defendant to the Claimant of the sums lent and lost. I have set out above the principles applicable to such a claim. I am entirely satisfied that if the Defendant had fully and fairly explained the nature of each proposed transaction and his interest in it, then Claimant would not have embarked on either. In relation to the Portuguese project, there is in my judgment a fundamental difference between a transaction under which the Claimant considered that he was investing in a vehicle that was to acquire land which would then be developed and sold by others for reward and which would be supervised by the Defendant on behalf of two investors introduced by the him and what in fact took place. Had the Defendant suggested that the Claimant lend £1.2 million to the Defendant on an unsecured basis in order to allow the Claimant the opportunity to make a profit of the sort that was thought possible at the time without any risk to the Claimant, I have no doubt that the Claimant would have sought alternative advice – the whole foundation of the relationship between the Claimant and the Defendant was a belief on the part of the Claimant that he was receiving independent advice from the Defendant in relation to matters that he was not equipped by knowledge or experience to manage himself. It would have been entirely apparent to the Claimant that such could not be the case where the loan was to benefit the Defendant. The Claimant told me in the course of his evidence and I accept that had he been told that he was being invited to lend £1.2 million to an entity controlled by the Defendant that was going to raise the further funds needed by a secured loan from a bank, he would not have done so. The Defendant ought in conscience to have advised the Claimant to seek advice from someone else with full disclosure of what was proposed. Aside from the general point, it seems to me clear beyond doubt that once advice had been received from counsel relating to the tax issue, the Defendant came under a duty to advise him in clear terms of what had happened so as to allow the Claimant the opportunity to make a fully informed choice as how best to proceed. In fact as I have found, the Defendant did not do so.

107. Similarly I have no doubt that the Claimant would not have proceeded with the loan in relation to the Spanish project had he known what in reality was happening. There is a clear and obvious difference between a secured loan made by an offshore entity managed on

behalf of the lender by someone in whom trust and confidence is reposed and a loan that is wholly unsecured and is advanced to an offshore entity controlled by the fiduciary in order to give the supposed fiduciary an undisclosed interest in a transaction that was different to that which the principal thought was being financed. Again, it seems to me if the transaction was to proceed in this manner at all, it could only do so on the basis of very full disclosure of precisely what was intended and for whose benefit. Had such disclosure been given I see no prospect of the Claimant being willing to invest in this manner.

108.     There is no other evidence from which it can be inferred that some other outcome than the one referred to above would have been the result had the Defendant not acted in breach of fiduciary duty. In the result, and subject to one point that I mention below, I conclude that the Claimant is entitled to recover the sums loaned in relations to each of the transactions together with some interest.

109.     The single point that remains is the amount of the equitable compensation. In principle, the Claimant is entitled on the findings I have made to recover the amount he was persuaded to part with together with interest for at least some of the period since he parted with it. However, I have concluded that the funds that the Claimant was persuaded to part with may have been perhaps even probably were sums that Geoff Bell Limited was beneficially entitled to. I draw attention to this point when I circulated the draft version of this judgment and invited submissions in relation to it. Those were delivered prior to the first date fixed for the hand down of this judgment. In the event, I was not able to hand down the judgment then because of the material produced by the Defendant from Mr Pina referred to above. In the result I was able to add to this judgment my conclusions in relation to the effect of the ownership of the leasehold interests on the equitable compensation claim.

110.     In summary, as I have said above, the issue concerning whether the Claimant was in truth the beneficial owner of the leasehold interests who was induced to part with them by an error on the part of his then advisors or whether what happened subsequently gave rise to an estoppel was not investigated before me nor could it be for the point was plainly collateral to the issues that I had to decide. This is so because as Mr Cawson points out, correctly in my judgment, it has never been part of the Defendant's case in these proceedings that the Claimant is not entitled to equitable compensation because he held the proceeds of sale of the leasehold interests on trust for the company. The issue would have been resolved in the proceedings brought by the company (by then controlled by the Defendant) against the Claimant referred to above but as I have said above, those proceedings never proceeded to trial. The company has itself now been wound up (on a petition presented by the Defendant) and was dissolved on 2$^{nd}$ November 1996, prior to the bankruptcy of the Claimant. All of this leads me to conclude that my initial inclination was correct. As between the Claimant and the Defendant, the Claimant is entitled to recover the full amount of the equitable compensation mentioned above. Whether the company could be restored to the register to make a claim against the Claimant or whether as Mr Cawson maintains, the ability of the company to make a claim (even if it could be restored for that purpose) has been lost because the claim could have been but was not made in the Claimant's bankruptcy are interesting questions but they are not for me to decide in the context of these proceedings.

111.     The remaining questions concern interest and costs. I had intended to deal with the interest issue in this Judgement. However, the Defendant does not address this issue at all in his written submissions lodged after the draft of this judgment was circulated. At the hearing before me at which this judgment was meant to be but was not handed down, the Defendant made clear that he wanted to reserve his submissions as to costs until he had seen my conclusions on the equitable compensation issue addressed in paragraphs 98-99 above. Mr Cawson has made it clear that (a) he seeks interest on a compound basis for the whole of the

period since the date of the making of the various payments and (b) costs on an indemnity basis against the Defendant. In view of the fact that the Defendant has not addressed these issues, I direct as follows:

i)  The Defendant is to serve and file written submissions in relation to (a) the principle of interest being awarded on a compounded basis and (b) the period in respect of which interest should be awarded (whether assessed on a simple or compounded basis) and (c) on whether he should be required to pay the costs of these proceedings and if so whether they should be assessed on the standard or indemnity basis by no later than 4pm on 1st May 2009; and

ii) The Claimant is to serve and file any submissions in reply to those served and filed pursuant to (i) above by no later than 4pm on 6th May.

I will then deliver a separate written ruling on interest and costs. I intend that this judgment be handed down prior to that. There is no need for the parties to attend that hearing unless they wish to do so. At the hand down hearing, after handing down the judgment, I will adjourn the hearing down to the date to be fixed for the hand down of the interest and costs ruling for the purpose of enabling any party who wishes to do so to apply for permission to appeal in accordance with CPR 52.3(2)(a) at that hearing.

oooooooooooooooooooooooooooooooooooooo.

**IN THE HIGH COURT OF JUSTICE**     <u>Claim No: 94B10474</u>

**CHANCERY DIVISION**

**MANCHESTER DISTRICT REGISTRY**

**HIS HONOUR JUDGE PELLING QC**
**SITTING AS A JUDGE OF THE HIGH COURT**
**WEDNESDAY 27 MAY 2009**

**BETWEEN:**

IAN GEOFFREY BELL

<u>Claimant</u>

and

MICHAEL JAMES BLAND                    <u>Defendant</u>

---
### ORDER
---

**UPON** this action coming on for trial on 30, and 31 March, and 1-3, and 6-8 April 2009, and judgment on issues apart from interest and costs having been handed down on 27 April 2009

**AND UPON** hearing leading Counsel for the Claimant and the Defendant in person

**AND UPON** reading the documents on the Court file recorded as having been read

**AND UPON** hearing oral evidence

**IT IS ORDERED THAT**:

1.    The Defendant do pay to the Claimant the sum of <u>£1,450,035.00</u> by way of equitable compensation;

2.    The Defendant do pay to the Claimant the sum of <u>£4,663,750.10</u> by way of interest on the said sum of £1,450,035 (calculated at 1% over base rate from 31 July 1989 to 27 May 2009 compounded annually);

3.    Save as otherwise already provided for by previous orders made in this action, the Defendant do pay to the Claimant his costs of this action, and the costs of the Claimant's trustee in bankruptcy, John Lee, incurred whilst the claims herein were vested in him,

including the Claimant's costs of the Claimant's application dated 7 March 2008 and the Defendant's application dated 7 August 2008 reserved by the Order dated 30 October 2008 ("the 2008 Application Costs");

4.  The costs awarded in favour of the Claimant referred to in paragraph 3 above shall be assessed in default of agreement by way of detailed assessment on the indemnity basis save that the 2008 Application Costs shall in default of agreement be assessed by way of detailed assessment on the standard basis;

5.  The Defendant shall have permission to enforce the costs awarded in his favour by the Order dated 30 January 2009 by way of set-off against the costs awarded in favour of the Claimant as aforesaid, and such costs shall in default of agreement be assessed by way of detailed assessment on the standard basis;

6.  The Defendant shall on or before 29 June 2009 pay to the Claimant the sum of £100,000 on account of the costs awarded in favour of the Claimant as aforesaid;

<u>Claim No: 94B10474</u>

**<u>IN THE HIGH COURT OF JUSTICE</u>**
**<u>CHANCERY DIVISION</u>**
**<u>MANCHESTER DISTRICT REGISTRY</u>**

**HIS HONOUR JUDGE PELLING QC**
**SITTING AS A JUDGE OF THE HIGH COURT**
**WEDNESDAY 27 MAY 2009**

**B E T W E E N:**

**IAN GEOFFREY BELL**

<u>Claimant</u>

**and**

**MICHAEL JAMES BLAND**    <u>Defendant</u>

---

**ORDER**

---

Linder Myers LLP
Phoenix House
45 Cross Street
MANCHESTER
M2  4JF

Ref: Anthony Robinson

# Appendix 3

On the following pages is the Judgment which was brought by Kevin Mawer, Michael Bland's Trustee, for not cooperating with his (Bland's) bankruptcy. You will see all the tricks that Michael Bland got up to.

No: 4711 of 2009

IN THE HIGH COURT OF JUSTICE
IN BANKRUPTCY

Royal Courts of Justice
Fetter Lane, London, EC4A 1NL

Date: 10 May 2012

Before:

**Mr Registrar Baister**

- - - - - - - - - - - - - - - - - - - -

Between :

|  |  |
|---|---|
| **KEVIN ROY MAWER**<br>**RICHARD JOHN HILL**<br>(Trustees in Bankruptcy of Michael James Bland)<br>- and - | **Applicants** |
| **MICHAEL JAMES BLAND** | **Respondent** |

- - - - - - - - - - - - - - - - - - - - -
- - - - - - - - - - - - - - - - - - - - -

Miss  Karen Troy (instructed by **Cobbetts LLP**) for the **Applicants**
Professor Mark Watson-Gandy (instructed by **direct access**) for the **Respondent**

Hearing date: 2 & 3 April 2012
- - - - - - - - - - - - - - - - - - - - -

# Approved Judgment

I direct pursuant to CPR PD 39A para 6.1 that no official shorthand note shall be taken of this
Judgment and that copies of this version as handed down may be treated as authentic.

Mr Registrar Baister

240

No: 4711 of 2009

IN THE HIGH COURT OF JUSTICE
IN BANKRUPTCY

Royal Courts of Justice
Fetter Lane, London, EC4A 1NL

Date: 10 May 2012

Before:

**Mr Registrar Baister**

--------------------------
Between :

KEVIN ROY MAWER        <u>Applicants</u>
RICHARD JOHN HILL
(Trustees in Bankruptcy of Michael James Bland)
- and -
MICHAEL JAMES BLAND        <u>Respondent</u>

--------------------------
--------------------------

**Miss Karen Troy** (instructed by **Cobbetts LLP**) for the **Applicants**
**Professor Mark Watson-Gandy** (instructed by **direct access**) for the **Respondent**

Hearing date: 2 & 3 April 2012
--------------------------

# Approved Judgment

I direct pursuant to CPR PD 39A para 6.1 that no official shorthand note shall be taken of this Judgment and that copies of this version as handed down may be treated as authentic.

*[signature]*

Mr Registrar Baister

241

**Mr Registrar Baister :**

1.  The respondent bankrupt, Michael James Bland, was made bankrupt on his own petition on 9 June 2009. The applicants were appointed as his trustees in bankruptcy on 1 July 2009.

## The applications

2.  On 24 May 2010 the trustees applied for the suspension of Mr Bland's discharge, and Mr Deputy Registrar Schaffer ordered interim suspension of the running of the discharge period on 7 June 2010. The applicant trustees seek the continuation of such suspension. Mr Bland opposes; indeed he applies for the suspension of his discharge period to be lifted forthwith.

## The background

3.  Mr Bland qualified as a chartered accountant in 1984. He became a partner in a firm called Dodd & Co in Carlisle. In about 1988 he became involved in or interested in property investment in Spain and Portugal, as a result of which he put a client of Dodd & Co for whom he acted, a Mr Ian Bell, in touch with a Mr Martin Corlett, apparently on the basis of a newspaper advertisement he had seen seeking investors. In 1989 he relinquished his partnership in Dodd & Co and went to live in Portugal and/or Gibraltar, primarily to assist or advise Mr Corlett in connexion with the development of land called Aldeia das Ferrarais in a place called Almancil on the Algarve coast in Portugal. Mr Bell invested £1.25 million in the development in the form of a loan to Mr Corlett, but at some stage, according to Mr Bland, Mr Corlett "ran off to Africa" (see bundle 5/tab 14/page 2038).

4.  That venture involved Mr Bland and others in a bewildering range of companies incorporated in a number of jurisdictions through which the property business or related business was transacted. I will try to deal with some of them in greater detail later but I am by no means sure that I fully grasp what went on. The trustees do not either. Indeed that is one of their concerns.

5.  The venture was not a success. Mr Bland says that he was paid very little. He was supposed to be paid £60,000-£70,000 a year but in fact earned no fixed salary. He says that he lived very cheaply in rented accommodation and that between 1989 and 2005 he was "permanently broke" (5/14/2039).

6.  In 1994 Mr Bell brought proceedings against Mr Bland, essentially for breach of fiduciary duty, although the detail no longer matters. The trial eventually took place before His Honour Judge Pelling QC in late March/early April 2009. Judgment was given against Mr Bland on 27 April 2009 for £1.5 million and for £6 million odd on 27 May 2009. On 29 May 2009 Mr Bell obtained a worldwide freezing order against Mr Bland. All that precipitated Mr Bland to petition for his own bankruptcy. In paragraph 11.2 of his affidavit in support of his petition he attributes his insolvency to Mr Bell's judgment and his non-receipt of remuneration in excess of €600,000 "due to Mr Corlett running off to Africa" (5/14/2024).

7.  Central to the property development project was a company called Epiette Ltd. It was incorporated in Jersey on 9 January 1989. Mr Bland says that it was a holding

company, which I understand to mean that it held the shares in a number of single purpose companies formed to acquire the various plots into which the development site was divided. The shares in the individual companies were sold (or intended to be sold) rather than the land itself, because, I am told, this is a tax efficient way of conducting business of this kind.

8.  Mr Bland's evidence is that he was a director of Epiette between 9 June 2004 and 9 June 2009 (see paragraph 29 of his eleventh witness statement of 31 March (7/4/8).

9.  The shareholding in Epiette is confusing. Minutes of a board meeting held on 21 January 1995 record the transfer of 7,500 shares from TCB Nominees Ltd and to Mr Bland and of 2,500 from TCB Facilities Ltd to Mr Corlett, so that, it would seem, at an early stage Mr Bland held 75% of the shares and Mr Corlett 25% (see the board minutes of 21 January 1995 at 6/14/2331). In 2003 he became the sole shareholder. However, in an interview with the trustee held on 22 October 2009 Mr Bland said that Mr Corlett owned Epiette, or at least had a 75% interest in it (5/14/2040). So, according to Mr Bland, Mr Corlett owned or controlled Epiette which owned or controlled the development (5/14/2040). Later, at some stage, again according to Mr Bland, two new companies were formed, Crashpast Ltd and Homestrike Ltd (both Gibraltar companies) which in some way took over the shares in Epiette, leaving Epiette a shell (5/14/2040-2041). That, at least, was the position as I understood it from earlier hearings. As we shall see, there was much more to it than that and in fact Mr Bland controlled Epiette and probably still does.

10. Other companies of which Mr Bland was a director during the same period as he was a director of Epiette are the following:

> Rainy Day Holdings Ltd (Turks and Caicos Islands);
>
> Atlantic House Holdings Limited (Turks and Caicos Islands);
>
> Atlantic House Limited (Gibraltar);
>
> Iberian Development Corporation Limited (Gibraltar);
>
> Waburn Investments Limited (Gibraltar);
>
> Sandwell Properties Limited (Isle of Man);
>
> Holgate Corporation (USA); and
>
> Aldeia das Ferrarias (Portugal) (again see paragraph 29 of his eleventh witness statement).

11. A number of other companies feature in the evidence:

> Aldeburgh Enterprises Limited (Gibraltar), a company which it is said the court in Gibraltar has found to have been owned by Mr Bland (1/3/52) but about which I know very little;
>
> Hampshire Cosmetics Limited, a UK company the shares of which are owned by Wystan Holdings Inc (Turks and Caicos)

243

(1/3/53) which the trustees suspect Mr Bland owns or controls but in which Mr Bland says he has no interest (1/4/60);

New Capital Management Limited, a company which Mr Bland was able to sign for but in which he says he has no interest (1/3/53; 1/4/60; 1/4/57);

Rosewood Associates Limited, about which again I know little;

Rosewood Consultants Limited, which Mr Bland says is/was his business through which he provided accountancy services (1/13/1948, 1958);

Aston International Limited (Isle of Man), a management company from which the trustees have recently obtained some 10,000 pages of documents and with which Mr Bland has had extensive dealings; and

Blenheim Trust BVI, which was intended to take over from Aston (it may in fact have done so) and which, like Aston, provides what might be described as corporate services.

The foregoing lists are not comprehensive.

12. It is unsurprising that, faced with the £6 million bankruptcy of an accountant, a failed property development in Portugal, allegations of wrongdoing and complex international corporate arrangements (many offshore) involving Mr Bland and people with whom he has had a business connexion of one kind or another the trustees (Mr Mawer in particular, so henceforth I shall refer to him alone) should have felt it appropriate to conduct a searching investigation of the bankrupt's affairs. Mr Bland's initial conduct was disappointing. Mr Mawer sought a meeting with Mr Bland as early as 2 July 2009, but Mr Bland prevaricated, and it was not until October 2009 that an interview took place. Matters were not improved by the fact that Mr Bland refused initially to provide an email address or a telephone number to ease communication. (I shall assume that better lines of communication are now in place.) He has made complaints about Mr Mawer's conduct to the police and the Institute of Chartered Accountants. I do not know the detail of the complaints and make no comment about their merits, but I note that Mr Bland also complained to the Bar Council about the conduct of Mr Mark Cawson QC in the *Bell* proceedings. Mr Mawer thinks that Mr Bland is trying to deflect him from his real job. Mr Bland has now written a great deal and has attended interviews and so on, as a result of which a great deal of paper has been generated; but when one examines it closely it soon becomes apparent that the quality of the information provided from time to time leaves much to be desired. Mr Bland has produced virtually no documents relating to 17 years of his business affairs. Mr Mawer has not had an easy time.

13. The inevitable result of this initial lack of co-operation was an application for a private examination which took place before me on 7 April 2011 (see the transcript at 5/14/2072-2222). Mr Bland was not wholly co-operative then either, and I remarked adversely on aspects of his evidence. I gave certain directions as to the information he was to provide and adjourned the hearing. It came back before Mrs Registrar Derrett

244

on 8 December 2011 but had to be adjourned further in circumstances in which costs were awarded against the trustees and in favour of Mr Bland.

14. The application to suspend the running of the discharge period came on for substantive hearing, again before me, on 22 June 2011. The proceedings rapidly became bogged down in detail, as a result of which I adjourned them and ordered the preparation of a Scott schedule setting out (with references to documents) precisely what information the trustee required at that time and ordering Mr Bland to provide replies, again by reference to documents. The result has not been as helpful as I had hoped. Several Scott schedules have indeed been prepared and more or less answered, but the parties have bickered over form and content, the timetable has slipped, and the scope of the trustee's inquiries has mushroomed. A further difficulty arose in the run up to this adjourned hearing because the trustee obtained an order in the Isle of Man courts which resulted in the production of 17 lever arch files containing some 10,000 pages of documents belonging to Aston International Limited. All this meant that by 2 April 2012 I had before me seven files of documents relied on by the trustee and two from Mr Bland, most of it provided late and some at the start of the hearing. Skeletons were late, as a result of which I was guided as to what to read very late. Counsel for both sides had only recently been instructed so were themselves catching up as the application proceeded. I commend them for what they did manage to achieve in the short time available to them, but I write this judgment with unease about the level of assistance I have received.

15. I think the foregoing is sufficient to outline the basic facts of the bankruptcy and how it has proceeded. Further detail appears from the helpful chronology which Miss Troy prepared for the hearing (and updated in the course of it) which I gratefully adopt as an appendix to this judgment.

## The evidence

16. The written evidence is extensive. Directions given provided for the cross-examination of Mr Mawer and Mr Bland. On 2 April 2012, to my surprise, Miss Troy said she did not wish to cross-examine Mr Bland. I was surprised because Mr Bland's truthfulness has been an issue throughout these proceedings and indeed before them. In his evidence the trustee refers to the conclusions of His Honour Judge Pelling QC in the *Bell* actions. In paragraph 89 of his judgment the learned judge observed:

> "As will be apparent from the conclusions that I have reached so far, I consider that the Defendant has sought dishonestly to mislead me as he has sought in the past dishonestly to mislead others about the events with which I am concerned. In summary, he is not a witness who in my judgment can be trusted to tell the truth other than to the extent the truth is perceived by him in the needs of the moment. Having observed him both as a witness and advocate in his own cause for some 8 days, I have concluded that where and when he claims not to be able to recall something, that invariably meant that he could not think of an answer to the point in issue at that moment."

17. In the course of his private examination on 7 April 2011 I warned Mr Bland that I did not believe he was being truthful when he said that he could not remember anything

245

about relatively recent events (2/7/691). Later in the course of the same examination Mr Bland accepted that he had given misleading information about the storage of documents at a mail forwarding address, accepting with the benefit of hindsight that what he had told the official receiver was incorrect and explaining his behaviour by saying that he "probably just panicked" (1/7/754-756). Yet later Mr Bland was evasive when he was asked about attempts the trustee believed he had made to stop a bank in Portugal providing the trustee with information. The following exchange took place (2/7/778-779):

> "Q.   Have you taken any steps to write to the bank in Portugal to stop them providing me with information?
>
> A.    Not that I can recall.
>
> Q.    Mr Bland -
>
> Reg:  Well, it is not the sort of thing you would forget, is it?
>
> A.    Well, I remember, I remember... I remember you asked me for the letters of authority -
>
> Mawer: And you signed it and I submitted it.
>
> A.    Yes.
>
> Q.    And they gave me a closing statement.
>
> A.    I've also written to them and that is all they would give me.
>
> Q.    Have you written to them saying do not give any information to the Trustee in Bankruptcy?
>
> A.    I may have written to them -
>
> Q.    A "yes" or a "no" would suffice.
>
> A.    Well I think probably yes.
>
> Q.    Why?
>
> Q.    Because it became apparent that you were not going to let me have copies of the bank statements but you were asking about entries on them.
>
> Q.    That is not -
>
> Reg.  It is not up to Trustees to provide you with information, it is a one-way flow. You do things. Look, I strongly suggest if you get a continuation of this behaviour you do not waste my time; you go to the

> judge and say that this man is in contempt and have
> him put in prison which is -
>
> Mawer. He has done the same in Guernsey.
>
> Reg. - manifestly where he belongs.
>
> Mawer. He has done the same in Guernsey, sir.
>
> Reg. Yes, well, you have got to teach him a lesson, I am
> afraid. You have got to get him locked up. People like
> this never understand.
>
> Bland. Well, I apologise, sir.
>
> Reg. Your apology is no good."

18. I mention these matters as illustrative of the fact that Mr Bland has conducted himself before this court in much the same way as he conducted himself before His Honour Judge Pelling. I warned Mr Bland about trying to be more clever then he was (1/7/801) and about being untruthful when it suited him (2/7/810).

19. I do not propose to go into further detail. Mr Watson-Gandy submitted that Mr Bland had now recognised the error of his ways and was intent on co-operating. He invited me to look at matters afresh, as they now stood, untainted by Mr Bland's past behaviour. There is something in that, indeed it is consistent with Miss Troy's submission that for the purposes of this judgment I should concentrate on the recent evidence, primarily Mr Mawer's eighth witness statement and the two most recent witness statements of Mr Bland. By and large I agree with that and propose to approach the matter as I am invited to, although it also seems to me that I must consider and decide whether Mr Bland has changed tack or whether he simply continues now in the same vein as earlier.

20. If Mr Bland was not cross-examined, Mr Mawer was. A criticism Mr Watson-Gandy makes of Mr Mawer is that there is bad blood between him and Mr Bland so that he will now not believe Mr Bland no matter what he says. Mr Watson-Gandy cross-examined the trustee about this and other matters. He demonstrated that the trustee was at times prone to exaggeration and was wrong in some of the evidence he has given. It is plain, for example, that Mr Bland did store documents with a storage company in Carlisle and that there was a flood, so that on the balance of probability it is likely that documents were destroyed in January 2005. The trustee remains sceptical about that, but I think it is a fact that he must now accept. It is also an exaggeration to say, as the trustee has, that Mr Bland has not disclosed a single document to him. He has for example disclosed some probate documents, as Mr Watson-Gandy demonstrated. However, the exaggeration is not much of an exaggeration. Miss Troy tempered the trustee's position in her closing submissions, contending that Mr Bland has not disclosed a single email relating to his affairs. Mr Watson-Gandy did not challenge that proposition directly. He said that there was no requirement in the Scott schedules to do so. He said that one of Mr Bland's computer servers had "lapsed" and referred to other difficulties with computer stored information. For reasons to which I shall come, I do not accept that Mr Bland has not

247

had access to emails and a host of other documents which he could and should have made available to the trustee.

21. Mr Watson-Gandy put to Mr Mawer that his aim in bringing his application was to punish Mr Bland for the past. He also complained about the late provision of papers for the hearing and referred to Mrs Registrar Derrett's criticism of the trustee's team for oppressive behaviour at an earlier hearing.

22. Mr Mawer frankly said he could not explain the dilatory conduct of his solicitors. He pointed, however, to the difficulty he had experienced in obtaining documents and information about a complex bankruptcy. He denied that he had any desire to punish Mr Bland.

23. Although Mr Watson-Gandy hit home on a number of points, they were in fact small points. I do not believe that the trustee is intent on punishing Mr Bland, nor is he seeking to be oppressive, nor yet is his conduct coloured by some improper animus. The picture I have is of a trustee trying to do a proper job of investigating a bankruptcy of some complexity with little assistance from the bankrupt in terms of the provision of documents, the giving of reliable and truthful information, and of a trustee being impeded by conduct designed to defeat or delay his proper avenues of enquiry.

## The law and submissions

24. The jurisdiction to suspend the running of the discharge period of a bankrupt arises under section 279 Insolvency Act 1986 which provides as follows:

> "(1) A bankrupt is discharged from bankruptcy at the end of the period of one year beginning with the date on which the bankruptcy commences.
>
> (2) If before the end of that period the official receiver files with the court a notice stating that investigation of the conduct and affairs of the bankrupt under section 289 is unnecessary or concluded, the bankrupt is discharged when the notice is filed.
>
> (3) On the application of the official receiver or the trustee of a bankrupt's estate, the court may order that the period specified in subsection (1) shall cease to run until—
>
> > (a) the end of a specified period, or
> >
> > (b) the fulfilment of a specified condition.
>
> (4) The court may make an order under subsection (3) only if satisfied that the bankrupt has failed or is failing to comply with an obligation under this Part.
>
> (5) In subsection (3)(b) "condition" includes a condition requiring that the court be satisfied of something.

(6)   In the case of an individual who is adjudged bankrupt
on a petition under section 264(1)(d) —

(a)   subsections (1) to (5) shall not apply, and

(b)   the bankrupt is discharged from bankruptcy by
an order of the court under section 280.

(7)   This section is without prejudice to any power of the
court to annul a bankruptcy order".

25.   The jurisdiction was considered by the Chancellor in *Shierson v Rastogi (a bankrupt)*
[2007] EWHC 1266 (Ch) who, in paragraph 8 of his judgement, explained the
obligations of a bankrupt in the following terms:

"Section 291 of the Act imposes duties on a bankrupt to deliver
possession of his estate to the official receiver and to deliver up
to him all books, papers and other records 'which relate to his
estate and affairs'. [...] The trustee is required to take
possession of all books, papers and other records which relate
to the bankrupt's estate and affairs and which belong to him or
are under his control (s. 311) and the bankrupt is obliged to
deliver them up to him (s. 312)".

The Chancellor went on in paragraph 9 to say that section 333 imposed on the
bankrupt an obligation to give to his trustee "such information as to his affairs...as the
trustee may for the purposes of carrying out his functions...reasonably require". In
paragraph 65 he considered the nature of the jurisdiction conferred by section 279:

"It is clear from the terms of s 279 that postponement of
discharge is linked to a failure to comply with the obligations
imposed on a bankrupt by Pt IX. But is the purpose of the
power to postpone a discharge to provide an incentive to full
compliance? Or is it that the disabilities arising from being an
un-discharged bankrupt should, in the public interest, continue
until there has been full compliance? I doubt whether, on the
facts of this case, it is necessary to reach a final conclusion on
those questions. But in my view the purpose of the power is the
latter, even though its effect may be to achieve the former.
Were it otherwise I would have expected Parliament to have
made discharge conditional on full compliance."

26.   *Shierson v Rastogi* concerned the conduct of a bankrupt who, it was said, had failed to
explain or account for the disparity between the amount of a judgment and the value
of assets disclosed by him, had failed to disclose or account for the proceeds of sale of
shares in a company, had failed to disclose a beneficial interest in various companies
and whose affairs were unclear as a result of what the Chancellor described as "a lack
of information on matters which ought to be within the knowledge of the bankrupt".

27.   The Chancellor dealt with the extent to which the trustees in that case were entitled to
rely on findings of Hart J in prior proceedings (which I mention  because of the

reliance in this application on the judgment of His Honour Judge Pelling QC, if only by way of background). It is plain from paragraph 40 of the Chancellor's judgment that such reliance is permissible. The Chancellor, hearing the case on appeal, criticised the court below for having taken too narrow a view of a bankrupt's obligations. He said, in paragraph 51 of his judgment, that, "the duties of the bankrupt extend beyond matters relating to his estate to matters relating to his financial affairs generally". This is important because Miss Troy submits that Mr Bland is taking a narrow view of the scope of the information he is required to provide. She relies on the broad meaning of the word "affairs" in section 333.

28. The Chancellor noted in paragraph 7 of his judgment that discharge from bankruptcy did not affect the continuing obligations of a bankrupt to assist the official receiver or his trustee with the provision of information and the recovery of assets. It is important that I note that too since one of Mr Watson-Gandy's submissions is precisely that: Mr Bland will be obliged to continue to co-operate with the trustee whether or not the latter's application succeeds.

29. Mr Watson-Gandy also relies on *Official Receiver v Milborn*, an unreported decision of His Honour Judge Rich QC (sitting as a deputy High Court judge) of 6 July 1999. The brief report says,

> "When considering whether to exercise the power under s. 279 of the Insolvency act 1986 to suspend the discharge of a bankrupt, the court had to be satisfied of the bankrupt's non-compliance with his obligations under the Act: reasonable suspicion of non-compliance was not sufficient".

Mr Watson-Gandy submits that that is apposite here, and that much of the trustee's case rests on suspicion rather than fact.

30. Relevant to the question of delay and leaving matters to the last minute was also, he said, *Bagnall v Official Receiver* [2004] EWCA Civ 1925 where the Court of Appeal said that the late making of an application could in certain circumstances warrant not granting the order sought by the trustee. He relies on the following passage from the judgment of Arden LJ:

> "There are two further points. Trustees who leave it to the very last moment run the risk that the court will not exercise its discretion to make the suspension order. It is a judicial discretion. As the judge said, the interests of the creditors whom the Official Receiver represents have to be balanced with those of the bankrupt. Circumstances may arise where a trustee has been so dilatory that the consequences to the bankrupt are so unfair that the court might take the view that it was not appropriate to exercise its powers under s 279(3) despite the bankrupt's past or current failure to co-operate."

He submits that delay is a relevant consideration in this case and is a factor which should weigh in his client's favour.

31. Mr Watson-Gandy helpfully summarises the key principles in his written closing submissions as follows:

    i)    Deferment of discharge is at the discretion of the court.

    ii)   In exercising that discretion the court may have regard to:

        a)    whether the bankrupt needs to be incentivised in order to comply with his duties to the trustee;

        b)    what is in the interests of the creditors;

        c)    what is in the interests of the bankrupt;

        d)    how the trustee has conducted himself and whether there has been any delay by him.

    (see paragraph 10).

32. He submits that Mr Bland has learned his lesson and has now fully co-operated. In paragraph 14 of his closing submissions he lists a number of matters to support that claim, pointing to (a) the fullness and promptness of replies to requests for information in correspondence, (b) the timing of responses to the Scott schedules, (c) the provision of data from a number of computers, (d) the provision of letters of authority, (e) the carrying out of research by Mr Bland and (f) the offer of a further meeting which has been rejected. Mr Watson-Gandy gives detailed references to documents which I do not think I need to repeat here.

33. As regards Mr Bland's interests, Mr Watson-Gandy relies on his wish to rebuild his life (including his professional life), the fact that the interim order has been on foot since 2010 and the fact that Mr Bland is at present living on the goodwill of his friends and family (paragraph 15-18 and 33 of his closing submissions).

34. Mr Watson-Gandy deals with the interests of creditors in paragraphs 19-26 of his written submissions. I have already dealt with some of the points he makes, notably the fact that discharge does not prevent the trustee from pursuing his inquiries and does not release a bankrupt from his obligations to assist his trustee.

35. He points out that a number of companies about which the trustee has made inquiries are now dormant, dissolved or struck off, have no known assets or "appear to be owned directly or indirectly by Mr Waite" (paragraph 24). As to Hampshire Cosmetics Limited (which does have some value), he points out that Mr Mawer did not adopt the proceedings in which Mr Bell sought a freezing order in support of his judgment against Mr Bland.

36. He goes on,

    "Commercially it is difficult to see how this [application] could be in the interests in the creditors. After 2 ½ years and something in the region of £3/4 m spent and with 24 files of papers amassed (not counting the 10 boxes of papers on the section 366 case) chasing an estate with disclosed assets of

£9,747, the Trustees have recovered [only small sums]"
(paragraph 26).

37. He then deals with the conduct of the trustee (paragraphs 27-32) to which I have
already made brief reference, criticising his "sweeping accusations", his suggestion
that four bank accounts had not been disclosed when they were referred to in the
statement of affairs and his failure to supply documents to Mr Bland to enable him to
assist and so on.

38. He concludes,

"In all the circumstances, Mr Bland seeks that no further
extension of his discharge be made. Normally he would have
had his discharge in 2010. He is unable to seek reinstatement in
his former profession as an accountant until discharge. Mr
Bland has now shown that he is prepared to fully engage with
his Trustees and the reason for suspending his discharge no
longer applies."

39. All those are powerful points, well made.

## Conclusions

40. In spite of them, looking at matters as they now stand, and doing so with a cautious
eye on the history of the dealings between Mr Bland and Mr Mawer, I conclude that
there are ample reasons on the facts of this case for exercising the discretion to grant
the trustees the relief they seek on the basis that Mr Bland has failed and continues to
fail properly or at all to comply with his obligations in a number of significant
respects. Although this application has generated a great deal of paperwork and Mr
Bland has provided answers to questions, as Miss Troy submits, the quality, as
opposed to the quantity, of the information he has provided is inadequate. His affairs,
which the trustee needs to understand, remain shrouded in confusion. This can, I
accept, be attributed in part to the passage of time, but that is not a complete answer;
for I remind myself that Mr Bland is qualified as a chartered accountant, was and still
appears to engage in what might loosely be called accountancy advisory work, and
would therefore be acutely aware of the need to keep proper records of his business
and personal financial and other dealings at least for some period of time. Indeed one
of the points made on his behalf by Mr Watson-Gandy is, as we have seen, that he
needs to put this bankruptcy behind him so that he can try to resume practice as a
chartered accountant.

41. In my view, the reality is as Miss Troy submits, namely that Mr Bland seeks to give
the appearance of co-operation, but what he actually provides falls short of actual co-
operation.

42. I turn, then, to the specific matters upon which Mr Mawer relies and which, in my
view, warrant the granting of relief. I do not pretend that what I set out in the
following paragraphs is necessarily exhaustive: it is illustrative of Mr Bland's failures
rather a comprehensive account of them.

43. In his eighth witness statement Mr Mawer marshals his material under the following broad headings:

> loss of records (paragraphs 13-48);
>
> use of computers (paragraphs 49-51);
>
> concealment of property (paragraphs 52-64);
>
> inconsistencies in evidence (paragraphs 78-79).

Important sub-categories, in my view, are the matters that arise out of the disclosure of the Aston documents (see paragraphs 37-48) and the light that those documents throw on Mr Bland's involvement with and shareholding in Epiette and the implications of the latter for other companies with which Mr Bland has had dealings. I deal with those matters using different categories from those adopted by Mr Mawer, although there is necessarily a heavy degree of overlap.

## (a) Inadequate disclosure of documents

44. As I have already remarked, it is untrue to say that Mr Bland has disclosed nothing. It is, however, true that he has disclosed nothing of consequence, as Miss Troy says: not a single email and, as far as I can ascertain, virtually no documents dealing with his financial and business affairs relating to his time in Portugal/Gibraltar or the time immediately prior to or after the making of the bankruptcy order. It is simply incredible that an accountant of Mr Bland's experience, qualification and sophistication can have been conducting or advising on business of the nature and extent he has been involved in without keeping records.

45. As I have already indicated, I am prepared (because there is independent corroboration of the fact) to accept that Mr Bland stored documents at Scott Self Storage in Carlisle and that those documents were destroyed in a flood of 8 January 2005. However, his explanation as to what has become of other sources of information is less satisfactory, indeed so unsatisfactory as, to my mind, to be incredible. I have already mentioned a contention that documents were stored at the address of a mail forwarding company, which Mr Bland accepted, under some pressure, was untrue. Other computer discs are said to have become corrupted and sent to a retrieval specialist in California who Mr Bland is wholly unable to identify. That too seems remarkable. In the course of his private examination on 7 April 2011 Mr Bland said that he had handed a CD containing the books and records of Epiette to Mr Thomas Waite (who he claims is now the ultimate owner of Epiette) in the summer of 2008. However, by 21 April 2011 Mr Bland was already constrained to write to Mr Mawer to say that he had since spoken to Mr Waite who did not recall a DVD (*sic*). "It would seem therefore that I was mistaken since I do not have the accounting records it would appear that they have been lost". Again that is remarkable. When one considers all these matters cumulatively Mr Bland's position becomes incredible.

46. There are other indications that Mr Bland must have had documents. As Mr Mawer rightly observes, the January 2005 flood does not explain what has become of documents coming into existence since that date. It is clear from an interview which

Mr Bland had with Mr Mawer on 22 October 2009 (1/4/186 ff.) that Mr Bland continued to undertake advisory work because he raised with Mr Mawer the issue of client confidentiality (1/4/191). On his own evidence he traded through Rosewood Consultants Limited between 1 January 2001 and 31 March 2009. As Mr Mawer notes in paragraph 8 of his eighth witness statement Mr Bland's sole (or possibly principal) client has been Mr Waite. For reasons to which I shall come, it is plain that Mr Bland continues to do work for or in conjunction with Mr Waite. If he does so he must have books and records. It is incredible that none have been produced. I should also note that Mr Bland used the name of Rosewood Consultants Limited in connection with an appeal in the *Bell* case (see 1/4/89). Furthermore, as Mr Mawer points out in paragraph 36 of his eighth witness statement, a vast amount of correspondence was entered into using that company's notepaper. Mr Mawer notes, "The bankrupt has yet to produce one page of evidence in relation to the business and dealings of Rosewood Consultants, albeit it is now his case that Rosewood Consultants never traded and never had a bank account". This too is remarkable. As the trustee points out, if the company was not trading why was it sending letters and emails and so on? Even if it was not trading in the sense of generating money, the company was active or purporting to be active, so documents coming into existence are plainly relevant to Mr Bland's affairs within the meaning of the Insolvency Act.

47.    For reasons already canvassed, as I understand it, no documents have been produced in respect of Epiette. However, Mr Bland has recently produced a summary of Epiette's main expenditure from 1 June 2008 to closure compiled from bank statements. I presume that the bank statements came from the trustee, but if they did not then either Mr Bland has an extraordinary recollection that has enabled him to construct an income and expenditure account (which would be at odds with his general inability to recollect information) or alternatively he has access to documents that have prompted his recollection.

48.    However, perhaps the strongest indication of all that Mr Bland has not been straightforward with his trustee regarding documents and information is the recent development regarding Aston International Limited. On 22 March 2011 the trustee made an application for Aston to disclose documents which has resulted in the disclosure of the documents to which I have already referred. The documents held by Aston included statutory books and records, share registers, members' registers, accounts and details of directorships and share transactions. Plainly these are documents over which Mr Bland exercised control. I take a serious view of his conduct in relation to those documents. Although Mr Bland says that he signed an authority to enable the trustee to gain access to those documents it is plain that in fact Mr Bland, directly or indirectly, has sought to frustrate the trustee's access to those documents. The existence of the Aston documents is also a strong indication that there are likely to be other documents in relation to which Mr Bland has behaved similarly. Again the fact that they have been uncovered points, to my mind, to a pattern of behaviour designed to deprive the trustee of information and documents to which he is manifestly entitled.

*(b) The Aston International Limited documents*

49.    The trustee asserts that Mr Bland and/or Mr Waite have sought to procure the destruction of documents held by Aston. The details are set out in paragraphs 41-48 of Mr Mawer's eighth witness statement.

50.     As I have mentioned, Aston is an Isle of Man company that provides corporate services. Mr Bland and/or Mr Waite, who until very recently had been using its services, decided to instruct a company in the British Virgin Islands called Blenheim Trust in its place. There can be little doubt that they wanted to cover their tracks, because elaborate enquiries were made about the obligations of Aston under Isle of Man law to retain documents, largely, it seems, by Mr Bland. Those enquires appear to have begun on 1 March 2010 when Mr Bland emailed Mr David Griffin of Aston asking, "If you are no longer instructed to act as an intermediary…and a request is made for you to deliver up all those records … that you hold to your client, without retaining copies, what records are you obliged to retain under IoM law, and for how long".

51.     I do not think it is necessary to repeat the sequence of events described in Mr Mawer's witness statement. Suffice it to say that Aston held records for New Capital Management Limited which were covered by a freezing order made on 12 June 2009. That, at least, is what Mr Mawer says, and I did not understand the point to be challenged. The exchange of correspondence between Aston and Mr Bland culminated in a letter of 22 March 2010 sent by email apparently from Mr Waite to Mr Griffin:

> "Dear Mr Griffin
>
> Re:     New Capital Management Limited
>
> I'm writing in my capacity as director of and owner of the above company.
>
> Following the change of the registered local agent dealing with the administration of the company for me, and your ceasing to be involved, please accept this letters [*sic*] as my request and instruction for you to delete and destroy any and all records you hold in relation to the company which are more than 6 years old, other than those records which you are obliged to retain in accordance with you local laws.
>
> I would be grateful if you could acknowledge receipt of this letter and confirm that you have complied with my request.
>
> I would like to take this opportunity of thanking you for your assistance and support whilst involved with the company.
>
> Yours sincerely
>
> Thomas Waite".

In fact the documents were not destroyed.

52.     Technically the trustee is wrong when he says in paragraph 41 of his witness statement that the bankrupt and Mr Waite arranged for and ordered the destruction of the records. The order actually came from Mr Waite. However, the preceding exchange of emails makes it abundantly clear that Mr Waite and Mr Bland were

255

acting together to achieve a common goal. Mr Bland was firmly back in the driving seat by April 2010: on 20 April Catherine Jackson wrote to Mr Bland rather than Mr Waite confirming that the transfer was complete and that the company documents would be delivered to the new BVI agent "tomorrow at the latest" (6/14/2322).

53.     Mr Bland's involvement, whilst an undischarged bankrupt, in an attempt to destroy documents plainly relevant to his affairs speaks volumes and substantially undermines Mr Watson-Gandy's submission that he has learned a salutary lesson.

## (c ) The relationship between Mr Bland and Mr Waite and others

54.     The relationship between Mr Bland and Mr Waite remains unclear. I do not know, nor as far as I am aware does the trustee, whether Mr Bland works for Mr Waite or whether Mr Waite is simply a front for Mr Bland's activities. As I have commented, the Aston documentation appears to indicate that Mr Bland took the lead in dealing with it but that he and/or Mr Waite felt that the final instruction as to dealing with documents had to come from the latter. The question remains, is or was Aston controlled by Mr Bland or Mr Waite? For that matter, there is now a further question, namely who is able to instruct the BVI trust that has replaced Aston?

55.     The position as regards Mr Bland's role in Epiette is similarly unclear. I have already set out something of what I think I understood about Epiette from the early stages of these proceedings based on the evidence as it then stood; but we know more now as a result of the Aston disclosure.

56.     In his first witness statement the trustee said that the annual return of Epiette showed that Mr Bland was the registered shareholder of 100% of the ordinary shares in the company and was thus the sole shareholder. (1/2/52). He was also a director (see paragraph 8 above).

57.     On 3 July 2009, shortly before petitioning for his own bankruptcy, Mr Bland wrote to Aston asking it to record his resignation as a director of Epiette and the appointment of a Mr Philip Crone as a director in his place with effect from 30/31 May 2009 (6/14/2371).

58.     Mr Bland had also been trying to dispose of his shares in Epiette. On 29 April 2009, two days after His Honour Judge Pelling gave judgment against him for £1.5 million, he asked Aston to prepare the forms required to transfer his shares to Northpoint Venture Partners Inc (6/14/2441). I note in passing (because Epiette is not the only company about which questions remain to be answered) that Mr Bland also said "ie the same as for Sandwell". Mr Bland then asked for confirmation as to who in fact held the shares in Epiette and repeated his instruction regarding the transfer (6/14/2359). Mr Oates of Aston confirmed that he did own them(6/14/2362). Again the reference to Sandwell should be noted: Mr Oates was seeking instructions in relation to that company too.

59.     (Pausing there, briefly, it is hardly surprising that many of us involved in this case have been confused about the shareholding in Epiette when Mr Bland himself appears to have been uncertain about the position. On the other hand, I should also say that Mr Bland's documented confusion gives some support to the proposition that he may

256

not always be being untruthful in every case where he gets something wrong or confused.)

60.    On 18 June 2009, very shortly after the making of the bankruptcy order, Aston confirmed that it was proceeding with the share transfer. On 5 August 2009, after the bankruptcy order had been made, Mr Oates was still dealing with Mr Bland: he asked him to arrange for a questionnaire to be filled in by Mr Waite "in order to complete the shareholder change" (6/14/2371). On 30 October 2009 Mr Oates wrote asking Mr Bland to sign and return a stock transfer form (6/14/2376). Mr Bland appears to have returned a copy on 2 November 2009 (6/14/2377). He says in his letter that he executed it in August 2008 and that the original was handed to Northpoint Venture Partners Inc. It is hard to see how the share transfer form could have been executed in August 2008 (before Mr Bland's bankruptcy) in circumstances in which Mr Bland refers on 2 November 2009 to Mr Oates's "recent email". The recent email must surely be that of 30 October 2009. All this was going on around the time that Mr Bland was giving the trustee wholly different information about the shareholding in Epiette (see paragraph 7 above).

61.    Here too Mr Waite's name figures. On 21 March 2010 Mr Waite wrote to Aston on behalf of Northpoint Venture Partners Inc stating that on that date it had sold its entire shareholding in Epiette to Northpoint Ventures Inc. He asked Aston to record the change of ownership.

62.    The thrust of Mr Bland's initial case, at least as I understood it, was that Epiette had effectively been taken over by Mr Waite, albeit indirectly through companies which he owned or controlled. That fits in with Mr Bland's initial statement that he handed the books and records to Mr Waite on a CD or DVD.

63.    Some fairly obvious inferences can be drawn. Plainly on the date the bankruptcy order was made the shares in Epiette were held by Mr Bland. Equally plainly the shares were still Mr Bland's on 30 October 2009. The purported reference to the share transaction having been completed on 5 August 2008 (see the email of 2 November 2009 at 2377 to 2379) was an attempt by Mr Bland (possibly with the assistance of Mr Waite) to conceal a bankruptcy asset and/or dispose of it after its vesting in the trustees. This gives rise to the question why Mr Bland would go to so much trouble if Epiette was merely a shell. The obvious inference is either that Epiette, whether directly or indirectly, has in fact valuable assets, alternatively has information that will assist the trustee properly to understand how Mr Bland has been conducting his business affairs in the recent and not so recent past. Mr Bland's unsatisfactory explanations given to his trustee at a time when he was playing around with the shareholding of Epiette is, in my view, the plainest possible proof of non co-operation, breach of bankruptcy obligations, indeed downright dishonesty in Mr Bland's dealings with Mr Mawer. It is the source of Mr Mawer's justified frustration, and Mr Bland knows that all too well.

64.    Further evidence of Mr Bland's control of or intimate connexion with Epiette is the transfer of funds to him on 29 May 2009 and 3 June 2009.

*(d) Concealment/disposal of a bankruptcy asset*

65.    Mr Bland's attempted or actual disposal of his shares in Epiette after the making of
       the bankruptcy order and the vesting of them in his trustees constitutes an independent
       ground justifying the continuation of the suspension of the discharge period. I leave
       to one side the fact that the disposal or purported disposal is void. The matter is very
       serious.

*(e) Other companies*

66.    At paragraphs 65-73 of his eighth witness statement Mr Mawer gives details of other
       companies with which Mr Bland appears to have had dealings and which are now said
       to be beneficially owned by Mr Waite. In the context I have described it is plain that
       the trustee needs to investigate the affairs of these companies and that Mr Bland has
       provided inadequate assistance. I do not propose to set out the detail because I do not
       believe that I can satisfactorily add anything to what Mr Mawer says.

*(f) Mr Bland's evidence*

67.    At paragraph 78 of his witness statement Mr Mawer sets out a number of problems he
       identifies in relation to the consistency of Mr Bland's evidence. Again I do not think
       there is anything I can usefully add. I have myself referred in this judgment to a
       number of similar problems I have found with Mr Bland's evidence.    These
       inconsistencies need to be explained comprehensively and satisfactorily.

68.    I appreciate the pressure under which Mr Bland found himself when he made his
       eleventh witness statement of 31 March 2012. It consists of 57 paragraphs, but in
       common with a lot of what Mr Bland puts before the court and tells his trustee offers
       very little of substance. I cannot identify a single document Mr Bland exhibits which
       throws any real light on his affairs. He makes no attempt to explain his conduct in
       relation to Aston.    His tenth witness statement is argumentative rather than
       informative.

69.    As part of her closing submissions Miss Troy made the point that although Mr Bland
       had answered the questions put to him the Scott schedules many of his answers
       remained unhelpful. She directed my attention to a few examples:

            "The Trustee's Question:

            During the examination you stated you had sent the executed
            share transfer form to North Point Venture Partners in August
            2008. Please explain why, if that was indeed the case, you
            waited until May 2009 to query whether the shares were still
            held in your name and enquire as to whether they had been
            transferred. Presumably you are still able to access email
            exchanges with Mr Waite in relation to the purported transfer
            or can obtain from him copies of contemporaneous exchanges.
            Please do so and forward copies to us. If you had provided Mr
            Waite with the signed share transfer form why would you
            believe in May 2009 that you might still be the registered
            shareholder of Epiette?

258

The Bankrupt's Response:

During the period August 2008 to May 2009 I was preoccupied with the preparations for the Bell trial and was not paying proper attention to checking that other documentation had been dealt with properly. I am not able to access any of my historic emails. In order to properly respond to this question can you please provide me with copies of all the documentation you have received from Aston's in the Isle of Man in relation to Epiette Limited so that I can review the entirety of my correspondence with them. The only reason I can think of without sight of the Aston's documentation is that I could not recall seeing the signed stock transfer come back to me from Mr Waite for me to send on to Aston's and queried whether Mr Waite had send this to them directly" (1/6/551).

The question is answered only in a tentative way. The burden of providing information is thrown back on the trustee.

"The Trustee's Further Questions:

(1)     The Bankrupt is requested to explain why he cannot access any of his historic emails.

(2)     Please answer the question by reference to the email exchange with Aston.

The Bankrupt's Further Response:

(1)     I do not know where they are, or if they are still stored on any e-mail server. I refer to the notes in relation to Computer Records generally (Pages B1456 to B158) as to why these records are no longer available.

(2)     I refer to the notes in relation to Epiette generally (Page B164 to B169)

I am unable to add anything further" (1/6/552)..

This is remarkable given the quantity of emails to and from Mr Bland which the Aston discovery process has unearthed.

"The Trustee's Question:

Please detail what has happened to the books and records of Epiette.

The Bankrupt's Response:

This question does not relate to my assets or affairs. The questions relate to the affairs of Epiette, a company of which I am not a director and of which I am not a shareholder. Insofar

259

as you wish to have information in relation to the affairs of this company you should address your questions to the company directly. However in respect of the records, these have been lost due to the backup disk going missing. In respect of the statutory books I expect that these will be held by Astons in the Isle of Man" (1/6/556).

It will be recalled that the trustee was told that the books and records of Epiette went to Mr Waite but then that explanation was then retracted. I am not aware of any alternative explanation that has been given as to what has become of the papers. It is disingenuous of Mr Bland to say that a question about the books and records of a company with which he was involved for a significant period of time and of which he was both a shareholder and director does not relate to his assets or affairs. The response is calculatedly unhelpful.

70.     Mr Bland took a similar approach to other questions:

"The Trustee's Question:

At page 391 is a letter from you dated 3 December 2007 to Aston in which you advised Aston that you were opening a new bank account for Epiette with the National Westminster Bank in Guernsey. Please explain:

(i) Why was this new account to be opened.

(ii)     Was it opened.

(iii)    If so where were the bank statements sent to.

(iv)    Please can you provide copy bank statements.

The Bankrupt's Response:

(i)      This question does not relate to my assets or affairs. The questions relate to the affairs of Epiette, a company of which I am not a director and of which I am not a shareholder. Insofar as you wish to have information in relation to the affairs of this company you should address your questions to the company directly.

(ii)     Not as far as I can recall.

(iii)    N/A.

(iv)    No, I do not have them" (1/6/574).

Again the answer is unhelpful.

"The Trustee's Question

At Pages 395 and 396 is an email of 26 March 2009 sent by you to Attlas & Levy Gibraltar in relation to Waburn which states:

(i)     the shares were held to your order;

(ii)    That Waburn owned the shares of Atlantic House Limited and Iberian Development Corporation Limited;

(iii)   that you wanted to transfer that shareholding to Northpoint Venture Partners Inc.

By email on the same day (at page 397) Attlas & Levy confirmed that you were the beneficial owner;

Please clarify:

(i)     that you acknowledge you were the beneficial owner of the shares;

(ii)    why you suggested a transfer to either Northpoint or Sandwell;

(iii)   the consideration paid for the transfer of shares to you or in fact by anyone.

The Bankrupt's Response:

(i)     No, I held the shares as nominee for Atlantic House Holdings Limited. The company was previously administered by Jordans in Gibraltar and their documentation confirmed that the shares were owned by Atlantic House Limited. When I discovered that Mr Corlett had run off with the proceeds or sale of two plots of land, owned within the Atlantic House Holdings Limited Group, and refused to account to the company, or its creditors, I took steps, as a director of Atlantic House Holdings Limited to put all other assets of the Group outside reach of Mr Corlett until he accounted for the Group for the monies he had stolen. As part of these steps I moved the administration of Waburn from Jordans and Attlas and Levy, and rather than record the owner of Waburn as Atlantic House Holdings Limited, requested that he shares be held to my order so that Mr Corlett could have no influence over them until matters had been resolved.

(ii)    please provide the supporting documentation for the reference to Sandwell. In relation to the transfer to Northpoint, the Atlantic House Holdings Limited was

261

indebted to Mr Waite and as part repayment of the liabilities owed to him, and guaranteed by the Group, the shares in Waburn were transferred to Mr Waite's company, Northpoint, as part repayment of amounts due.

(iii)   No consideration was paid to me as I was not the beneficial owner of the shares, Atlantic House Holdings Limited was, hence the wording that the shares were "held to my order". In relation to the consideration paid to Atlantic House Holdings Limited for the transfer, the question does not relate to my assets or affairs. The questions relate to the affairs of Atlantic House Holdings Limited, a company of which I am not a director and of which I am not a shareholder. Insofar as you wish to have information in relation to the affairs of this company you should address your questions the company directly." (1/6/578 to 579).

71.   Miss Troy's point was that these answers demonstrated that Mr Bland had not learned his lesson and was still intent on providing as little information as possible. The point is well made. I agree.

72.   There are parallels between the situation in this case and that in *Shierson v Rastogi* which are too obvious to require spelling out. Manifestly Mr Bland's conduct is linked to failures on his part to comply with his obligations under Part IX of the Insolvency Act. As in *Rastogi*, this is a case where the trustee needs information and elucidation and is hampered by "a lack of information which ought to be within the knowledge of the bankrupt". That information goes to the bankrupt's affairs, which term should be construed broadly to include his dealings with companies. It is not good enough to direct the trustee to the companies without more. Whilst I accept that the bankrupt will continue to be bound by his obligations after discharge, this is plainly a case where the need to incentivise is one (but by no means the only) factor relevant to the exercise of the discretion. Whilst I accept that parts of the trustee's case are founded upon suspicion, his suspicions are grounded in reality. The Aston disclosure demonstrates that his earlier suspicions about what Mr Bland may have had access to are amply justified. The trustee's delay is, as Mr Watson-Gandy says, a factor to be taken into account, but much of the delay can, in the end, be laid at Mr Bland's door; in any event, such delay as there has been is not sufficient to outweigh the other factors to be taken into account. Similarly, this is plainly a case where the interests of the creditors outweigh those of the bankrupt.

73.   Subject to submissions as to the form of the order I should make, I would propose to continue the suspension of Mr Bland's discharge period not to the end of a specified period but until the trustee confirms to the court that he has properly and fully co-operated in all respects reasonably required of him by his trustee.

262

## Chronology

| DATE | EVENT | REFS. |
|------|-------|-------|
| 00.11.88 | Having replied to a newspaper advertisement seeking investors, Mr Bland put Mr Bell (then living in Spain) in contact with Mr Corlett in Portugal | 193-194 |
| 00.00.89 | Mr Bland went to work for Mr Corlett in Portugal, living in Portugal and/or Gibraltar for purposes of that work | 190-191 |
| 21.01.95 | Mr Bland acquired a 75% shareholding in Epiette (25% to Mr Corlett) | 2331 |
| 05.09.98 | Mr Bland ceased to hold a practising certificate from the ICAEW | 149 |
| 14.01.03 | Mr Bland became sole shareholder of Epiette | 2334; 2346 |
| 28.09.04 | Mr Bland rented storage space in Carlisle from Scott Self Storage | 2245 |
| 08.01.05 | Flooding in Carlisle, which is said to have destroyed records that Mr Bland had placed in storage at Scott Self Storage | 2245 |
| 13.02.05 | Mr Bland ceased to rent storage space in Carlisle | 2251 |
| 09.02.06 | Mr Bland obtained an interim injunction against Mr Corlett in Gibraltar covering assets up to €800,000 | 1982, ¶ 67 |
| 08.01.08-02.04.08 | Documents were prepared for an abortive transfer of Mr Bland's shares in Epiette to Mr Crone for £10,000 | 2355-2357 |
| 05.08.08 | Date entered on Stock Transfer Form transferring Bankrupt's shares in Epiette to Northpoint and director's approval resolution | 2378-2379 |
| 05.11.08 | Mr Bland requested Aston to process his resignation as a director of Epiette and appoint Mr Crone in his stead w.e.f. 31.10.08 (but this instruction was cancelled on 18.12.08) | 2433 (2434) |
| 01.01.09 | Mr Bland stated to be sole member of Epiette in its annual return | 2439 |
| 09.01.09 | Aston confirmed to Mr Bland, in response to his request for information, that he was the sole director and sole shareholder of Epiette | 2442 |
| 06.04.09 | Mr Bland gave evidence in the Manchester proceedings, Bell v Bland, about the role of Epiette Ltd and his relationship with that company | 229-231 |
| 27.04.09 | HH Judge Pelling QC gave judgment in Bell v Bland for a principal amount of equitable compensation of around £1.5 million and gave directions for the assessment of interest and costs. The Judge described Mr Bland, who had represented himself, as "highly articulate and highly intelligent" and noted that his cross-examination "would have done credit to a junior barrister of some years call" (but also treated Mr Bland as someone who had repeatedly "sought to dishonestly mislead" the Court – Judgment, ¶ 89, 91 & 92) | 1970, ¶ 59.18; 2609, ¶ 13 |
| 29.04.09 | Mr Bland asked Aston to prepare for him forms to record the transfer of the entire shareholding in Epiette from himself to Northpoint | 2441 |
| 29.04.09 | Mr Bland signed Epiette accounts for 2008 as having been approved by the Board on 29.04, which showed that he had been the sole director for 2008 and had held all of the shares in Epiette | 2427-2428 |

| DATE | EVENT | REFS. |
|---|---|---|
| | as at 31.12.08 and 01.01.09 | |
| 20.05.09 | Mr Bland requested confirmation from Aston as to who currently held the shares in Epiette and, if it was him, to prepare the necessary paperwork to transfer the shares to Northpoint | 2359 |
| 20.05.09 | Aston confirmed that Mr Bland was the sole shareholder of Epiette | 2362 |
| 20.05.09 | Date on Stock Transfer Form that appears to have been prepared by Aston for transfer of Mr Bland's shares in Epiette to Northpoint | 2364 |
| 20.05.09 | Mr Bland also wrote to Aston indicating that he would not be able to find another director for Epiette and therefore was considering winding it up | 2366 |
| 27.05.09 | HH Judge Pelling QC gave Judgment against Mr Bland in Bell v Bland Manchester proceedings for the principal sum of equitable compensation previously awarded, together assessed interest and costs, in a total of £6,113,785 | 45, ¶ 3 |
| 29.05.09 | Epiette paid £6,000 into Mr Bland's account at HSBC (into which a total of £487,000 had been paid since 15.08.02) | 50-51, ¶ 15 |
| 29.05.09 | Mr Bell obtained a worldwide freezing Order against Mr Bland | 45, ¶ 3; 119-124 |
| 03.06.09 | Epiette transferred funds into a Jersey bank account with Barclays Bank in the name of Mr Bland | 51, ¶ 16 |
| 09.06.09 | Bankruptcy Order made on petition of Bankrupt | 8 (29; 56) |
| 09.06.09 | Bankrupt filed questionnaire with OR | 1999-2025 |
| 09.06.09 | Bankrupt completed Statement of Affairs | Supp. 4, ex. 63 |
| 16.06.09-17.06.09 | In email exchanges with Aston, Bankrupt instructed Aston to proceed with preparing documents for the transfer of his shares in Epiette to Northpoint, despite his bankruptcy, as "I had agreed with TW to transfer the shares in Epiette to Northpoint on 20 May" | 2368-2369 |
| 17.06.09 | Bankrupt wrote to Trustees to disclose that he was the sole shareholder of Rosewood Consultants (Belize), but that the shares were worthless | 2644 |
| 18.06.09 | Aston informed the Bankrupt that it had received the documents for Northpoint and Mr Waite, requested a change of beneficial ownership indemnity from him and confirmed that the transfer of his shares in Epiette to Northpoint would be processed as soon as possible, provided that all documents were in order | 2370 |
| 01.07.09 | Trustees appointed | 9 (30; 57) |
| 02.07.09-24.09.09 | Trustees made numerous requests to Bankrupt to meet with Mr Mawer in London or Leeds, which all were fruitless until Bankrupt agreed in a phone conversation on 24.09.09 to meet with Mr Mawer in London on 01.10.09 | 46-47, ¶ 10; 65-63, 62-63, 60-61 & 71-99 Supp. 4, ex. 49 |
| 02.07.09 | Hugh G O'Neill of Turks & Caicos confirmed to Trustees that Wystan Holdings was acquired by Mr Waite in 2002 and that Bankrupt had never been a shareholder in or director or officer of Wystan | Supp. 1, ex. 58 |
| 03.07.09 | Bankrupt wrote to Aston requesting it to record his resignation as | 2448 |

| DATE | EVENT | REFS. |
|------|-------|-------|
| | director of Epiette and the appointment of Mr Crone in his stead w.e.f. 31 and 30.05.09 respectively | |
| 06.07.09 | Bankrupt responded in brief to email queries from Trustees but declined meetings in Leeds on the basis that the Trustees had been appointed because they had an office in London | 2498 |
| 30.07.09 | Bankrupt responded to a letter from Trustees dated 27.07 with initial points, e.g. as to numbering of questions put to him | 2500-2501 |
| 05.08.09 | Aston asked Bankrupt to arrange for Mr Waite to complete Personal Questionnaire so that Epiette share transfer could be completed | 2371 |
| 05.08.09 | Bankrupt responded further to Trustees' letter of 27.07, requiring that all future communications be by letter and stating that he retained no accounting records and he did not own a computer | 2506-2508 |
| 06.08.09 | Trustees addressed written questions to Bankrupt, including in relation to Hampshire Cosmetics, New Capital Management, Epiette, Rosewood and Mr Corlett | See, 2223 |
| 06.08.09 | Bankrupt provided further responses to Trustees' queries of 27.07, in two letters, subject to the caveat that he was concerned about disclosing information about parties such as Hampshire Cosmetics that was not in the public domain because information had been provided to him in his capacity as a chartered accountant and there might be a breach of confidentiality. Bankrupt also required Trustees to set out the basis on which their queries included queries about third parties, so that he could take legal advice on whether this was permissible | 2509-2516 |
| 13.08.09 | Bankrupt wrote to Barclays Bank instructing the Bank to pay to him in Portugal any funds remaining in a specified account | 49, ¶ 12.11 |
| 21.08.09 | Trustees repeated their initial written queries to Bankrupt | See, 2230 |
| 26.08.09 | Bankrupt provided Trustees with his initial responses to queries arising out of materials in relation to the freezing Order granted in Bell v Bland | 2517-2518 |
| 27.08.09 | Bankrupt provided Trustees with 3 letters of authority in relation to bank accounts he held in Gibraltar (Barclays), Guernsey (Barclays) and Portugal (Millenium BCP) | 2519-2522 |
| 28.08.09 | Bankrupt provided initial responses to Trustees, but also declined to communicate other than by letter and stated reasons for his failure to maintain any records since 2005 | 2223 |
| 03.09.09 | Bankrupt reiterated and elaborated on his initial responses to Trustees' written queries and stated that he could be available to meet with Trustees in London at any time during weeks commencing 14 or 21.09 | 2230-2240 |
| 14.09.09 | Bankrupt indicated to Aston "from memory" that Northpoint was the sole shareholder of Epiette and he was still the sole director and asked about the procedure for having the company re-domiciled in Delaware | 2449 |

| DATE | EVENT | REFS. |
|------|-------|-------|
| 15.09.09 | Bankrupt emailed Aston that he had noticed that Epiette's 03.09 accounts (this appears to have been a reference to the 2008 annual accounts) were incorrect, asked whether these had been filed yet and, if not, for deletion of those accounts | 2451 |
| 15.09.09 | Aston stated (incorrectly) that Northpoint was sole shareholder of Epiette, reminded the Bankrupt that Mr Crone had been appointed as a director of Epiette on 30.05 and he had resigned on 31.05 and stated that the accounts of Epiette were only held on file and could be updated. Aston also advised that re-domiciliation of Epiette would be extremely expensive | 2451 |
| 15.09.09+ | Revised 2008 accounts for Epiette showed that the Bankrupt had continued as a director of Epiette throughout the period but had held "Nil" shares in the company for the year ended 31.12.08 | 2443-2444 |
| 01.10.09 | Bankrupt met with Mr Mawer of the Trustees, who conducted an initial interview with the Bankrupt, *inter alia* on his relationship with Epiette | 47, ¶ 10.13; 50-52,¶¶14-22; 131-171 (also @ 2026-2071) |
| 10.10.09 | Bankrupt made a written enquiry as to the location of Epiette share certificate no. 21 (which would need to be surrendered for cancellation before the share transfer to Northpoint could complete and a share certificate could be issued to Northpoint) | 2372-2373 (see, 2360) |
| 13.10.09 | Trustees sent Bankrupt a list of bank transactions requiring explanation, together with questions on those transactions | 100 |
| 16.10.09 | Trustees sent Bankrupt issues regarding Mr Waite, Mr Corlett and Epiette on which further information was required | 101-102 |
| 26.10.09 | Bankrupt requested copies of all documents in the Trustees' possession that could assist him in responding to their questions (still, to date, not a single document emanating from or addressed to the Bankrupt (including in that description emails) has been produced by the Bankrupt) | 103 (1947, ¶ 5-8) |
| 27.10.09 | Bankrupt, on behalf of Mr Waite, asked Aston if it could act as director and company secretary for Epiette and also asked for a copy of the last set of accounts filed with Aston | 2375 |
| 27.10.09 | Aston sent the Bankrupt a copy of the last set of Epiette accounts filed with it and information about fees due and formalities to be completed if it was to act as agent for Epiette on behalf of Mr Waite | 2375 |
| 28.10.09 | Bankrupt acknowledged receipt of information from Aston for Mr Waite and indicated it was likely to be early December before changes would be effected | 2374 |
| 30.10.09 | Aston requested Bankrupt to complete a Stock Transfer Form in relation to Epiette (the actual Form referred to has not been disclosed or located) | 2376 |
| 02.11.09 | Stock Transfer Form and directors resolution for transfer of Bankrupt's shares in Epiette to Northpoint, both dated 05.08.08, sent to Aston by Bankrupt | 2377-2379 |
| 15.12.09 | Bankrupt emailed Aston to instruct that its annual return for 2009 | 2496 |

| DATE | EVENT | REFS. |
|------|-------|-------|
| | should not be filed without prior confirmation from him | |
| 21.12.09 | CA refused permission to appeal against Judgment in Bell v Bland | 109 |
| 23.12.09 | Trustees chased for a response to their letter of 13.10.09, clarifying that providing the Bankrupt with copies of the bank statements that had given rise to the questions would not assist him in responding to them | 105 |
| 06.01.10 | Bankrupt again requested copies of all bank statements in the Trustees' possession plus an electronic copy of the spread sheet file prepared by the Trustees and by reference to which their questions had been posed | 106-107 |
| 08.01.10 | Bankrupt notified the Trustees of CA decision refusing permission to appeal in Bell v Bland on paper application and that he had requested an oral hearing of the application | 108 |
| 12.01.10 | Trustees responded to various communications from Bankrupt | 160-163 |
| 19.01.10 | Trustees wrote to Bankrupt by registered post raising further questions, but also enclosing, on disc, copies of the bank statements then available to them, their summary schedule of account transactions by reference to which questions had been posed to the Bankrupt and a transcript of Mr Mawer's initial interview with the Bankrupt and informing the Bankrupt that the Trustees held no other documents or information relating to his financial affairs (Bankrupt refused to sign for this letter) | 48, ¶ 12.5; 112-116 |
| 22.01.10 | Bankrupt informed Aston that Mr Waite wanted to move Epiette to Delaware | 1966, ¶ 58.1 |
| 28.01.10 | Bankrupt continued to correspond with Aston about the proposed change in domicile of Epiette and noted that he had forgotten to ask prior to 31.12.09 whether Aston directors could be appointed with retrospective effect, to appear on Epiette's return to 31.12.09 | 2464 |
| 03.02.10 | Trustees chased for a response to their letter of 19.01.10, enclosing copy | 126 |
| 03.02.10 | Aston confirmed to the Bankrupt that it would accept appointment as director of Epiette w.e.f. 31.12.09 | 2465 |
| 11.02.10 | Bankrupt informed Trustees that he had not received their letter of 19.01.10 and requested the enclosure to the original letter | 127 |
| 12.02.10 | Trustees again chased for a response to their letter of 19.01.10 (this letter evidently crossed with the Bankrupt's letter of 11.02.10) | 128 (129) |
| 19.02.10 | Trustees wrote to Bankrupt to inform him that a further copy of the disc sent to him on 19.01.10 had been sent to their London offices for him to collect and proposed a further meeting for 09.03.10, to follow his review of the materials and the provision of his responses (Bankrupt did not collect the forwarded disc) | 130 (49,¶ 12.10) |
| 26.02.10 | Bankrupt wrote to Trustees stating that he did not have a computer and that those who let him use their computers were concerned about him using their computers to access encrypted files received from the Trustees, so that he required paper copies of the relevant documents. He also asked the Trustees to explain the legal basis on which they had asked questions relating to third parties and stated that he was unable to meet the Trustees on 09.03.10 | 137-138 |

| DATE | EVENT | REFS. |
|---|---|---|
| 01.03.10-20.04.10 | Bankrupt assisted Mr Waite in correspondence with Aston for the purpose of procuring the transfer of administration of New Capital Management to a new local agent in the BVI and the destruction of records held by Aston for the period 1993-2003 | 1959, ¶ 42 – 1964, ¶ 48; 2273-2323 |
| 03.03.10 | Mr Mawer hand delivered a copy of the disc containing copies of all documents then held by the Trustees to the Bankrupt's address at 20 Montefiore Street, where Mr Dominic Bland took delivery and told Mr Mawer that the Bankrupt did not in fact live at that address | 49, ¶ 12.10; 139 |
| 04.03.10 | Trustees wrote to Bankrupt to chase for provision of all information and explanations previously requested from him and expressed frustration at the Bankrupt's failure to provide information requested from him. Trustees also asked Bankrupt additional questions, including in relation to his instruction to Barclays Bank on 13.08.09 and his withdrawal of funds after his bankruptcy.* The Bankrupt was informed that unless he confirmed that he would respond to all outstanding questions within 14 days Trustees would instruct solicitors to apply for a s. 366 examination | 139-142 *399-400 Contd. |
| 05.03.10 | Bankrupt wrote to Trustees that he would endeavour to respond to them within 14 days of receipt of copies of all documents requested, including copies of statements for the Barclays Bank account referred to | 143-144 |
| 08.03.10 | Trustees confirmed receipt of Bankrupt's letter of 05.03 but also confirmed that copies of all documents requested were on the disc delivered to 20 Montefiore Street and chased for a substantive response to their letter of 04.03 | 145-146 |
| 16.03.10 | Trustees sent the Bankrupt hard copies of the documents previously provided to him on CD and requested his responses to all outstanding queries within 14 days | 147 |
| 21.03.10 | Mr Waite wrote to inform Aston of a transfer of the entire shareholding in Epiette from Northpoint to a different Northpoint company and requested Aston, as nominee shareholders, to record this change | 1975, ¶ 59.43 |
| 22.03.10 | Trustees wrote to Bankrupt requesting confirmation of receipt of the documents sent to him on 16.03 and information as to when the Bankrupt would be providing the responses requested from him. Bankrupt was also asked further questions about his co-director of Hampshire Cosmetics Ltd and his interest in Aldeburgh Enterprises Ltd | 148-149 |
| 29.03.10 | Trustees sent Bankrupt a further copy of their letter of 16.03 and its enclosures (which the Bankrupt said he had not received), asked for an email address for the Bankrupt to expedite communications and again pressed for confirmation as to when responses would be provided | 154 |
| 31.03.10 | Bankrupt responded to queries from Trustees about Mr Watson-Clark, Aldeburgh and his practising as a chartered accountant | Supp. 4, ex. 93 |
| 01.04.10 | Trustees requested confirmation of receipt of their letter of 29.03 and again pressed for confirmation as to when responses would be provided | 156 |

| DATE | EVENT | REFS. |
|------|-------|-------|
| 01.04.10 | Bankrupt confirmed receipt of Trustees' letter of 29.03 but requested further documents to test the veracity of the documents supplied to him prior to providing responses | See, 162 |
| 12.04.10 | Trustees wrote to Bankrupt regarding the intended appeal in Bell v Bland, and the reasons the scope of their enquiries was so broad | Supp. 4, ex. 96 |
| 27.04.10 | Trustees confirmed receipt of letters from Bankrupt dated 20.04, 21.04 and 22.04 relating to the Bell v Bland appeal and other matters, noting that he still had not provided any of the information and explanations requested from him | 164-165 |
| 29.04.10 | Bankrupt wrote to Trustees regarding the Bell v Bland appeal and asking for clarification of references to Hampshire Cosmetics | 50, ¶ 12.19; 166-168 |
| 04.05.10 | Trustees wrote to inform Bankrupt that neither of his letters of 29.04 provided any response to any of the issues raised with him but providing clarification regarding references to Hampshire Cosmetics | 171-172 |
| 04.05.10 | Bankrupt wrote to Trustees regarding the Bell v Bland appeal, raising questions about the funding of the Trustees' costs and comments about provision of copies of trial bundles in historic Hampshire Cosmetics litigation | 173-177 |
| 04.05.10 | Bankrupt wrote to Trustees confirming that he had received outstanding documents requested by him and that he would endeavour to respond to their queries by 14.05 | 179 |
| 10.05.10 | Trustees wrote to the Bankrupt noting that he had stated that he would endeavour to respond to the questions addressed to him by 14.05 and indicating willingness to meet to discuss the Bell v Bland appeal and other issues raised by the Bankrupt on 04.05 | 180 |
| 14.05.10 | Bankrupt wrote to Trustees stating that it was taking him longer than expected to go through the documents forwarded to him but that he hoped to respond to their questions by 21.05 | 181 |
| 18.05.10 | Trustees wrote to note that Bankrupt had failed to provide his responses by the agreed deadline and gave notice that, pending his responses and in view of the approaching anniversary of his bankruptcy, an application for suspension if his discharge would be prepared | 182 |
| 19.05.10 | In the context of re-domiciliation of Epiette, Bankrupt told Aston that he thought it had provided nominee shareholders since 31.12.09 | 2469-2470 |
| 20.05.10 | Aston stated that it had not previously been asked to provide nominee shareholders and that the shares would need to be transferred from (the original) Northpoint in order for it to do so | 2471 |
| 20.05.10 | Bankrupt requested Aston to send him a share transfer form backdated prior to 31.12.09 for completion | 2471 |
| 20.05.10 | An internal Aston email indicated that it intended to prepare an undated stock transfer form in response to the Bankrupt's request and would record the share transfer in its records at the date the signed stock transfer form was received | 2472 |
| 24.05.10 | Aston informed the Bankrupt that the shareholder could date the requested stock transfer form and sent the Bankrupt a stock transfer | 2473 (1977, |

| DATE | EVENT | REFS. |
|------|-------|-------|
| | form for completion to effect the transfer of Epiette shares from Northpoint to Tanwood (an Aston entity) (the Stock Transfer Form appears on Aston's file together with a director's resolution signed on 21 and 24.05.10, which confirmed that the stock transfer form was dated 30.12.09) | ¶59.48) |
| 24.05.10 | Trustees applied for interim suspension of discharge of Bankrupt from bankruptcy | 1-3 |
| 25.05.10 | Mr Waite sent Aston "the signed Stock Transfer Form as requested". It is not clear whether the Form enclosed was a further copy of the form transferring Epiette's shares from the Bankrupt to Northpoint (as appears to be the case from Aston's files) or a copy of a form transferring Epiette's shares from Northpoint to Tanwood (which, however, is not on Aston's files). | 2474-2477 |
| 25.05.10 | Trustees consented to the dismissal of Bankrupt's application for permission to appeal to CA in Bell v Bland | Supp.1/ex. 27 |
| 27.05.10 | Application Notice for s. 279(3) application for suspension of discharge | 26-27 |
| 27.05.10 | Report of Mr Mawer on failure of Bankrupt to comply with his obligations to the Trustees | 44-53 |
| 28.05.10 | Aston requested Bankrupt to provide completed stock transfer form for purposes of re-domiciliation of Epiette (i.e. from Northpoint to Tanwood) | 2477 |
| 01.06.10 | Bankrupt informed Aston that it should have the completed Northpoint to Tanwood STF by the middle of the following week | 2477 |
| 07.06.10 | Deputy Registrar Schaffer granted interim suspension of discharge of the Bankrupt from bankruptcy, pending full hearing of s. 279(3) application | 43 |
| 07.07.10 | Aston requested the Bankrupt's urgent attention to provision of a director's resolution dated 19.05.09 confirming the transfer of the Bankrupt's shares in Epiette to Northpoint | 2478 |
| 07.07.10 | Bankrupt stated that he was "out of the office" until 18.07.10 but would respond to Aston's request on his return and queried where the date of 19.05.09 came from as he thought that he had transferred his shares on 05.08.08 | 2478 |
| 13.07.10 | Aston responded (incorrectly) that 19.05.09 was when it had received the STF between the Bankrupt and Northpoint but stated that the Bankrupt could use 05.08.08 as the date for the resolution since that was the date on the STF | 2481 |
| 13.07.10 | Bankrupt confirmed that, on instructions from Mr Waite, he would amend the resolution as suggested and also confirmed that Aston should file Epiette's annual return in Jersey | 2482-2483 |
| 13.07.10 | Aston issued an internal instruction for Epiette's annual return to be filed the following day | 2484 |
| 22.07.10 | Aston received STF between Bankrupt and Northpoint and share certificate no. 22 in favour of Northpoint | 1979, ¶ 59.58 |
| 23.07.10 | Original return date for hearing of s. 279(3) application adjourned (by consent), due to overlap with Manchester hearing in Bell v Bland (eventually to 23.06.11) | Supp.3, WS10, ¶ 19-21 |

| DATE | EVENT | REFS. |
|------|-------|-------|
| 10.08.10 | Application Notice for s. 366 examination of Bankrupt, with return date of 07.04.11 | Supp. 3, ex. 19-20 |
| 13.10.10 | Chief Registrar Baister granted Order for s. 366 examination of Bankrupt, extending to a wide range of companies and requiring production of documents, with examination date of 03.03.11 | Supp. 3, ex. 21-23 |
| 25.10.10 | Trustees entered into Order for dismissal by consent of appeal against Judgment in Bell v Bland | Supp. 1, ex. 27 |
| 18.01.11 | Epiette gave public notice of its intention to seek continuance as a Delaware corporation | 2336 |
| 24.01.11 | Bankrupt, for Epiette, instructed Epiette's former Bank to send bank statements for period 01.09.09 to closure of account to Aston | 2337 |
| 03.03.11 | Order for s. 366 examination was amended to increase its scope and examination date was moved to 07.04.11 | Supp. 3, ex. 25-30 |
| 22.03.11 | First disclosure Order made against Aston in Isle of Man (resulting in disclosure of one lever arch file of documents) | 1958, ¶ 38 |
| 07.04.11 | s. 366 examination of Bankrupt part-heard before Chief Registrar Baister and adjourned to 03.11.11 (in the event, due to listing confusion, 08.12.11) with ELH of 1 day and Bankrupt directed to respond by WS within 14 days to Trustees' questions, as set out in a table for the hearing of 07.04, and to provide access to all documents of his stored on any computer, including providing access (under supervision of independent solicitor) to his email accounts | 2072-2222; Order @ Supp. 3, ex. 31-32 |
| 20.04.11 | Bankrupt filed his 8th WS, responding in an Appendix to the questions contained in the table produced during his s. 366 examination | Supp. 2, App. |
| 21.04.11 | Bankrupt wrote to Trustees to correct a statement made during his s. 366 examination, after a conversation with Mr Waite, that he had handed a disc containing the records of Epiette to Mr Waite at the time of sale of the shares of Epiette – it was said that Mr Waite did not recall any such disc and that it seemed therefore that the Bankrupt had been mistaken and that it would appear that the accounting records must have been lost | 2494 |
| 26.04.11 | Bankrupt provided responses to queries that the Trustees had raised in relation to his bank accounts as long ago as 13.10.09 and indicated that he believed he had now dealt with all of Trustees' outstanding requests | 2523-2543 |
| 06.05.11 | Bankrupt requested copies of the letters of authority signed by him at his s. 366 examination on 07.04 | 2535 |
| 03.06.11 | Bankrupt issued cross-application for his discharge and/or clarification of the conditions on fulfilment of which he would be discharged | Supp.3, ex. 15-16 |
| 20.06.11 | Trustees wrote to Bankrupt setting out a list of 94 questions for response | see, 2543 |
| 23.06.11 | s. 279(3) application came before Chief Registrar Baister, when Trustees relied, in part, upon Bankrupt's failure to respond adequately to questions put to him in advance of and at commencement of s. 366 examination as evidence of his failure to | 267; 2072-2222; 2548 (Order) |

| DATE | EVENT | REFS. |
|------|-------|-------|
| | cooperate. To address this concern, Trustees were directed to draw up a Scott Schedule of s. 366 questions (cross-referenced to documents) by 16.07.11, to which Bankrupt was to provide answers by 03.08.11, and application was adjourned to 02-03.04.12 with ELH of 2 days | |
| 01.07.11 | Bankrupt wrote to Trustees in response to their letter of 20.06 requesting that all future questions be cross-referenced to underlying documents, that copies of the documents referred to be provided and that the Trustees provide him with a set of the document bundles used during his s. 366 examination | 2543-2544 |
| 14.07.11 | Bankrupt wrote to Trustees to indicate that, because he had not been self-employed in the 2 years preceding his bankruptcy he should have left section 2 of his Statement of Affairs blank and thus no assumption should be made that he/Rosewood Consultants Ltd had conducted any "business" during that period | 2536-2539 |
| 15.07.11 | Bankrupt wrote to Trustees about Bell v Bland appeal | 2540-2542 |
| 16.07.11 | Directed deadline for Trustees to produce Scott Schedule | 267 |
| 29.07.11 | First draft of Scott Schedule supplied to Bankrupt in pdf format, incorporating questions included in a letter from the Trustees also dated 29.07 and without cross-references to documents but suggesting that the Bankrupt have until 05.09 to respond | 2612 |
| 01.08.11 | Bankrupt reserved his position on whether the Trustees had complied with the Court's Order in relation to the Scott Schedule but requested Word copy of Scott Schedule with cross-references and copies of the documents referred to | 2613 |
| 16.08.11 | Bankrupt wrote to Cobbetts asserting that the hearing of deferment application on 23.06 had been adjourned largely due to Mr Whittle's failure to prepare for it and to have documents available to evidence alleged failures to cooperate and/or provision of inconsistent answers and complained of the manner in which the Scott Schedule had been constructed and failure to supply copies of underlying documents | 2615-2617 |
| 16.08.11 | Bankrupt noted that Trustees or their solicitors had been in touch with Mr Corlett and asked what steps had been taken to recover monies due from him to Bankrupt's estate, in excess of €600,000 | Supp. 4, ex. 50 |
| 16.08.11 | Trustees agreed to consent Order directing that Bankrupt's application for discharge and/or clarification of the conditions for discharge be listed for hearing with the s. 279(3) application | Supp. 3, ex. 38-39 |
| 18.08.11 | Bankrupt noted that Mr Whittle and his assistant were both be away on holiday and that the Scott Schedule thus would not be provided to him until September | 2618 |
| 06.09.11 | Second draft of Scott Schedule supplied to Bankrupt in Word format but without cross-references to documents | see, 2545; 2619 |
| 07.09.11 | Bankrupt reminded Trustees' solicitors that he should have received the Scott Schedule by 16.07 and requested a revised copy of Scott Schedule with document references and supporting evidence within 14 days, failing which an application to strike out the Trustees' suspension application was threatened | 2545-2546; 2619-2621 |

272

| DATE | EVENT | REFS. |
|------|-------|-------|
| 26.09.11 | Mr Whittle wrote to Bankrupt pointing out that many of the questions in the second draft Scott Schedule did contain document references and/or arose out of documents provided to the Bankrupt and suggested that the Bankrupt address these questions whilst references were prepared for other questions | 2622-2623 |
| 27.09.11 | Bankrupt indicated that he would respond to questions in Scott Schedule from memory and the documents provided and hoped to provide his response within 3 weeks | 2624 |
| 29.09.11 | Cobbetts provided an updated version of the Scott Schedule with further document references added, supplied further copy documents and suggested that the Bankrupt provide his responses by 14.10.11 | 2625 |
| 05.10.11 | Bankrupt wrote to Mr Hill requesting confirmation as to who his Trustees now were and details of the circumstances in which Mr Mawer had left KPMG | 2549 |
| 17.10.11 | Bankrupt wrote again to Mr Hill, elaborating concerns about the conduct of Mr Mawer | 2550-2553 |
| 21.10.11 | Bankrupt asked Trustees to provide written consent for him to obtain documents from Aston and Attias & Levy in Gibraltar | 2554 |
| 24.10.11 | Bankrupt provided responses to Scott Schedule in a separate document and proposed that when the Schedule had been updated it be returned to him to enter his own references and documents that he wanted included in the application hearing bundle | 2567; 2626 |
| 24.10.11 | Bankrupt invited Trustees to remove from the Scott Schedule questions that did not relate to his affairs but to the affairs of companies or other individuals, noting that he had "not been in practice as a Chartered Accountant for many years" | 2627 |
| 26.10.11 | Trustees' solicitors indicated that Scott Schedule would be re-formatted, questions would be clarified to ensure that the Bankrupt's answers would be more responsive and cross-references would be added | 2568; 2628 |
| 27.10.11 | Bankrupt wrote to Trustees' solicitors to point out that Trustees were not permitted to amend the Scott Schedule with a further Court Order | 2569; 2629 |
| 01.11.11 | Bankrupt wrote to Mr Hill suggesting a meeting with Trustees | see, 2560 |
| 04.11.11 | Mr Hill wrote to Bankrupt declining consent to communications by him with Aston and Attias & Levy, on the basis that this was not appropriate as Trustees were already in direct communication with these parties, and indicating that he did not think that a meeting with the Bankrupt would serve any useful purpose in light of the Bankrupt's continued failure to provide information required of him | 2559-2560 |
| 18.11.11 | Bankrupt wrote to Trustees indicating that it was his understanding that the Scott Schedule ordered in the s. 279(3) application superseded the continuation of his oral s. 366 examination and inviting the Trustees to agree to adjournment of the s. 366 examination scheduled to take place before Registrar Derrett on 08.12.11 to 02-03.04.12, to be heard with the s. 279(3) application, | Supp. 3, ex. 42 |

| DATE | EVENT | REFS. |
|------|-------|-------|
| | which it was said to duplicate, and in the meantime to provide any further questions for him in writing | |
| 25.11.11 | Trustees informed Bankrupt that they intended to proceed with s. 366 examination to clarify some answers given in the Scott Schedule and to cover other matters | Supp. 3, ex. 40 |
| 29.11.11 | Bankrupt reiterated his view that it would be an abuse of process for Trustees to proceed on 08.12.11 and again requested that any further questions to be put to him be put in writing | Supp. 3, ex. 44 |
| 30.11.11 | Mr Waite procured his appointment as a director of Epiette in order to intervene in the Trustees' application in Jersey for copies of Epiette's bank records | 1979, ¶ 59.61 |
| 02.12.11 | Bankrupt wrote to Mr Hill suggesting that KPMG held a Memorandum from the Trustees' lawyers that stated that none of Mr Mawer's testimony in this matter was accurate, and requesting confirmation of this and disclosure of the Memorandum | 2561 |
| 06.12.11 | Bankrupt invited Trustees to agree to adjournment of the continuation of the s. 366 examination on 08.12.11 to save the costs of an application | Supp 3, ex. 49 |
| 06.12.11 | Bankrupt filed his 10th WS in relation to the continuation of the s. 366 examination on 08.12, in which he applied for the examination to be adjourned to 02-03.04.12 | Supp. 3 |
| 08.12.11 | On application of Bankrupt Mrs Registrar Derrett further adjourned continuation of s. 366 examination to 02-03.04.12, with Trustees ordered to pay costs of Bankrupt's counsel | Transcript @ Supp. 4, ex. 99-107; Order @ Supp. 5 |
| 09.12.11 | Trustees assured Bankrupt that revised Scott Schedule was in preparation | see, 2562 |
| 21.12.11 | Bankrupt chased Trustees for a copy of the revised and cross-referenced Scott Schedule | 2562 |
| 05.01.12 | Trustees informed Bankrupt that Scott Schedule was being updated to include further questions arising out of information received since the Schedule had been compiled | 2564 |
| 12.01.12 | Trustees were granted Order permitting the disclosure of information acquired during the bankruptcy for use as evidence in a pending application in the Manchester Bell v Bland proceedings, with provision made for the Bankrupt to review a draft of the Trustees' intended WS for the Manchester application and for any objections that he had to its content to be determined by the Court, if not resolved by agreement | 268-270 |
| 23.01.12 | Bankrupt wrote to Trustees about Bell v Bland appeal | 2570 |
| 30.01.12 | Hearing of further disclosure application against Aston in Isle of Man | 1958, ¶ 38 |
| 01.02.12 | Trustees' solicitors apologised to Bankrupt for not reverting to him on his Scott Schedule responses, due to being busy with applications in Jersey, Isle of Man, London and Manchester and indicated that this would be done soon | 2631 |
| 08.02.12 | 2nd disclosure Order made against Aston in Isle of Man | 1958, ¶ 38 |

| DATE | EVENT | REFS. |
|---|---|---|
| 08.02.12 | Bankrupt wrote to Trustees' solicitors requiring information on whether Cobbetts had advised Trustees on appeal in Bell v Bland | 2579 |
| 09.02.12 | Trustees sent the Bankrupt a draft of their intended WS for the Manchester application, running to about 200 pages with 5 lever arch files of exhibited documents, explaining that and why it had not been possible to finalise the WS in the time allowed | 2582 |
| 13.02.12 | Trustees provided updated information on their costs to date | 2574-2575 |
| 13.02.12 | Bankrupt wrote to Trustees requesting an explanation of why their proposed WS for the pending Manchester application in Bell v Bland had not been served in final form | see, 2586 |
| 14.02.12 | Trustees provided further information on their own costs and the costs of their solicitors in relation to the preparation of a WS for use as evidence in the pending Bell v Bland Manchester application and noted that an explanation for delay in finalising the Trustees' proposed WS already had been provided | 2576-2578; 2586 |
| 15.02.12 | Bankrupt asked the Trustees to comment on whether Mr Bell was paying the Trustees' costs for preparation of evidence for use in the pending Manchester application | 2587 |
| 17.02.12 | Bankrupt's solicitors provided a revised, cross-referenced third draft Scott Schedule to Bankrupt, which included additional questions, explaining in detail their reasons for revising the Schedule and indicating also matters on which Bankrupt might need to obtain documents from third parties | 2632-2634 |
| 22.02.12 | Trustees received 17 lever arch files (some 10,000 documents) of disclosure from Aston in Isle of Man | 1948, ¶ 11 |
| 23.02.12 | Bankrupt provided his responses to the second draft of Scott Schedule | See, 2497 |
| 23.02.12 | Mr Whittell of Cobbetts informed Bankrupt that he did not intend to respond, without his client's instructions, to enquiries regarding any advice given to the Trustees in relation to the Bell v Bland appeal but also that he did not recall having given such advice | 2580 |
| 27.02.12 | Bankrupt suggested that the Scott Schedule be divided into two parts, to separate questions originally posed from questions recently added but suggested that he would in any event seek to update the Scott Schedule as best he could over the next 2 weeks | 2635-2366 |
| 01.03.12 | Mr Whittle wrote to Bankrupt requesting that he explain why he had instigated the destruction of records of New Capital Management | 2604 |
| 01.03.12 | Mr Whittle wrote to Bankrupt about arrangements for the hearing of the s. 279(3) application and noted that the Trustees' understanding of his affairs had developed as a result of the recent disclosure from the Isle of Man and that new questions would therefore be raised with him | 2639 |
| 02.03.12 | 2nd and 3rd Scott Schedules served on the Bankrupt posing new questions arising out of recent third party disclosure on payments made to Aston and Epiette accounts | see, 2641; 2643 |

| DATE | EVENT | REFS. |
|------|-------|-------|
| 02.03.12 | Bankrupt wrote to Mr Hill raising further concerns about Mr Mawer's conduct and the veracity of his statements to the Court and suggesting that Mr Hill should take independent advice about the content of Mr Mawer's draft WS for use in the Bell v Bland Manchester application | 2588-2589 |
| 03.03.12 | Bankrupt requested that, if Trustees wished him to respond to questions arising out of the 10,000 pages of disclosure received from the Isle of Man they should provide him with copies of those 10,000 pages or confirm that any document not provided would not be used against him at any stage | 2637-2638 |
| 07.03.12 | Bankrupt wrote to Mr Hill raising a number of questions about the role of Mr Whittell of Cobbetts in the conduct of his bankruptcy | 2590-2591 |
| 08.03.12 | Bankrupt again wrote to Mr Hill, raising for comment a number of respects in which Mr Hill's evidence to the Court was asserted to be inaccurate | 2592-2594 |
| 09.03.12 | Bankrupt wrote to Mr Whittle stating that it was his understanding that no documents of New Capital Management had been destroyed and asking Mr Whittle to provide evidence of his allegation that the Bankrupt had instigated the destruction of records | 2605-2606 |
| 10.03.12 | Bankrupt wrote to Mr Hill to complain of Mr Whittell's conduct, namely in writing a letter concerning the Isle of Man disclosure as to New Capital Management that was said to contain false allegations about destruction of documents, which the Bankrupt stated had not occurred | 2602-2603 |
| 15.03.12 | Trustees received disclosure of bank statements from Jersey | 1948, ¶ 11 |
| 15.03.12 | Cobbetts declined to provide Bankrupt with copies of 10,000 pages of disclosure received from Isle of Man but offered facilities for inspection and otherwise dealt with arrangements for hearing on 02-03.04 | Supp. 4, ex. 16 |
| 19.03.12 | HH Judge Hodge QC made Order at telephone hearing extending time for service on Bankrupt of draft of evidence intended for Bell v Bland Manchester application, to 26.03.12 | see, Supp. 4, ex. 32 |
| 22.03.12 | Bankrupt provided his answers to the updated original Scott Schedule and to 2nd and 3rd Scott Schedules, together with documents B1-B176 (now in the hearing bundles at 2498-2673) and asked that hearing bundles be lodged and provided to his Counsel at least 5 days before the hearing on 02-03.04 | 1947, ¶ 9; Supp. 4, ex. 31 2497 |
| 22.03.12 | Bankrupt requested Cobbetts to provide s. 279(3) application hearing bundle to his Counsel "today" to allow sufficient time for preparation | Supp. 4, ex. 28 |
| 22.03.12 | Cobbetts informed Bankrupt that Trustees hoped to provide final version of WS intended for use in the Bell v Bland Manchester Application on 26.03.12 and asked when Bankrupt would be in a position to respond to outstanding Scott Schedule queries | Supp. 4, ex. 32 |
| 22.03.12 | Mr Mawer met with, and interviewed, MD of Aston on Isle of Man on instructions sent to Aston by Bankrupt requesting destruction of records of New Capital Management, when it was confirmed that Aston had not acted on that instruction | 1959, ¶41 |

276

| DATE | EVENT | REFS. |
|------|-------|-------|
| 26.03.12 | Trustees served final draft of Mr Mawer's proposed WS for use as evidence in Manchester application, running to 250 pages with 9 lever arch files of exhibited documents | 1948, ¶ 11 |
| 27.03.12 | Bankrupt noted that he had provided his answers to the Scott Schedule on 22.03 and asked for any further evidence that the Trustees intended to file for the hearing of the s. 279(3) application on 02-03.04 | Supp. 4, ex. 34 |
| 27.03.12 | Cobbetts emailed Bankrupt proposed list of contents for hearing bundles for 02-03.04, assuming that both s. 279(3) application and s. 366 examination would proceed | Supp. 4, ex. 6 |
| 27.03.12 | Bankrupt agreed to adjournment of continuation of s. 366 examination from 02-03.04 but wanted s. 279(3) application to proceed | Supp. 4, ex. 38 |
| 28.03.12 | Trustees served 4th Scott Schedule | Supp. 4, WS11, ¶ 20 |
| 28.03.12 | Cobbetts offered to deliver electronic copies of hearing bundles to Bankrupt and his counsel and also gave notice that a WS from Mr Mawer would be served later in the day | Supp. 4, ex. 39 |
| 28.03.12 | Bankrupt requested hard copies of hearing bundles for both himself and Counsel with e-copies in the interim | Supp. 4, ex. 40 |
| 28.03.12 | Bankrupt requested Cobbetts to include in the hearing bundles all of his own and of the Trustees' WS and exhibit filed in relation to the s. 279(3) application | Supp. 4, ex. 41 |
| 28.03.12 | Bankrupt requested Cobbetts to include in the hearing bundles Mr Mawer's WS in relation to an 02.10 hearing in Bell v Bland on the freezing Order | Supp. 4, ex. 42 |
| 28.03.12 | Bankrupt requested disc copy of electronic version of hearing bundles | Supp. 4, ex. 43 |
| 28.03.12 | Bankrupt requested clarification as to the arrangement of the hearing bundles | Supp. 4, ex. 44 |
| 29.03.12 | Supplementary WS of Mr Mawer in support of the s. 279(3) application | 1946-1996 |
| 29.03.12 | S. 279(3) hearing bundles filed and provided to Bankrupt | Supp. 4, ex. 47 |
| 29.03.12 | Bankrupt repeated his request for a disc copy of the electronic version of the hearing bundles as the volume of emailed documents had caused his email account to crash | Supp. 4, ex. 48 |
| 30.03.12 | Bankrupt provided his answers to 4th Scott Schedule | Supp. 4, WS11, ¶ 20 |
| 01.04.12 | Bankrupt served, through Counsel, copy of WS dated 31.03.12 and exhibit (numbered 10th but in fact 11th) | BWS 11 |
| 01.04.12 | Trustees are continuing to review the Bankrupt's recent responses to the Scott Schedules, and contemplating contempt proceedings | 1948, ¶ 12 |

KPMG were the Trustees for Michael Bland. Kevin Mawer was a partner and you can read all the court work he and his solicitor Mark Whittell, a partner at Cobbett's of Manchester, have done. They proved in court that Michael Bland had siphoned money from the Portugal Project into offshore companies. Kevin Mawer put the figure near to £10 million.

# 1 Background

## 1.1 Bell and the commencement of the bankruptcy

1.1.1      Michael Bland (**the Bankrupt**) was a Chartered Accountant, originally based in Carlisle.

1.1.2      One of the Bankrupt's clients was Geoffrey Bell (**Bell**). Bell sold his business in Carlisle for £1.9m in 1987. The Bankrupt advised Bell on a scheme to reinvest the money off-shore purportedly for tax saving purposes. In fact, the Bankrupt diverted the money to The Village Project (see below) and defrauded Bell. Bell subsequently commenced proceedings against the Bankrupt and in May 2009 secured a judgment against him for in excess of £6m. Bell also secured a Freezing Order against the Bankrupt's property.

1.1.3      On 9 June 2009, very shortly following the Bell judgment, the Bankrupt petitioned for his own bankruptcy. On 1 July 2009 Kevin Mawer (**KM**) and Richard Hill, then both of KPMG, (the **Trustees**) were appointed as the Bankrupt's joint trustees in bankruptcy. KM subsequently transferred to Begbies Traynor (Leeds) and is the lead trustee in the case.

## 1.2 Corlett and The Village Project

1.2.1      In the meantime, the Bankrupt had engaged in a number of other nefarious ventures. He had used the money defrauded from Bell to invest in a development project in Portugal called "The Village". The Bankrupt's partner in that project was an individual called Martin Corlett (**Corlett**). The Bankrupt and Corlett subsequently fell out. The Bankrupt alleges that in or about 2005, Corlett absconded with the proceeds of sale of 2 (out of 80) of the plots at The Village. The Bankrupt subsequently commenced proceedings against Corlett and secured a judgment against him for €800,000 together with a Freezing Order against the property of Corlett.

1.2.2      The Trustees believe that between £5m and £6m were extracted by the Bankrupt from The Village Project through various means and remain unaccounted for.

## 1.3 Hampshire

1.3.1      Another business with which the Bankrupt was involved historically was Hampshire Cosmetic Laboratories Ltd (**Laboratories**) and (its originally wholly owned subsidiary), Hampshire Cosmetics Ltd (**Cosmetics**). This was a highly successful and cash generative business. The shares in Laboratories were originally held in the following proportions:-

25% - Mike Duffell (**Duffell**);

25% - Michael Belcher (**Belcher**);

50% - Paul Younger (**Younger**).

1.3.2        The Bankrupt originally acted for Duffell and Belcher. Laboratories was subject to an HMRC investigation and the Bankrupt advised Duffell and Belcher to transfer their shares to another client of his, Thomas Waite (**Waite**), to protect themselves. This occurred in or about March 1994. The Bankrupt then ceased to act for (or show any concern for) Duffell and Belcher and instead aligned himself with Younger against them.

1.3.3        Proceedings were subsequently commenced by Duffell and Belcher, initially against the Bankrupt and Waite. Through a series of further developments and proceedings the Duffell and Belcher shares were moved about between various parties over a period of time but eventually ended up in the hands of a Gibraltarian Company called Aldeburgh Enterprises Ltd (**Aldeburgh**). It is the Bankrupt's case that Waite is the beneficial owner of Aldeburgh. It is the Trustees' case that the Bankrupt is the beneficial owner of Aldeburgh.

1.3.4        In the meantime, in or about November 1994 Laboratories hived down the whole of its assets to Cosmetics. Subsequently, in March 1996, Laboratories transferred 25% of its shares in Cosmetics to a BVI Company called New Capital Management Ltd (**NCM**). It is the Bankrupt's case that Waite (and his partner, Audrey Hardy) are the beneficial owners of NCM. It is the Trustees' case that the Bankrupt is the beneficial owner of NCM.

1.3.5        When the 25% shareholding in Cosmetics was transferred to NCM, the other 75% shareholding was transferred to Younger. Subsequently, the shares held by NCM were transferred to a Turks and Caicos Islands company called Wystan Inc (**Wystan**). At a later date Cosmetics bought out Younger's 75% shareholding in itself, leaving Wystan owning all of the shares in Cosmetics. It is the Trustees' case that the Bankrupt is the beneficial owner of Wystan. The value of the whole of the Laboratories/Cosmetics business is thought to be in excess of £6m.

1.4     Epiette

1.5     Another company in which the Bankrupt was heavily involved is a Jersey company called Epiette Ltd (**Epiette**). The Bankrupt was certainly the 100% shareholder of Epiette from 2003 onwards. The Bankrupt seeks to argue that he disposed of his shares at a later date but the Trustees apparently have evidence that this was not the case.

1.6     Epiette was used for money laundering purposes generally. It was the vehicle through which money was invested into The Village Project. It is also the vehicle through which monies have been paid to and from Waite and it can be shown that Epiette was used to pay the outgoings on Flat 3 (see below).

1.7     Caldew Beck

1.7.1        The Bankrupt is an unmarried man. He has a sister, Jennifer Bland (**Jennifer**) It is alleged by the Bankrupt that following the death of his parents, the estate passed to Jennifer (and a brother?) and that he was excluded. Included in the estate is the family home at Caldew Beck, Welton, Carlisle (**Caldew Beck**) which is vested in the sole name of Jennifer. The Bankrupt has boasted privately to others that the arrangements regarding the distribution of his parents estate is a sham and that he does have a beneficial interest in Caldew Beck.

1.8     Flat 3

1.8.1        The Bankrupt purports to live at 20 Montefiore Street, London S19 3TL, a property owned by an individual called Dominic Bland, who purports to be the Bankrupt's landlord. Whilst it is known that the Bankrupt visits that property occasionally, the Trustees believe that he lives principally at another address in London, Flat 3, Kipling House, 43 Villiers Street, London WC2N 6NE (**Flat 3**).

1.8.2    Flat 3 was purchased in or about January 2005 for a price of around £775,000. The purchaser and registered proprietor was a Turks and Caicos Islands company called Rainy Day Holdings Ltd (**Rainy Day**). The Bankrupt claims that Waite is the beneficial owner of Rainy Day and therefore Flat 3. Waite's solicitors have produced evidence (which TLT has not seen) of the alleged source of the purchase price – a bank statement in respect of an account allegedly in Waite's name. However the Trustees contest the reliability of that, first because they are of the view that the Bankrupt and Waite are not averse to manipulating or forging documents when required (and therefore the authenticity of this statement is in doubt), secondly because there is no clear evidence of the original source of the money anyhow and thirdly because the claimed original source ( the sale of Waite's business) is known to have produced no more than £484,000, just under £300,000 less than the purchase price of Flat 3.

1.8.3    Flat 3 is also subject to a charge dated 22 December 2011 in favour of Barclays Private Clients International Ltd (the **Barclays Wealth Charge**). The Trustees do not know how much is secured by the Barclays Wealth Charge and accordingly how much equity there is in Flat 3. They suspect that this may have been the source of funds to meet Waite's and the Bankrupt's legal fees over the last couple of years.

1.8.4    The Trustees have extensive evidence to show that the Bankrupt resides regularly at Flat 3 and pays all the utilities and other outgoings. Waite maintains that Flat 3 is his home but in fact he lives in the Turks and Caicos Islands where he has a plumbers' merchant's business. He visits the UK very rarely and when he does, he visits family in Carlisle. He has no need of a property in London. The Trustees think it inconceivable that Waite is really the beneficial owner of Rainy Day (and therefore Flat 3). They maintain that the Bankrupt is the beneficial owner.

1.8.5    The Trustees believe that Flat 3 is currently worth about £1m, subject to the Barclays Wealth Charge.

1.9    The Bankrupt's conduct

1.9.1    The Bankrupt has been remarkably unco-operative with the Trustees. Despite the huge complexity of his affairs he has failed to produce any documentary or other records in respect of any of his dealings. He claims that these have all been destroyed or lost.

1.9.2    The Trustees regard the Bankrupt as an inveterate liar. They have been supported in that view by various judges in various sets of proceedings. There is no doubt that the Bankrupt's credibility in any proceedings will be seriously limited.

1.10    Waite

1.10.1    Waite was originally one of the Bankrupt's clients. He now runs a plumbers' merchants business after the failure/disposal of his former business. He was not a man originally of significant personal wealth or substance.

1.10.2    It is the Trustees' case that Waite is simply the Bankrupt's front-man and that he has conspired with the Bankrupt to hide the Bankrupt's assets through a web of companies in various jurisdictions, of many of which Waite now (falsely) claims to be the beneficial owner.

1.10.3    Waite (and the various relevant companies) have been represented throughout by Kit Sorrell of Pannone, Manchester, together with Michael Booth QC. They have adopted an aggressive and unco-operative style towards the Trustees.

1.11  <u>Trustees' legal representation and funding to date</u>

1.11.1    Following their appointment, the Trustees engaged Mark Whittell (**MW**) formerly of Cobbetts, Manchester to act for them. After the failure of Cobbetts, MW moved to DWF Manchester.

1.11.2    MW has used Karen Troy, Counsel of Exchange Chambers Manchester from time to time in connection with the case.

1.11.3    Cobbetts/DWF have acted throughout on an informal (unwritten) CFA. This has been backed by an Investment Agreement between the Trustees and Harbour Litigation Investment Fund LP (**Harbour**) dated 19 May 2011 to cover defined disbursements and (in certain circumstances) adverse costs. The funding available under that agreement is currently limited to £300,000.

1.11.4    Huge amounts of work have been undertaken by Cobbetts/DWF, primarily of an investigative/evidence gathering nature. They have issued no substantive applications or proceedings for the recovery of any property. The proceedings actually taken to date have included proceedings under Section 366 of the Insolvency Act 1986 in the High Court for the examination of the Bankrupt (and possibly others). Proceedings have also been commenced in the Isle of Man and in Jersey against third parties to try to piece together further evidence. In the Isle of Man, proceedings were taken against Aston International Ltd (**Aston**), a company registration agent based there and used by the Bankrupt for many of his companies.

1.11.5    It appears that MW is about to leave, or has already left DWF. DWF say that they have a conflict in continuing to act for the Trustees because of a previous involvement with one of the companies which is the subject of the Trustees' investigation. DWF have accordingly given notice of ceasing to act.

1.11.6    The Trustees have been told that Cobbetts/DWF have run up WIP of around £800,000. They believe that DWF would be prepared to assign the benefit of this WIP either to Harbour or to any new solicitors appointed to act – possibly for nil consideration (given the difficulties which the Trustees now face, some of which may be of their or their counsel's making – see below) or against a commitment for some return in the event of the case ultimately being successful.

1.11.7    DWF have informed TLT that they have 139 boxes (files?) of papers relating to the case. The impression is that this may not be well ordered; MW was seemingly not always very fastidious.

1.11.8    Significant disbursements have been run up – primarily paying Counsel's fees and the fees of lawyers and agents in other jurisdictions. The disbursements paid out by Harbour to date stand at £210,000 leaving just £90,000 available under the existing agreement.

1.11.9    There have been problems with Karen Troy (see below). More recently and at the suggestion of Harbour, the Trustees consulted with Felicity Toube QC of 3-4 South Square regarding a possible substantive application in relation to Flat 3. She has worked on a witness statement in support of such an application, which TLT has seen (without the exhibit). TLT has not spoken with Felicity Toube QC or seen any advice from her on the merits of that application. Harbour has been told that the anticipated fees of Felicity Toube QC (and a junior) to proceed with the application would be of the order of £90,000 – wiping out the rest of the available budget under the Investment Agreement.

1.12    The Costs Orders

1.12.1    The proceedings in the Isle of Man in relation to Aston were successful and on 17 February 2012, a costs order was made in the Trustees' favour against four companies associated with the Bankrupt/Waite including Epiette and NCM. The Bill of Costs has been prepared in respect of that costs order and puts the Trustees' costs in relation to that application at a figure of £64,910.53. The costs figure has not been finalised by the Isle of Man Court because the Respondents have objected on the grounds of non disclosure of the Trustees' funding arrangements, including the terms of the CFA under which Cobbetts/DWF were operating and the Investment Agreement with Harbour.

1.12.2    In the proceedings taken by the Trustees to date as against the Bankrupt himself (namely of Section 366 proceedings), the Bankrupt has seemingly represented himself, although the Trustees suspect that he is receiving advice in the background. However, in the proceedings for information from the various companies allegedly beneficially owned by Waite, Waite and those companies have been represented by Pannone.

1.12.3    In the course of one of the Section 366 hearings before Chief Registrar Baister, TLT understands that a particular point was established or conceded and Baister was persuaded to make a Declaration to that effect. It is understood that Cobbetts subsequently tried to use that Declaration as a substantive finding as against the relevant Waite company. At this point, TLT has not had full disclosure of the relevant details, but it appears that Pannone objected to this on the grounds that of course the relevant company had not been a party to the application and had not had the proper opportunity to respond. They issued an application for an order that the Declaration was not binding on the relevant Waite company and, for reasons that are not entirely clear (because the point was conceded), an order to this effect was eventually made with a costs order against the Trustees personally.

1.12.4    TLT has seen two costs orders against the Trustees dated 5 March 2013. The first of these appears to be in favour of Northpoint Ventures Inc (a Delaware company which is also part of the Bankrupt's web of companies, again allegedly under the beneficial ownership of Waite). This refers to costs being summarily assessed against the Trustees in the sum of £21,958. The second appears to be in favour of Waite personally and refers to a detailed assessment hearing (with an estimate of 1 day) to take place on 26 June 2013. There is provision in this order for an interim costs certificate in the sum of £30,000.

1.12.5    It is the Trustees ' case that the making of these costs orders against them was due to the negligent handling of these applications by Cobbetts/DWF or, more particularly, Counsel, Karen Troy.

1.13    Discharge

1.14    In the meantime, the Bankrupt has made an Application to challenge the decision to suspend his discharge. There is apparently a Court of Appeal hearing in relation to this floating over 11 to 14 June 2013. Whilst the Trustees accept that the granting of the discharge will not affect their right to continue their work, they are concerned that the granting of the discharge might undermine their attacks on the Bankrupt's credibility and encourage the Bankrupt and Pannone to have more confidence generally in their position. Tactically, they feel that it would be better if the Bankrupt continued to be denied his discharge pending the completion of all their investigations.

## 2 The Trustees' potential claims in the bankruptcy

The Trustees have identified potential claims as follows:-

2.1 They believe that the Bankrupt is the beneficial owner of the Laboratories/Cosmetics business (through Aldeburgh and/or Wystan and/or NCM). They believe it to be worth in excess of £6m. The Bankrupt denies his beneficial ownership and has failed to account for anything.

2.2 The Trustees believe that the Bankrupt is the beneficial owner of Epiette. They believe that Epiette has been the recipient of significant funds from a variety of sources. . The Bankrupt denies his beneficial ownership and has failed to account for anything.

2.3 The Trustees believe that the Bankrupt has (directly or indirectly) received sums in the region of £5m to £6m from The Village Project. The Bankrupt has failed to account for any of these monies.

2.4 The Trustees believe that the Bankrupt has an interest in the family estate inherited from his parents, including Caldew Beck. He denies any such interest and has failed to account for any of it.

2.5 The Trustees believe that the Bankrupt is the beneficial owner of Rainy Day and accordingly Flat 3. The Trustees believe that Flat 3 is worth around £1m (subject to the Barclays Wealth Charge). The Bankrupt denies beneficial ownership of Rainy Day and has failed to account for any such interest.

## 3 TLT's involvement to date

3.1 TLT was approached by Harbour on Wednesday 24 April 2012 to see if TLT would consider stepping in to act for the Trustees in place of DWF. TLT was sent copies of two long draft witness statements in the proceedings (with no exhibits) and invited to attend a meeting with KM to discuss the case. That meeting took place on Tuesday 30 April 2013 (Philip May and Tessa Glover in attendance). KM gave a general account of the history of the case at that meeting and it was at that point that more of the detail emerged.

3.2 Stephen O'Dowd of Harbour subsequently joined the meeting and explained Harbour's perspective. He confirmed that further funding under the existing agreement was very limited and that without a clear and acceptable strategy to take the matter forward generally Harbour would withdraw support. He invited TLT to put together proposals for taking the case forward (probably on a phased basis – see below) if TLT felt able to act. Philip May made it clear that, whilst TLT would like to help, the matter would require careful review and he could not commit TLT to anything at that stage.

3.3 TLT subsequently spoke with DWF; DWF and KM then sent through to TLT some further papers, including the costs orders referred to above and some documents purporting to be exhibits to various witness statements; these are not the exhibits to the two draft witness statements originally sent to TLT by Harbour.

3.4 KM has since emailed through to TLT copies of letter received by him from Gateley Waring acting for KPMG and some correspondence with Cains - Isle of Man lawyers representing Aston.

3.4.1 TLT has carried out a high level review of the case. This has not involved a full review of all the documents actually sent through to TLT to date (let alone all the other material retained by DWF) and so this review may contain errors or omissions.

**4 Proposals for TLT further involvement**

4.1 It was originally indicated to TLT that this case might proceed on a limited basis, focussing exclusively (in the short term) on the Flat 3 application. At the meeting with KM on 30 April 2013, it became apparent that there were several other pressing matters to attend to, including in particular the costs order against the Trustees (in respect of which over £50,000 is now seemingly payable by the Trustees personally forthwith), the costs order against NCM, Epiette et al in favour of the Trustees, the negligence claim against Cobbetts/DWF/Karen Troy and the Court of Appeal discharge hearing.

4.2 In the light of these developments, TLT was invited to make a proposal for dealing with the matter on a phased basis as follows (Harbour's words) :-

*Phase 1*

 *Deal with existing costs orders in the Trustees' favour; potentially using a small and controlled portion of the remaining budget to close those issues off.*

 *Deal with impact of adverse costs orders against the Trustees personally and what options they have; what impact not dealing with these issues could have on the Flat 3 application and wider.*

 *Deal with the Bankrupt's appeal re the bankruptcy order.*

 *Firm up Flat 3 application with a view to sending it to Pannone in draft, with TLT confirmed as acting, and asking direct question about charge over Flat 3 etc.*

*[n.b. Harbour will want to understand costs and timing of this phase]*

*Phase 2*

 *Issue and pursue Flat 3 application.*

*[same as above re costs and timing]*

*Phase 3*

 *Consider remaining avenues of investigation if Flat 3 successful.*

4.3 Harbour has made it clear that in any substantive proceedings Harbour would expect TLT to act on a CFA basis with disbursements' and adverse costs' funding from Harbour. Harbour has also made it clear that in that eventuality Harbour would want the waterfall arrangement in the event of success to give them priority out of the proceeds, - possibly up to as much as £500,000 out of the Flat 3 application. Clearly, if the net recoveries did not reach that mark, then there would be no return for TLT (or KPMG/Begbies Traynor) whatsoever.

**5 Pros and Cons for TLT**

5.1 Pros

5.1.1    This is a high profile, high value, interesting and complex matter of a type which TLT would ordinarily welcome.

5.1.2    KPMG, Begbies Traynor and Harbour are all highly valued clients of TLT and TLT would welcome the opportunity to work further with them on a case of this nature.

5.1.3     TLT has not previously worked with KM or Begbies Traynor Leeds/Manchester; this case would present an opportunity to extend relationships.

5.1.4     The evidence and information considered by TLT to date suggests that there is an overwhelming case against the Bankrupt for having secreted or failed to account for very substantial sums of money and other assets of considerable value. In a case like this it would ordinarily be expected that, with sufficient determination and the exertion of sufficient pressure, the Bankrupt would eventually be forced to capitulate and disgorge something of what he had squirreled away. In this case it would not be unreasonable to expect recoveries ultimately running to several million pounds.

5.1.5     Whilst pursuing all the various claims at this stage might be a tall order, the Flat 3 application is arguably a discrete assignment, which has already been worked on by Felicity Toube QC of 3-4 South Square (leading insolvency set) and has been described as being more or less "ready to go". TLT should be able to pick this up fairly quickly and get on with it.

5.1.6     If successful, the Flat 3 application could be worth as much as £1m. Whilst Harbour may be looking for priority for the return of its investment, if the net proceeds were of this order the potential return to TLT under a CFA could be significant.

5.1.7     If a win could be achieved in relation to Flat 3 this might create a fighting fund and/or level of confidence to press on with further applications which if successful could return several million pounds to the Bankrupt's estate and TLT could expect a significant return on its further CFA work.

5.1.8     TLT's return would potentially be enhanced if it were able to acquire the Cobbetts/DWF WIP, said to have a value of around £800,000.

5.1.9     There is already some funding for disbursements and adverse costs in place from Harbour. If TLT takes the case on, it is possible (but not guaranteed) that Harbour might extend its cover – at least to enable the Flat 3 application to proceed.

5.2 <u>Cons</u>

5.2.1     The Trustees have been in office already for nearly 4 years and have carried out very extensive investigations into events going back many years before their appointment. The affairs of the Bankrupt are exceptionally complicated involving large number of companies and other associates spread across a variety of jurisdictions. As noted above, DWF have advised that they have 139 boxes (files?) of papers and clearly absorbing all this material and getting up to speed with all the intricate details will be no small task, particularly where it seems likely that the papers may not be in a very orderly state.

5.2.2     The Bankrupt and his associates (represented by Pannone) have shown remarkable resilience over this period and do not appear to be close to any sort of capitulation.

5.2.3     It is to be expected that the Bankrupt, Waite and Pannone, will make the most of the opportunity created by a change of solicitors to put extra pressure upon the Trustees and will certainly not extend any co-operation or assistance to newly appointed solicitors.

5.2.4     Even if the short term focus is simply upon the Flat 3 application the matter is not without significant difficulty. Although Felicity Toube QC has been engaged to review and amend the evidence in support of that application, TLT has been informed that this has been subjected to some further amendments by MW and TLT does not have the accompanying exhibit. DWF has not been immediately able to locate it. TLT has not seen any advice from Felicity Toube QC (or anyone else) on the merits of the application or its prospects of success and at present is being asked to form a view based on a very limited review of such evidence as there is.

5.2.5     The evidence which TLT has seen in relation to the Flat 3 application is largely inferential. There is plenty of evidence to show that the Bankrupt uses Flat 3 as though it were his own, but there is no <u>direct</u> evidence to show that he paid for it. The case appears to be that it is highly unlikely that Waite could, or would, ever have paid for it. If it turns out that Waite did pay for Flat 3, in whole or in part, then he is going to establish a beneficial interest in it and that is going to limit what may be recovered by the Trustees.

5.2.6     Furthermore, any sums due under the Barclays Wealth Charge are again going to reduce the equity available to the Trustees if the application is successful. Whilst at this point in time, the Trustees have no knowledge of how much might be secured by that Charge, the conduct of the Bankrupt and Waite to date in so many other respects would tend to suggest that everything possible will have been done to extract value out of the Flat 3 asset (being the one real estate asset in the jurisdiction which they have and on which they know the Trustees have been focussing) and put that beyond the immediate reach of the Trustees. Indeed the Trustees suspect that the Barclays Wealth Charge may well have been used simply to secure the funding of Waite's legal costs to date. If so the debt built up could be significant; Pannone has said that these costs run to hundreds of thousands of pounds.

5.2.7     The combined impact of the Barclays Wealth Charge, the possibility that Waite did put in some or all of the purchase price for Flat 3 and the priority claim of Harbour to any proceeds of any successful action means that there is a very real risk that there would be nothing (or very little) left for TLT/KPMG/Begbies Traynor even if the application was successful.

5.2.8     The suggestion is that TLT should simply send off the Flat 3 evidence to Pannone and see if this can be used as a lever either to drive a deal or extract information regarding the source of the purchase price and/or the debt outstanding under the Barclays Wealth

287

Charge.  Given all the above, however, it is unlikely that Pannone is going to be immediately (or convincingly) co-operative over any of this and may well simply call TLT's bluff to issue the application.  If the application has to be issued, permission will have to be sought to serve it out of the jurisdiction on Waite and Rainy Day and then attempts will have to be made to effect service on them in Turks and Caicos; this could be costly and time consuming.

5.2.9     In any event it is by no means clear that, if TLT takes the case on, it will be possible to adopt a limited approach to taking matters forward.  In particular:-

(a)     The Bankrupt's affairs are exceptionally complex; unravelling Flat 3 is going to involve tracing through many of his other dealings and the numerous companies with which he has been involved.

(b)     Whilst there are no formal claims extant, there are a couple of sets of proceedings for examination of parties under oath adjourned and it is possible that Pannone will start to put pressure on the Trustees to bring those matters to a conclusion.  They will certainly continue to bombard the Trustees or their advisors with various demands and counter allegations.

(c)     Cains are now pressing the Trustees to take substantive proceedings in relation to Epiette in Jersey.

(d)     In addition, the Trustees have to deal with the costs orders which have been made against them.  These are personal and the total sum already due under them exceeds £50,000; when finalised the further amount due could add significantly to that.  This matter is now critical.  What cannot be denied is that a significant liability now exists (it is too late for there to be any appeal) and so, apart from possibly arguing quantum in respect of the balance of the costs to be assessed (a job for a costs' lawyer or costs' draftsman, where TLT could probably add very little value anyhow) the Trustees have no alternative other than to pay up.  The Trustees would like to argue for a set off against the costs orders made in their favour in the Isle of Man proceedings, but the parties involved are not identical and the orders have been made in courts in different jurisdictions.  In any event, if a set off were agreed based on common beneficial ownership (which seems very unlikely) this would be tantamount to a concession on the part of the Trustees that Waite is indeed the beneficial owner of Epiette, NCM and the other companies against whom the costs order in favour of the Trustees has been made.  That would blow apart a number of the Trustees' arguments in relation to other aspects of the case.

(e)     The Trustees may have recourse against other parties in respect of their liability under the costs orders - including Cobbetts/DWF, Karen Troy, KPMG, Begbies Traynor and Harbour, all of whom have denied (or are likely to deny) responsibility.  Whilst TLT would have no difficulty acting against Cobbetts/DWF (if an appropriate funding arrangement were in place, bearing in mind that such ordinary professional negligence proceedings would be subject to the changes imposed by the Jackson reforms), TLT could not, for professional reasons, act against or advise KM in relation to claims which he or the Trustees might have against any of those other parties (or that he might have against Richard Hill).  Whatever happens the Trustees/KM are going to need independent advice in this respect.

(f)    The Bankrupt is pursuing an appeal in respect of the suspension of his discharge. Whilst KM feels strongly about this and TLT has not had the opportunity to investigate the merits, the risks are, as a matter of practicality, not insignificant; if the Trustees are successful, costs may be ordered in their favour but this will bring nothing by way of immediate return (because the Bankrupt is bankrupt) and certainly there will be no substantive recovery. If the Trustees are unsuccessful a further costs order will be made against them and if the case has been conducted by TLT on some form of CFA or similar arrangement without adverse costs insurance or coverage in place, TLT could be exposed to a third party costs order.

(g)    There are dates for hearings very soon in respect of the discharge appeal (11 to 14 June 2013) and in respect of the detailed assessment of one of the costs orders against the Trustees (26 June 2013). These are accordingly urgent matters which need to be dealt with.

5.2.10    There is insufficient headroom under the existing Harbour budget to cover all the disbursements and adverse costs risks associated with all the above, let alone relieve TLT of its CFA risk.

5.2.11    The possibility of picking up the Cobbetts/DWF WIP for nil consideration may not be as appealing as might at first sight be apparent. A significant amount of that WIP may be impaired or may otherwise not be recoverable as against any third parties given:-

(a)    The fact that a good deal of it may relate to investigatory work not likely to be susceptible to inter partes costs claims;

(b)    The fact that some of it has already been the subject of inter partes costs claims (both ways) and has therefore been "wiped out";

(c)    The suspicion that MW may not always have been very efficient or economic in his handling of the matter;

(d)    The fact that TLT would, in any event, have to read in and so there would be a good deal of irrecoverable duplication.


**Philip May**

Lightning Source UK Ltd.
Milton Keynes UK
UKHW021318241220
375828UK00007B/258

*Geoff Bell* revolutionised truck drivers' accommodation by building Carlisle Truck Inn and running it for 10 years.

He built up a fleet of 15 Volvo F86s running round the clock and thus helped forge the modern-day road haulage industry.

Then Michael James Bland, his trusted chartered accountant and a partner at Dodd & Co Carlisle, turned out to be a professional fraudster, who defrauded Geoff Bell out of his hard-earned money from the Carlisle Truck Inn, after he had sold out to BP Oil.

ISBN 978-1-78222-797-7

01899

9 781782 227977